Designing Web Interfaces

Bill Scott and Theresa Neil

O'REILLY®

Beijing · Cambridge · Farnham · Köln · Sebastopol · Taipei · Tokyo

Designing Web Interfaces
by Bill Scott and Theresa Neil

Published by O'Reilly Media, Inc., 1005 Gravenstein Highway North, Sebastopol, CA 95472.

O'Reilly books may be purchased for educational, business, or sales promotional use. Online editions are also available for most titles (*safari.oreilly.com*). For more information, contact our corporate/institutional sales department: 800-998-9938 or *corporate@oreilly.com*.

Editor: Mary Treseler	**Indexer:** Julie Hawks
Production Editor: Rachel Monaghan	**Cover Designer:** Karen Montgomery
Copyeditor: Colleen Gorman	**Interior Designer:** Ron Bilodeau
Proofreader: Rachel Monaghan	**Illustrator:** Robert Romano

Printing History:

January 2009: First Edition.

ISBN: 978-0-596-51625-3

[V]   [6/09]

Contents

Principle One: Make It Direct

Principle Four: Provide an Invitation

Principle Five: Use Transitions

Foreword

In architecture, *parti* refers to the underlying concept of a building.* Will it be an academic structure aimed at increasing cross-disciplinary collaboration or a theater flexible enough to support quick set changes? To bring a specific parti to life, architects must not only define its essence but also know how to manage the huge number of considerations that ultimately impact its construction.

Design principles are the guiding light for any architect's parti. They define and communicate the key characteristics of a building to a wide variety of stakeholders, including clients, builders, city planners, and engineers. Design principles articulate the fundamental goals that all decisions can be measured against and thereby keep the pieces of a project moving toward an integrated whole. But design principles are not enough.

Every aspect of a building from an attic to a Zen garden has a set of opportunities and limitations that can either add to or detract from the main concept or parti. These include standard dimensions, spacing requirements, aesthetics, physical limitations, and more. Architects who want to bring coherent visions to life need to learn the detailed ins and outs of these design considerations so they can select the best solutions from the options available.

This combination of design principles at the top and design considerations at the bottom is what allows architects to fill in the middle with meaningful buildings that enable people and organizations to interact, communicate, and get things done.

Those of us whose parti is bringing rich web applications to life can also benefit from a framework of design principles and considerations to guide us. In these pages, Bill Scott and Theresa Neil give us just that. Through 30 years of designing and developing software, Bill and Theresa have been the consummate taxonomists—naming, documenting, and sharing in loving detail what makes rich interactions succeed and fail.

---

* The term *parti* comes from Matthew Frederick's book *101 Things I Learned in Architecture School* (MIT Press).

The breadth of solutions they have encountered has given them a unique perspective on the design principles behind the most successful rich interactions on the Web. From "make it direct" to "react immediately," the principles he outlines in this book are your yardstick for measuring the value that rich interactions bring to your web application. Through in-depth descriptions of context and trade-offs, Bill and Theresa support each principle with the design considerations and best practices you need to make informed decisions. Engineers, product managers, marketers, and designers can rally around and continually return to these principles and considerations to ensure that everyone is evaluating the impact of design decisions the same way.

This combination of rich web interaction design principles at the top and design considerations at the bottom allows web designers to fill in the middle with meaningful structures that enable people and organizations to interact, communicate, and get things done. Just like our friends, the architects.

So, dive in and immerse yourself in the direction and details you need to bring your rich web application partis to life!

—Luke Wroblewski
October 2008
Senior Director, Product Ideation and Design, Yahoo! Inc.
Author, *Web Form Design: Filling in the Blanks* (Rosenfeld Media)
Author, *Site-Seeing: A Visual Approach to Web Usability* (Wiley)

Preface

What Happened

My (Bill's) first personal computer was a Radio Shack Color Computer (circa 1981)—complete with a chiclet-style keyboard. The first few months the main user interface was the command line, typing in COLOR BASIC code.

Later, an upgrade to an Apple IIe brought a nicer keyboard with lots of games. But the interface was basically the same. The command-line and text-driven menu systems ruled the day. When the IBM PC came on the scene it brought more of the same. Lotus 123, which was the state-of-the-art spreadsheet application at the time, was controlled by a set of cryptic keystrokes. Not much of a user experience.

Then an interface revolution started. The Macintosh arrived in 1984, and shortly after its introduction, I brought one home. The mouse opened the door to a brand-new world of interaction. Instead of having to learn archaic commands to navigate through text-based menus, interaction in this new environment happened naturally in a direct, intuitive manner.

OK, you are probably thinking, so what? That was 1984. This is now. What does this have to do with a book about designing web interfaces?

Everything.

For most of the history of the Web, sites and applications were marked by primitive interfaces—just like the early desktop era. Most sites were built from two events:

- Clicking hyperlinks
- Submitting forms

Try to create an interesting user experience from just those two events. And, to add insult to injury, every click and every submit was punctuated with a page refresh. Creating a seamless user experience was next to impossible.

Interestingly, the technologies have existed for many years to get around these limitations. But it was only after they became widely available across the most common browsers that developers could count on them in their everyday development. In 2004, Google launched Gmail and Google Maps using a set of techniques later dubbed Ajax by Jesse James Garrett.

The difference was dramatic. The Ajax-enabled Google Maps now interacted more like a desktop application with real-time pan-and-zoom—all with no page refresh. Mapquest, on the other hand, behaved like most other web applications at the time, refreshing the page each time the map was repositioned or zoomed. The contrast was clear between the old world of the Web and the new world as enabled by Ajax.

Why We Wrote This Book

While I got the chance to live through the first interface revolution for the desktop (even writing one of the first games for the Macintosh*), my coauthor Theresa Neil lived through the second revolution on the Web.

A few years ago our paths crossed at Sabre (parent company of Travelocity). Together we founded a user experience design team and worked to improve dozens of products, performing heuristic evaluations and participating in full web application redesigns. From that work, we distilled a number of user interface design patterns as well as anti-patterns (common mistakes to avoid).

From there I went to Yahoo! and got to play an active role in defining the Ajax interface revolution on the Web. One of my contributions at Yahoo! was to publicly launch the Yahoo! Design Pattern Library. As Yahoo!'s Ajax Evangelist, I met and brainstormed with many of Yahoo!'s best minds on what it means to take these new interactions and apply them to the unique context of the Web. As a result, over the last few years, I have given countless talks on this subject, sharing best practices with web developers and designers from around the world.

At the same time Theresa struck out as an interface designer in her own consultancy. In her work she has continued to refine the initial set of design patterns and principles while leading the design for 30+ live rich internet applications—enterprise applications as well as public-facing websites. These patterns have given Theresa and her clients a common vocabulary and a set of standards to work with for new application design and existing system redesign.

This book is an outgrowth of our experience—a distillation of the combined 30+ years that Theresa and I share. After repeated requests, we decided the best way to share this with a larger audience was to put the material into book form.

---

* *GATO* was published by Spectrum Holobyte in 1985.

What This Book Is About

This book is not about information architecture, although you will find information architecture principles alluded to throughout it. And this book is also not about visual design, although you will find that the backdrop of good visual design is assumed throughout.

This book is about *interaction* design: specifically, interaction design on the Web. And even more specifically, about *rich* interaction design on the Web. It is a distillation of best practices, patterns, and principles for creating a rich experience unique to the Web.

By *unique* I mean that the Web comes with its own context. It is not the desktop. And while over time the lines between desktop and Web blur more and more, there is still a unique aspect to creating rich interactions on the Web. Editing content directly on the page (e.g., In-Page Editing, as we discuss in Chapter 1) borrows heavily from the desktop—but has its own unique flavor when applied to a web page. This book explores these unique rich interactions as set of design patterns in the context of a few key design principles.

Design Patterns

What do we mean by design patterns?

Christopher Alexander coined the term "patterns" in his seminal work *A Pattern Language: Towns, Buildings, Construction* (Oxford University Press) to catalog common architectural solutions to human activities. He described a pattern as:

> *...a problem which occurs over and over again in our environment, and then describes the core of the solution to that problem...*

Patterns were later applied to software in the book *Design Patterns: Elements of Reusable Object-Oriented Software* (Addison-Wesley), by the Gang of Four (Erich Gamma, Richard Helm, Ralph Johnson, and John M. Vlissides). A few years later design patterns were extended to the realm of user interface design.[*]

It is the latter form of patterns that we present in this book: *interaction design patterns*. You will find 75+ patterns illustrating the most common techniques used for rich web interaction. Each design pattern is illustrated by examples from various websites. Since the patterns described are interactive, we use a generous amount of figures to explain the concept. We tease out the nuances for a given solution as well as identify patterns to be avoided (anti-patterns). Best practice sections call out suggestions along the way.

The patterns are presented in the context of six design principles, which form the framework for the book:

---

[*] See works such as Jenifer Tidwell's *Designing Interfaces: Patterns for Effective Interaction Design* (O'Reilly) and the pattern library of Martijn van Welie (*http://www.welie.com/*).

Principle One: Make It Direct

As Alan Cooper states: "Where there is output, let there be input." This is the principle of direct manipulation. For example, instead of editing content on a separate page, do it directly in context. Chapters 1–3 in this principle include patterns for "In-Page Editing," "Drag and Drop," and "Direct Selection."

Principle Two: Keep It Lightweight

While working on a redesign of Yahoo! 360 the designer, Ericson deJesus, used the phrase "light footprint" to describe the need to reduce the effort required to interact with the site. A primary way to create a light footprint is through the use of Contextual Tools. This principle explores the various patterns for these in Chapter 4, "Contextual Tools."

Principle Three: Stay on the Page

The page refresh is disruptive to the user's mental flow. Instead of assuming a page refresh for every action, we can get back to modeling the user's process. We can decide intelligently when to keep the user on the page. Ways to overlay information or provide the information in the page flow are discussed in Chapters 5 and 6, "Overlays" and "Inlays", respectively. Revealing dynamic content is discussed in Chapter 7, "Virtual Pages." In the last chapter of this section, Chapter 8, we discuss "Process Flows," where instead of moving from page to page, we can create in-page flows.

Principle Four: Provide an Invitation

Discoverability is one of the primary challenges for rich interaction on the Web. A feature is useless if users don't discover it. A key way to improve discoverability is to provide invitations. Invitations cue the user to the next level of interaction. This section, including Chapters 9 and 10, looks at "Static Invitations," those offered statically on the page, and "Dynamic Invitations," those that come into play in response to the user.

Principle Five: Use Transitions

Animations, cinematic effects, and various other types of visual transitions can be powerful techniques. We explore engagement and communication in Chapter 11, looking at a set of the most common "Transitional Patterns," and Chapter 12 is devoted to the "Purpose of Transitions." A number of anti-patterns are explored as well.

Principle Six: React Immediately

A responsive interface is an intelligent interface. This principle explores how to make a rich experience by using lively responses. In Chapter 13, a set of "Lookup Patterns" is explored, including Live Search, Live Suggest, Refining Search, and Auto Complete. In Chapter 14, we look at a set of "Feedback Patterns," including Live Previews, Progressive Disclosure, Progress Indication, and Periodic Refresh.

Who Should Read This Book

Designing Web Interfaces is for anyone who specifies, designs, or builds web interfaces.

Web designers will find the principles especially helpful as they form a mental framework, defining a philosophy of designing nuanced rich interactions. They will also find the patterns a welcome addition to their design toolbox, as well as find the hundreds of provided examples a useful reference. And of course the best practices should provide a nice checklist reminder for various interaction idioms.

Product managers will find the patterns and examples to be excellent idea starters as they think through a new business problem. Though this book does not provide programming solutions, web developers will nevertheless appreciate the patterns, as they can be mapped directly into specific code solutions. For everyone involved, the patterns form a vocabulary that can span product management, design, and engineering, which in the end forms the basis for clearer cross-team communication.

You'll also find that whether you are just starting out or you are a grizzled veteran, the wealth of real-world examples in the context of design principles and patterns will be a benefit to your daily work.

What Comes with This Book

This book has a companion website (*http://designingwebinterfaces.com*) that serves as an addendum containing updated examples; additional thoughts on the principles, patterns, and best practices; and helpful links to articles and resources on designing web interfaces.

All of the book's diagrams and figures are available under a Creative Commons license for you to download and use in your own presentations. You'll find them at Flickr (*http://www.flickr.com/photos/designingwebinterfaces/*).

Conventions Used in This Book

This book uses the following typographic conventions:

Italic
> Used for example URLs, names of directories and files, options, and occasionally for emphasis.

Bold text
> Indicates pattern names.

Tip

This indicates a tip, suggestion, or general note.

Using Examples

You can find all of the figure examples on our companion Flickr site (*http://flickr.com/ photos/designingwebinterfaces*). The figures are available for use in presentations or other derivative works provided you respect the Creative Commons license and provide attribution to this work. An attribution usually includes the title, author, publisher, and ISBN. For example: "*Designing Web Interfaces*, by Bill Scott and Theresa Neil, Copyright 2009 Bill Scott and Theresa Neil, 978-0-596-51625-3."

If you feel your use of examples falls outside fair use or the permission given above, feel free to contact us at *permissions@oreilly.com*.

We'd Like to Hear from You

We have tested and verified the information in this book to the best of our ability, but you may find that features have changed or that we may have made a mistake or two (shocking and hard to believe). Please let us know about any errors you find, as well as your suggestions for future editions by writing to:

> O'Reilly Media, Inc.
> 1005 Gravenstein Highway North
> Sebastopol, CA 95472
> 800-998-9938 (in the United States or Canada)
> 707-829-0515 (international or local)
> 707-829-0104 (fax)

We have a web page for this book where we list examples and any plans for future editions. You can access this information at:

> *http://www.oreilly.com/catalog/9780596516253*

You can also send messages electronically. To be put on the mailing list or request a catalog, send an email to:

> *info@oreilly.com*

To comment on the book, send an email to:

> *bookquestions@oreilly.com*

For more information about our books, conferences, Resource Centers, and the O'Reilly Network, see our website at:

> *http://www.oreilly.com*

Safari Books Online

When you see a Safari® Books Online icon on the cover of your favorite technology book, that means the book is available online through the O'Reilly Network Safari Bookshelf.

Safari offers a solution that's better than e-books. It's a virtual library that lets you easily search thousands of top tech books, cut and paste code samples, download chapters, and find quick answers when you need the most accurate, current information. Try it for free at *http://safari.oreilly.com*.

Acknowledgments

Bill's Acknowledgments

Writing this book was not just the effort of Theresa Neil and myself. There are many direct contributors but even more that indirectly inspired us.

Most importantly I wish to thank Ruth. You are my wonderful wife of 30 years, my friend, and an amazing mother. Without your patience and support I could not have gotten this book finished.

I am deeply indebted to my editors at O'Reilly. Double kudos go to Mary Treseler, who patiently cajoled Theresa and I to complete this work. You provided valuable feedback early in the process. Thanks to the rest of the team that brought this book to life: Rachel Monaghan, Marlowe Shaeffer, Ron Bilodeau, Colleen Gorman, Adam Witwer, and Robert Romano, to name a few.

Anyone who has written a book also knows that the technical reviewers are your critical test market. Thanks for the helpful praise and constructive criticism from Christian Crumlish, Dan Saffer, Luke Wroblewski, Juhan Sonin, Kevin Arthur, and Alan Baumgarten. Though I could not address every issue, I took each comment seriously and they had a significant impact on the finished product.

I owe a lot to my time at Yahoo!. Thanks to Erin Malone for sending me an email out of the blue, which eventually led to her hiring me at Yahoo!. There I was surrounded by brilliant people and given the opportunity to succeed. To Erin, Matt Leacock, and Chanel Wheeler for founding the Yahoo! Design Pattern Library. Thanks to Larry Tesler and Erin, who gave me the opportunity to lead and evangelize the launch of the public Yahoo! Design Pattern Library. It was in my role as pattern curator that I crystallized much of the thinking contained in this book. A special thanks to the many talented designers and developers who gave me continual feedback and inspired me with their craftsmanship.

The YUI team, and in particular Nate Koechley and Eric Miraglia, for the formulation of "Interesting Moments" grids and for the opportunity to tie the patterns to real-world code. My co-evangelists: Douglas Crockford, Iain Lamb, Julien Lecomte, and Adam Platti. My good friend, Darren James, who encouraged me along the way. Thanks to the many talented designers that I got the chance to collaborate with and whose thoughts are found sprinkled throughout this text: Karon Weber, Samantha Tripodi, Ericson deJesus, Micah Laaker, Luke Wroblewski, Tom Chi, Lucas Pettinati, Kevin Cheng, Kathleen Watkins, Kiersten Lammerding, Annette Leong, Lance Nishihira, and many others.

Outside of Yahoo!, my thinking was encouraged and matured by knowing/learning from Dan Saffer (Adaptive Path), Ryan Freitas (Adaptive Path), Aza Raskin (Humanized), Scott Robbins (Humanized), Peter Moerholz (Adaptive Path), and David Verba (Adaptive Path). A special debt of gratitude to those in the pattern community. Jenifer Tidwell for pointing the way to patterns. For Martijn van Welie for his excellent pattern library. For James Refell and Luke Wroblewski and their work on patterns at eBay. For Christian Crumlish, the current pattern curator at Yahoo! and his clear thinking. Jesse James Garrett, for not only giving Ajax a name, but inviting me to the first Ajax Summit and then taking me on tour with him. Teaching in the Designing for Ajax Workshops gave me the confidence to write this book and tested the material in front of a live audience.

And thanks to the many companies and conference coordinators that invited me to speak. Sharing this material with thousands of listeners was invaluable in determining what resonates with most designers and developers. In no particular order (listed with the company that they invited me to speak at): Jared Spool (UIE), Ben Galbraith and Dion Almer (Ajaxian/Ajax Experience), Kathryn McKinnon (Adobe), Jeremy Geelan (SysCon), Rashmi Sinha (BayCHI/Slideshare), Aaron Newton (CNET), Brian Kromrey (Yahoo! UED courses), Luke Kowalski (Oracle), Sean Kane (Netflix), Reshma Kumar (Silicon Valley Web Guild), Emmanuel Levi-Valensi (People in Action), Bruno Figueiredo (SHiFT), Matthew Moroz (Avenue A Razorfish), Peter Boersma (SIGCHI.NL), Kit Seeborg (Web-Visions), Will Tschumy (Microsoft), Bob Baxley (Yahoo!), Jay Zimmerman (Rich Web Experience), Dave Verba (UX Week). Other conferences and companies that I must thank: Web Builder 2.0, eBig, PayPal, eBay, CSU Hayward, City College San Francisco, Apple, and many others.

My deep appreciation goes to Sabre Airline Solutions, and especially Brad Jensen, who bet on me and gave me a great opportunity to build a UX practice in his organization; and to David Endicott and Damon Hougland, who encouraged me to bring these ideas to the public. And to my whole team there for helping Theresa and I vet these ideas in the wild. Many patterns in this book were born out of designing products there.

Finally, I want to thank Netflix, where I am now happily engaged in one of the best places to work in the world. Thanks for supporting me in this endeavor and for teaching me how to design and build great user experiences.

Theresa's Acknowledgments

I would like to gratefully acknowledge the following folks:

Aaron Arlof, who provided the illustrations for this book. They are the perfect representation of the six principles.

Brad Jensen, my vice president at Sabre Airline solutions, who had me interview Bill in the first place. Without Bill's mentoring and training I would not be in this field.

Damon Hougland, who helped Bill and I build out the User Experience team at Sabre.

Jo Balderas, who made me learn to code.

Darren James, who taught me how to code.

All of my clients who have participated in many a white board session, enthusiastically learning and exploring the patterns and principles of UI design, especially Steven Smith, Dave Wilby, Suri Bala, Jeff Como, and Seth Alsbury, who allowed me to design their enterprise applications at the beginning of the RIA revolution. A special thanks to my current colleagues: Scott Boms of Wishingline, Paulo Viera, Jessica Douglas, Alan Baumgarten, and Rob Jones.

Most importantly, I wish to thank my husband for his unwavering support, and my parents for their encouragement. And my son, Aaron, for letting me spend so many hours in front of the computer.

Make It Direct

On a recent trip to Big Sur, California, I took some photos along scenic Highway 1. After uploading my pictures to the online photo service, Flickr, I decided to give one of the photos a descriptive name. Instead of "IMG_6420.jpg", I thought a more apt name would be "Coastline with Bixby Bridge."

The traditional way to do this on the Web requires going to the photo's page and clicking an edit button. Then a separate page for the photo's title, description, and other information is displayed. Once on the editing page, the photo's title can be changed. Clicking "Save" saves the changes and returns to the original photo page with the new title displayed. Figure P1-1 illustrates this flow.

Figure P1-1. *Web applications have typically led the user to a new page to perform editing*

In Flickr you can edit the photo title just like this. However, Flickr's main way to edit photos is much more direct. In Figure P1-2 you can see that by just clicking on "IMG_6420.jpg", editing controls now encapsulate the title. You have entered the editing mode directly with just a simple click.

Editing directly in context is a better user experience since it does not require switching the user's context. As an added bonus, making it easier to edit the photo's title, description, and tags means more meta-information recorded for each photo—resulting in a better searching and browsing experience.

Figure P1-2. *In Flickr, clicking directly on the title allows it to be edited inline*

Make It Direct

The very first websites were focused on displaying content and making it easy to navigate to more content. There wasn't much in the way of interactivity. Early versions of HTML didn't include input forms for users to submit information. Even after both input and output were standard in websites, the early Web was still primarily a read-only experience punctuated by the occasional user input. This separation was not by design but due to the limits of the technology.

Alan Cooper, in the book *About Face 3: The Essentials of Interaction Design*, describes the false dichotomy.

> ...many programs have one place [for] output and another place [for] input, [treating them] as separate processes. The user's mental model...doesn't recognize a difference.

Cooper then summarizes this as a simple rule: *Allow input wherever you have output.*[*] More generally we should make the interface respond directly to the user's interaction: *Make it direct.*[†]

To illustrate this principle, we look at some broad patterns of interaction that can be used to make your interface more direct. The next three chapters discuss these patterns:

Chapter 1, *In-Page Editing*
: Directly editing of content.

Chapter 2, *Drag and Drop*
: Moving objects around directly with the mouse.

Chapter 3, *Direct Selection*
: Applying actions to directly selected objects.

---

[*] Cooper, Alan et al. *About Face 3: The Essentials of Interaction Design* (Wiley, 2007), 231.

[†] This is a restatement of the principle of *Direct Manipulation* coined by Ben Scheiderman ("Direct manipulation: a step beyond programming languages," IEEE Computer 16[8] [August 1983], 57–69).

Chapter 1

In-Page Editing

Content on web pages has traditionally been display-only. If something needs editing, a separate form is presented with a series of input fields and a button to submit the change. Letting the user directly edit content on the page follows the principle of *Make It Direct*.

This chapter describes a family of design patterns[*] for directly editing content in a web page. There are six patterns that define the most common in-page editing techniques:

Single-Field Inline Edit
Editing a single line of text.

Multi-Field Inline Edit
Editing more complex information.

Overlay Edit
Editing in an overlay panel.

Table Edit
Editing items in a grid.

Group Edit
Changing a group of items directly.

Module Configuration
Configuring settings on a page directly.

The most direct form of **In-Page Editing** is to edit within the context of the page. First, it means we don't leave the page. Second, we do the editing directly in the page.

---

[*] We use the term "design patterns" to denote common solutions to common problems. Design patterns originate from Christopher Alexander's book *A Pattern Language* (Oxford University Press). You can read a series of essays from me (Bill) and others on design patterns at *http://www.lukew.com/ff/entry.asp?347*.

The advantage of **Inline Edit** is the power of context. It is often necessary for users to continue to see the rest of the information on the page while editing. For example, it is helpful to see the photo while editing the photo's title, as explained in the next section, "Single-Field Inline Edit."

It is also useful when editing an element that is part of a larger set. Disqus, a global comment service, provides inline editing for comments (Figure 1-1). After posting a comment and before anyone replies to the comment, an edit link is provided. The editing occurs within the context of the rest of the comments shown on the page.

Tip ————————————————————————————————

If editing needs the context of the page, perform the editing inline.

Figure 1-1. *Disqus allows comments to editing inline within the context of other comments*

The first two patterns, **Single-Field Inline Edit** and **Multi-Field Inline Edit**, describe techniques for bringing direct inline editing into the page.

Single-Field Inline Edit

The simplest type of **In-Page Editing** is when editing a single field of text inline. The editing happens in place instead of in a separate window or on a separate page. Flickr provides us a canonical example of **Single-Field Inline Edit** (Figure 1-2).

Front Grounds

Non-editing state

Flickr chose to keep the title clear of any edit actions.

The title looks like a title. This provides the highest readability by not cluttering the interface with edit actions or an editable style.

This will lead to discoverability issues. An alternate approach is to place an "edit" link somewhere in line with the title that would start the editing process.

Invitation to edit

On mouse hover, the background is backlit with yellow. A tool tip invites the user to "Click to edit".

Invitations attempt to lead the user to the next level of interaction (from mouse hover to mouse click).

Invitations have to be discovered to be useful. Flickr's bet is that the user will drift his mouse over the title (of his own photo).

Editing

Once the user clicks on the title, it is placed into an edit mode. An edit box is switched into view immediately under the title text.

The "Save" and "Cancel" buttons make it clear we are editing the title by providing a familiar interface—the user input form.

A disadvantage to this approach is that the picture gets pushed down to make way for the additional interface elements.

Completion

There are a number of ways to signify that the text is being saved. In this example, the title text is temporarily replaced with the text "saving...". Upon completion, the new title is shown in the non-editing style.

An alternative approach is to show a busy progress indicator while the change is being made.

Figure 1-2. *Flickr provides a straightforward way to edit a photo's title directly inline*

Considerations

The flow is simple. Click on the title to start editing. When you are done, hit the "Save" button, and the title is saved in place. Flickr was one of the first sites to employ this type of in-page editing. As a testament to its usefulness, the interaction style first designed has not changed much over the last few years.

But there are some challenges to consider.

Discoverability

Just how discoverable is this feature? In this example, there are a number of cues that invite the user to edit. The invitations include:

- Showing a tool tip ("Click to edit")
- Highlighting the background of the editable area in yellow
- Changing the cursor to an edit cursor (I-beam)

But all these cues display *after* the user pauses the mouse over the title (mouse hover). Discoverability depends on the user hovering over the title and then noticing these invitations.*

To make the feature more discoverable, invitational cues could be included directly in the page. For example, an "edit" link could be shown along with the title. Clicking the link would trigger editing. By showing the link at all times, the edit feature would be made more discoverable.

But this has to be balanced with how much visual noise the page can accommodate. Each additional link or button makes the page harder to process and can lead to a feature not being utilized due to the sheer volume of features and their hints shown on the page.

Tip ───

If readability is more important than editability, keep the editing action hidden until the user interacts with the content.

Yahoo! Photos† took this approach for editing titles (Figure 1-3). When showing a group of photos, it would be visually noisy to display edit links beside each title. Instead, the titles are shown without any editing adornment. As the mouse hovers over a photo title, the text background highlights. Clicking on the title reveals an edit box. Clicking outside of the edit field or tabbing to another title automatically saves the change. This approach reduces the visual noise both during invitation and during editing. The result is a visually uncluttered gallery of photos.

---

* While the Yahoo! Design Pattern Library (*http://developer.yahoo.com/ypatterns/*) was being launched, this pattern was not included in the initial set of patterns due to an internal debate over this issue of discoverability. In fact, one of the reviewers, a senior designer and frequent user of Flickr, had only recently discovered the feature. As a result, we withheld the pattern from the public launch.

† Yahoo! Photos was replaced in 2007 with Flickr.

Figure 1-3. *Editing titles in Yahoo! Photos keeps visual clutter to a minimum; it simply turns on a visible edit area during editing*

Accessibility

Another concern that arises from inline editing is the lack of accessibility. Accessibility affects a wider range of users than you might first consider. Assistive technologies help those with physical impairments, medical conditions, problems with sight, and many other conditions.

Assistive technologies generally parse the page's markup to find content, anchors, alternate titles for images, and other page structure. If the inline edit feature does not contain explicit markup built into the page (such as an explicit, visible edit link), assistive technologies cannot easily discover the inline edit feature.

In a sense, relying on the mouse to discover features will prevent some users from being able to edit inline. As mentioned before, providing an explicit edit link helps with discoverability (as shown previously in Figure 1-1). But as a by-product it also makes the feature more accessible.

—— **Tip** —————————————————————————————

Providing an alternative to inline editing by allowing editing on a separate page can improve accessibility.

———————————————————————————————————

There is a natural tension between direct interaction and a more indirect, easily accessible flow. It is possible to relieve this tension by providing both approaches in the same interface. Flickr actually does this by offering an alternate, separate page for editing (Figure 1-4).

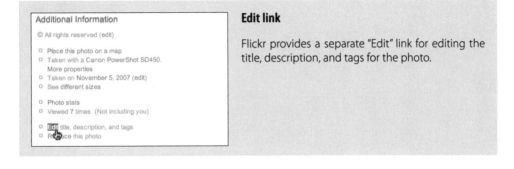

Edit link

Flickr provides a separate "Edit" link for editing the title, description, and tags for the photo.

Edit your photo

Title

Front Grounds

Description

Tags

Choose from your tags

SAVE CHANGES

Or, cancel and go back to the photo view.

Separate page for editing

The "Edit your photo" page provides a standard, form-based interface for editing. Assistive technologies work easily with static pages like this.

Figure 1-4. Flickr allows you to also edit a photo's title, description, and tags in a separate page

Multi-Field Inline Edit

In our previous example, a single value was being edited inline. What happens if there are multiple values, or the item being edited is more complex than a string of text and you still would like to edit the values inline?

The pattern **Multi-Field Inline Edit** describes this approach: editing multiple values inline.

37 Signal's Backpackit application uses this pattern for editing a note (Figure 1-5). A note consists of a title and its body. For readability, the title is displayed as a header and the body as normal text. During editing, the two values are shown in a form as input text fields with labeled prompts.

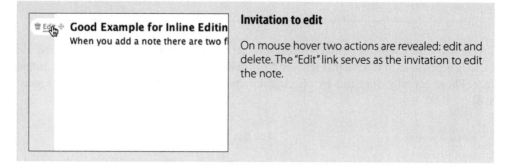

Good Example for Inline Editin

When you add a note there are two f

Invitation to edit

On mouse hover two actions are revealed: edit and delete. The "Edit" link serves as the invitation to edit the note.

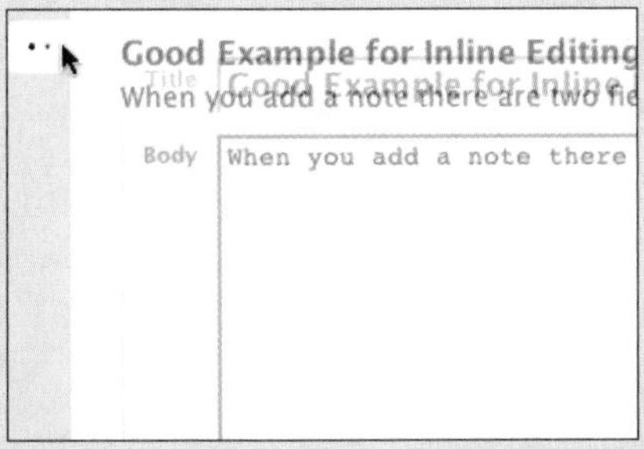

Transition to edit

Once you click the "Edit" link, a busy indicator is animated while an edit form for the title and body replaces the textual display of the note.

A slight cross-fade transition and a progress indicator are used to cue the user to this switch of context. This ties the textual display and the edit form together.

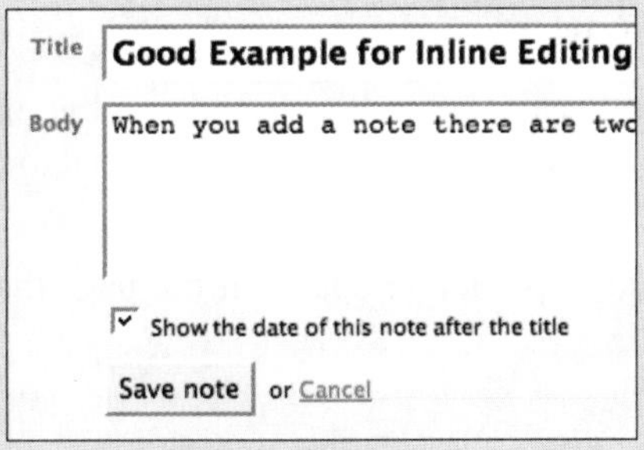

Editing

Editing is very straightforward since it uses a form. It provides the flexibility for other options to be placed in the editing form.

The "Save note" button completes the edit.

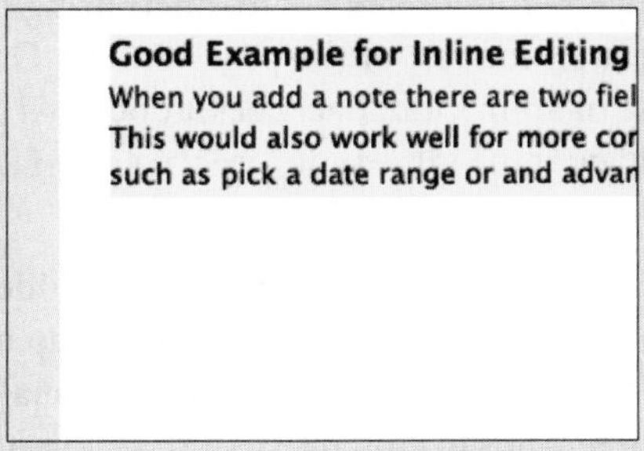

Completion

The edit form is replaced with the new title and body. To make it clear that a change occurred, the background is highlighted in yellow. After a few seconds the yellow is faded back down to the normal background color.

Contrast this with Flickr's technique of showing status while saving instead of after completion.

Figure 1-5. *Backpackit reveals a multi-field form for editing a note's title and body*

Considerations

In **Single-Field Inline Edit** the difference between display mode and edit mode can be more easily minimized, making the transition less disruptive. But when editing multiple fields, there is a bigger difference between what is shown in display mode and what is needed to support editing.

Readability versus editability

Readability is a primary concern during display. But the best way to present editing is with the common input form. The user will need some or all of the following:

- Edit controls
- Field prompts
- Help text for user input
- Error handling
- Assistive input (e.g., calendar pop up or drop-down selection field)
- Editing styles (e.g., edit fields with 3D sunken style)

The edit mode will need to be different in size and layout, as well as in the number and type of components used. This means that moving between modes has the potential to be a disruptive experience.

In our example, the form for editing the note takes up a larger space on the page than when just displaying the note.

Blending display and edit modes

Ideally you would like the two modes to blend together in a seamless manner. Bringing the edit form into the page flow will have an effect on the rest of the page content. One way to smooth out the transition is by a subtle use of animation. Backpackit does this by fading out the display view and fading in the edit view at the same time (see the cross-fade in Figure 1-5).

Another approach is to use the same amount of space for both display and edit modes. In Yahoo! 360, you can set a status message for yourself. Your current status shows up on your 360 home page as a "blast," represented as a comic book-style word bubble. Visually it looks like a single value, but there are actually three fields to edit: the blast style, the status, and any web page link you want to provide when the user clicks on your blast. Figure 1-6 shows the blast as it appears before editing.

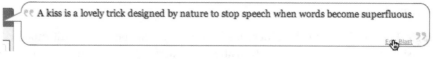

Figure 1-6. *Yahoo! 360 shows an "Edit Blast" link to invite editing*

Figure 1-7 shows how the blast appears during editing. Notice that the edit form is designed to show both modes (display and editing) in the same visual space.

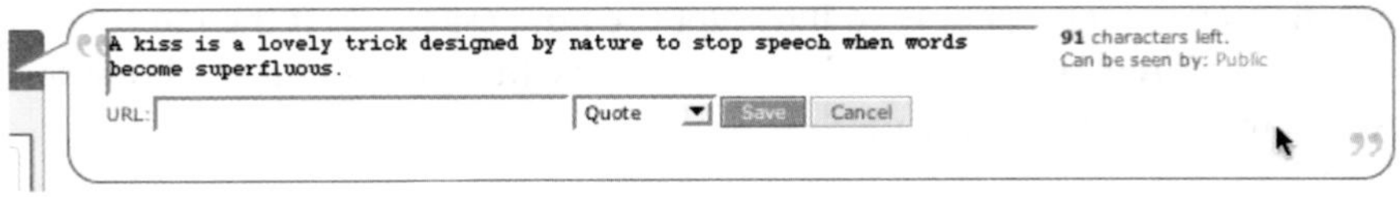

Figure 1-7. *Yahoo! 360 brings the editing into the displayed blast; the difference between display and edit modes is minimized*

The size similarity was not an accident. During design there was a concerted effort to make the display mode slightly larger without losing visual integrity, while accommodating the editing tools in the space of the bubble.

WYSIWYG*

If the two modes (display and editing) are in completely separate spaces, the user may lose a sense of what effect the change will have during display. In Yahoo! 360, you can change the type of bubble and immediately see what it will look like. Switching from a "quote" bubble to a "thought" bubble is reflected while still in editing mode (Figure 1-8). This would not be possible if editing happened in a separate edit form.

Figure 1-8. *Yahoo! 360 immediately displays the new blast type while still in edit mode*

Overlay Edit

The previous two patterns brought editing inline to the flow of the page. Inline editing keeps the editing in context with the rest of the elements on the page.

Overlay Edit patterns bring the editing form just a layer above the page. While still not leaving the page for editing, it does not attempt to do the editing directly in the flow of the page. Instead a lightweight pop-up layer (e.g., dialog) is used for the editing pane.

There are several reasons for choosing **Overlay Edit** instead of **Inline Edit**.

Sometimes you can't fit a complex edit into the flow of the page. If the editing area is just too large, bringing editing inline can shuffle content around on the page, detracting from the overall experience. A noisy transition from display to edit mode is not desirable.

---

* What You See Is What You Get: an interface where content displayed during editing appears very similar to the final output.

At other times you might choose to interrupt the flow, especially if the information be-ing edited is important in its own right. Overlays give the user a definite editing space. A lightweight overlay does this job nicely.*

Tip ──────────────────────────────────────
An **Overlay Edit** is a good choice if the editing pane needs dedicated screen space and the context of the page is not important to the editing task.

Yahoo! Trip Planner is an online place for creating and sharing trip plans. Trips contain itinerary items that can be scheduled. When scheduled, the itinerary contains the dates the item is scheduled. Each item can be edited in an overlay (Figure 1-9).

Non-editing state

Each itinerary item in Yahoo! Trip Planner can be scheduled.

You can add dates or edit an existing one. The dates scheduled are displayed in a simple read-able format.

Invitation to edit

The "[Edit]" link is the invitation to edit.

It is shown at all times.

---

* In the past, separate browser windows were used for secondary windows. Lightweight overlays simply map the secondary content into a floating layer on the page. The resulting overlay feels more lightweight. See Chapter 5.

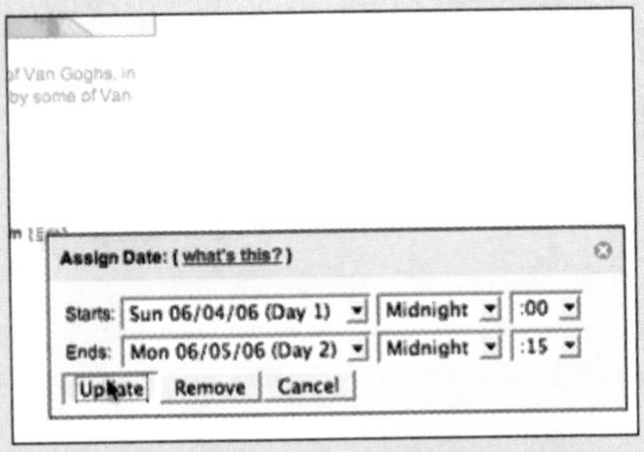

Editing

The edit form is shown in an overlay.

Since scheduling an itinerary item requires several fields of input, the overlay provides a nice place to contain this editing.

Completion

The itinerary item is scheduled after pressing the Update button.

No transitions are used. The presence of the scheduled date signifies that it has been added.

Figure 1-9. *Yahoo! Trip Planner provides a complex editor in an overlay for scheduling an itinerary item*

Considerations

"Sun Jun 4 12:00am—Mon Jun 5 12:00am" is easier to read than a format appropriate for editing (Figure 1-10). Using an editor prevents errors when entering the start and end dates for a specific itinerary item.

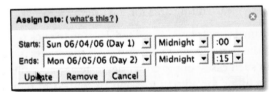

Figure 1-10. *Yahoo! Trip Planner provides an overlay editor for adjusting itinerary times*

Since the range of dates is known, Trip Planner uses a series of drop-downs to pick the start and end dates along with the time.

It should be noted that using multiple drop-downs for choosing the hour and minute is not the best experience. Although not in the context of an overlay, a better example of choosing an event time when creating an event can be found at Upcoming.org (Figure 1-11).

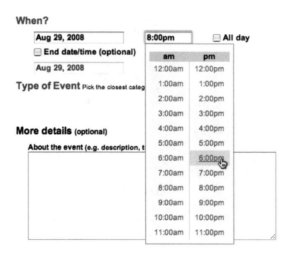

Figure 1-11. *Upcoming provides a better experience for choosing time of day*

The experience of picking a time from a single list (or typing the time in) is more direct than navigating multiple drop-downs.

Why an overlay?

An overlay should be considered when:

- The editing module is considerably larger than the display values.

- Opening an area on the page for the editing module would be distracting or push important information down the page.

- There is concern that the opened information might go partially below the fold. An overlay can be positioned to always be visible in the page.

- You want to create a clear editing area for the user.

- What you are editing is not frequently edited. Having to click on an edit link, adjust to the pop-up location, perform your edit, and close the dialog is a tedious way to edit a series of items. In such cases, opt to either dedicate a space on the page for each item as it is selected, or allow the editing to occur in context to remove some of the time required to deal with an overlay.

- What you are editing is a single entity. If you have a series of items, you should not obscure the other similar items with an overlay. By allowing the edit to occur in context, you can see what the other item's values are while editing.

Best Practices for Inline Edit and Overlay Edit

In-Page Editing provides a nice way to change displayed content and observe the change in context. Here are some best practices to consider:

- Keep the editing inline for single fields.
- Use inline when editing one of many in a set. This keeps the context in view.
- Keep the display and editing modes the same size when possible. This will avoid page jitter and reduce distraction when moving between the two modes.
- Make the transition between display and editing as smooth as possible.
- Use mouse hover invitations to indicate editing when readability is primary.
- Avoid using double-click to activate editing.
- Place a bracketed "[edit]" link near the item to be edited if editability is equally important or if the quantity of items that can be edited is small. This is a nice way to separate the link from the displayed text without creating visual distractions.
- Show the edit in place when editing one item in a series (to preserve context).
- Use an overlay when what is being edited needs careful attention. This removes the likelihood of accidentally changing a critical value.
- Do not use multiple overlays for additional fields. If you have a complex edit for a series of elements, use one overlay for all.
- When providing an overlay, use the most lightweight style available to reduce the disruptiveness of the context switch between render and editing state.
- Use buttons when it might be too subtle to trigger completion implicitly.
- Use explicit buttons for saving and canceling when there is room.
- Whenever possible, allow the overlay to be draggable so that obscured content can be revealed as needed.

Table Edit

Editing tables of data is less common in consumer web applications. In enterprise web applications, however, tables reign supreme. The most common request is for the table editing to work like Microsoft Excel, which long ago set the standard for editing data in a grid.

A good example of **Table Edit** is a Google Docs Spreadsheet (Figure 1-12).

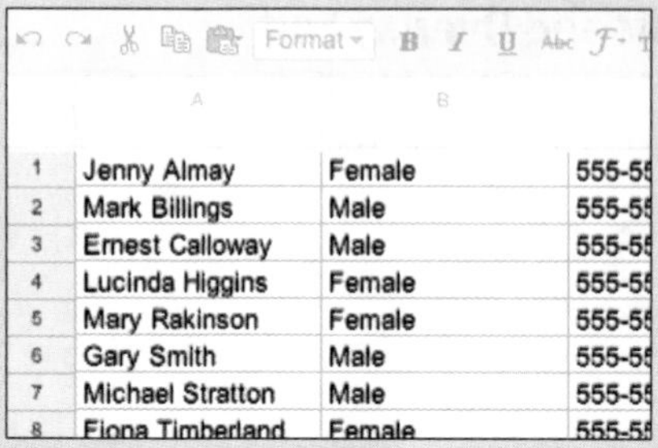

Non-editing state

Each cell is tuned toward readability. There are no editing clues while in this state.

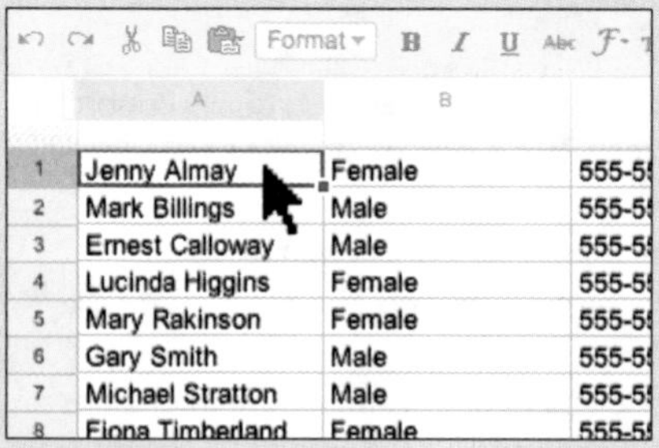

Invitation to edit

The invitation to edit comes after the cell is clicked.

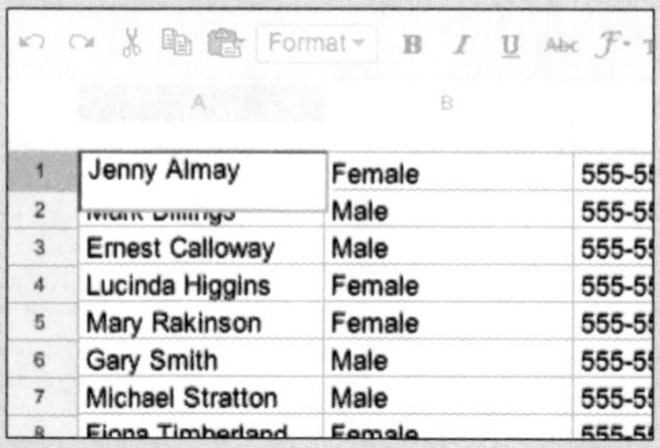

Editing

An edit box is overlaid on top of the cell being edited. This invites the user to actually type as much text as she needs into the cell.

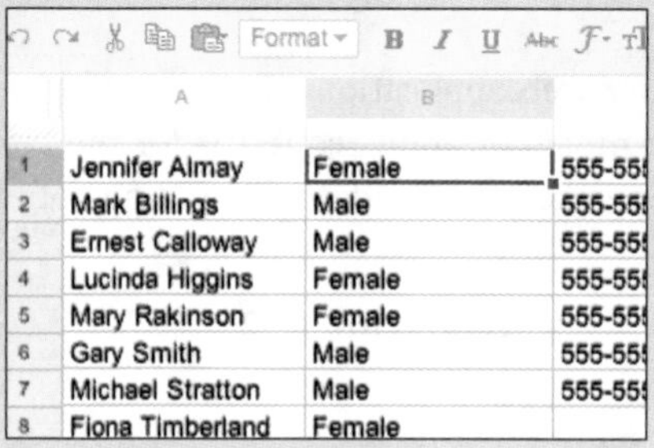

Completion

Completion occurs when the user tabs, clicks outside the cell, or presses Enter.

Figure 1-12. Editing a spreadsheet in Google Docs is very similar to editing a spreadsheet in Microsoft Excel

Considerations

Presentation is the primary consideration when displaying a table of data. Editing is secondary. As a result, the editing scaffolding is hidden and only revealed when it's clear the user wants to edit a cell.

Activation

A single mouse click is required to start editing a cell instead of a mouse hover. This is consistent with keeping the display of the grid uncluttered. Imagine how irritating it would be if every mouse motion revealed an edit box.

—— **Tip** ——
You should generally avoid double-click in web applications. However, when web applications look and behave like desktop applications, double-click can be appropriate.

Rendering versus editing. Google Spreadsheet displays the edit box slightly larger than the cell. This clearly indicates editability and lets the user know that input is not limited to the size of the cell (the edit box actually dynamically resizes as the user types into it). The only issue to consider is that the larger edit area covers other table cells. However, this works well in this case since editing is explicitly triggered by a mouse click. If activation had occurred on a mouse hover, the edit mode would have interfered with cell-to-cell navigation.

Best Practices for Table Edit

Here are some best practices for **Table Edit**:

- Bias the display toward readability of the table data.
- Avoid mouse hover for activating cell editing. It makes for the feeling of "mouse traps" and makes the interaction noisy.
- Activate edit with a single click. While using a double-click may not be totally unexpected (since it looks like an Excel spreadsheet), a single click is easier to perform.
- Consider allowing extra space during editing either through a drop-down editor or by slightly enlarging the edit cell.
- As much as possible, mimic the normal conventions of cell navigation that users will already be familiar with (e.g., in Microsoft Excel).

Group Edit

As mentioned before, it is a good idea to keep the differences between the edit mode and the display mode as minimal as possible. In fact, it is a good idea to minimize modes where possible. In honor of this principle, a former manager of mine sported a vanity plate with the phrase "NOMODES". However, modes cannot be avoided altogether, as they do provide necessary context for completing specific tasks.

If you want to keep the display of items on the page as uncluttered as possible while still supporting editing, consider using a single mechanism to enter a special editing mode: **Group Edit**.

On the iPhone's home screen, the icons are normally locked down. However, there is a way to switch into a special **Group Edit** mode that allows you to rearrange the icon's positions by drag and drop. You enter the mode by pressing down continuously on an icon until the editing mode is turned on (Figure 1-13).

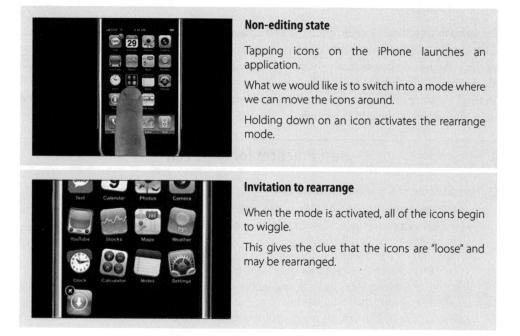

Non-editing state

Tapping icons on the iPhone launches an application.

What we would like is to switch into a mode where we can move the icons around.

Holding down on an icon activates the rearrange mode.

Invitation to rearrange

When the mode is activated, all of the icons begin to wiggle.

This gives the clue that the icons are "loose" and may be rearranged.

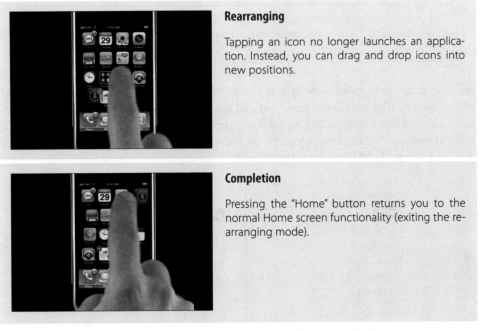

Rearranging

Tapping an icon no longer launches an application. Instead, you can drag and drop icons into new positions.

Completion

Pressing the "Home" button returns you to the normal Home screen functionality (exiting the rearranging mode).

Figure 1-13. *The iPhone has a special mode for rearranging applications on the home page—pressing and holding down on an icon places all the applications in "wiggly mode"*

Considerations

The Apple technique signifies that we have entered a special editing mode. When the icons become "wiggly," it is not a large intuitive leap that the icons have become loose and thus we can rearrange them.

Discoverability

Admittedly, the feature is not very discoverable. But it can be argued that it is straightforward once discovered. However, pressing the home button deactivates the rearranging mode. This really should operate more like a toggle. A better way to exit the "wiggly" mode would be to press and hold down on a wiggly icon. It follows the idea that you are pushing the icon back into its fixed place. Since deactivation is not the same mechanism as activation, it is a little hard to figure out how to go back into the normal display mode.

── Tip ──────────────────────────────

Activation and deactivation should normally follow the same interaction style. This makes it easy to discover the inverse action. This is a principle we call *Symmetry of Interaction*.

Another example of group editing is in the 37 Signals product, Basecamp (Figure 1-14). When sharing files with Basecamp, you can organize them into various categories. The categories are like folders. Clicking on a category link shows all the files in that "folder." What if you want to delete a category? Or rename it? At the top of the category section there is a single "Edit" link that turns on editing for the whole area.

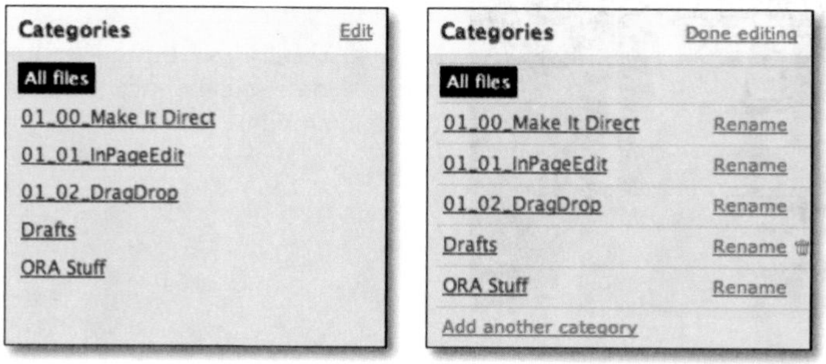

Figure 1-14. *37 Signals Basecamp provides a way to toggle a set of items into edit mode*

Once the **Group Edit** mode is entered, you can add another category, rename an existing category, or delete empty categories. Notice the "Edit" link toggled to read "Done Editing". Clicking this link exits the group-editing mode.

── Tip ──────────────────────────────

Switching between edit modes should happen instantaneously. There is no point in making the user wait on an animation to finish before he can start editing.

Discoverability versus readability

The advantage of providing a toggling edit mode is that it keeps the display uncluttered with the editing scaffolding. The disadvantage is that it is less discoverable. This tension between discoverability versus readability is common and must be balanced by the needs of the user.

Symmetry of Interaction

Unlike the iPhone example, you turn off editing in the same manner and location that you switched it on. The "Done Editing" link is in the same spot as the "Edit" link was. Since both are hyperlinks, they have the same interaction style. Interactions should be symmetrical wherever possible.

Module Configuration

Popular portal sites like Yahoo! and Google's interactive home page display specific content modules (e.g., Top Stories).

Module Configuration is a common pattern on these types of sites. Instead of modifying modules on a separate page, the sites provide ways to directly configure the amount and type of content that shows in each module. The My Yahoo! home page provides an "Edit" link that allows for **Module Configuration** (Figure 1-15).

Non-configuration state

A news module contains top news stories. Each module also has an "Edit" link.

Invitation to configure

The "Edit" link is the invitation to edit.

Activating edit slides in a mini-configuration panel in context with the news stories.

Configuration

The mini-form allows you to change the title and the number of stories that show. You can save the changes with the "Save" button. The "Close Edit" link forms a symmetrical interaction for edit activation and deactivation. However, there is ambiguity: does "Close Edit" do the same operation as "Save"?

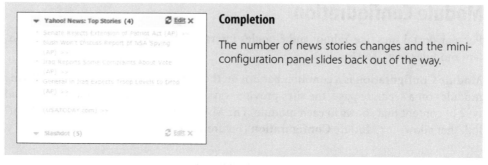

Completion

The number of news stories changes and the mini-configuration panel slides back out of the way.

Figure 1-15. *Configuring modules on the My Yahoo! page can be done directly in place*

Considerations

There are some issues to consider when using **Module Configuration**.

Visual noise

Putting edit links on each module can be visually noisy. An alternative approach is to use the **Group Edit** pattern (as we saw in Figure 1-14) to place an edit link at the page level that turns on edit links for each module. When the "Done Editing" link is clicked, the links for each module are hidden. Again the trade-off is between visual noise and discoverability.

Best Practices for Group Edit and Module Configuration

Here are some best practices to keep in mind:

- Use an edit toggle when there are a number of items to edit and showing edit scaffolding would make the display visually noisy.
- Make activation and deactivation as similar as possible (Symmetry of Interaction). Switching in and out of an editing mode should operate more like a toggle.
- Provide inline edit configuration for modules when configuration is an important feature.
- Provide a way to turn configuration on/off globally for module configuration when this is secondary to content display.

Guidelines for Choosing Specific Editing Patterns

In-Page Edit provides a powerful way to make interfaces direct. Here are some general guidelines to think about when choosing an editing pattern:

- Whenever you have a single field on the page that needs editing, consider using the **Single-Field Inline Edit**.

- For multiple fields or more complex editing, use the **Multi-Field Inline Edit**.

- If you don't need inline context while editing, or the editing is something that demands the user's full attention, use **Overlay Edit**.

- For grid editing, follow the pattern **Table Edit**.

- When dealing with multiple items on a page, **Group Edit** provides a way to balance between visual noise and discoverability.

- When providing direct configuring to modules, use the **Module Configuration** pattern.

Chapter 2

Drag and Drop

One of the great innovations that the Macintosh brought to the world in 1984 was **Drag and Drop**. Influenced by the graphical user interface work on Xerox PARC's Star Information System and subsequent lessons learned from the Apple Lisa, the Macintosh team invented drag and drop as an easy way to move, copy, and delete files on the user's desktop.

It was quite a while before drag and drop made its way to the Web in any serious application. In 2000, a small startup, HalfBrain,* launched a web-based presentation application, BrainMatter. It was written entirely in DHTML and used drag and drop as an integral part of its interface.

Drag and drop showed up again with another small startup, Oddpost,† when it launched a web-based mail application (Figure 2-1) that allowed users to drag and drop messages between folders.

---

* HalfBrain also created a full spreadsheet application written in DHTML prior to this. It included many of the features of Microsoft Excel.

† Some of the developers at Oddpost actually came from HalfBrain. Yahoo! later purchased Oddpost's mail application to form the basis for the current Yahoo! Mail product.

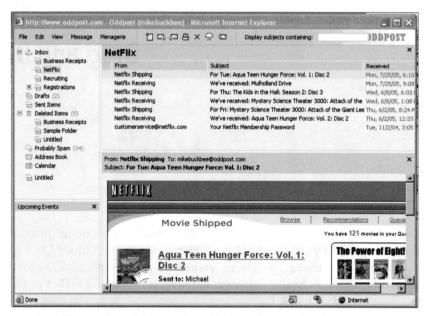

Figure 2-1. *The Oddpost web mail client performed like a desktop mail application and included drag and drop as a key feature*

The biggest hindrance was the difficulty in saving the user's state after a drag was completed without refreshing the page. It was possible, but the underlying technology was not consistent across all browsers. Now that the technologies underlying Ajax[*] have become widely known and a full complement of browsers support these techniques, **Drag and Drop** has become a more familiar idiom on the Web.

Interesting Moments

At first blush, drag and drop seems simple. Just grab an object and drop it somewhere. But, as always, the devil is in the details. There are a number of individual states at which interaction is possible. We call these microstates *interesting moments:*[†]

- How will users know what is draggable?

- What does it mean to drag and drop an object?

- Where can you drop an object, and where is it not valid to drop an object?

- What visual affordance will be used to indicate draggability?

---

[*] Jesse James Garrett, founder of Adaptive Path, originally defined the term *Ajax* as "Asynchronous JavaScript and XML." However, it generally means being able to retrieve information or save state without refreshing the page—an integral ability for any rich interaction.

[†] Bill Scott, author of this book, originally called these *interaction events*. Eric Miraglia, a former colleague of his at Yahoo!, coined the more colorful term *interesting moments*.

- During drag, how will valid and invalid drop targets be signified?
- Do you drag the actual object?
- Or do you drag just a ghost of the object?
- Or is it a thumbnail representation that gets dragged?
- What visual feedback should be used during the drag and drop interaction?

What makes it challenging is that there are a lot of events during drag and drop that can be used as opportunities for feedback to the user. Additionally, there are a number of elements on the page that can participate as actors in this feedback loop.

The Events

There are at least 15 events available for cueing the user during a drag and drop interaction:

Page Load
> Before any interaction occurs, you can pre-signify the availability of drag and drop. For example, you could display a tip on the page to indicate draggability.

Mouse Hover
> The mouse pointer hovers over an object that is draggable.

Mouse Down
> The user holds down the mouse button on the draggable object.

Drag Initiated
> After the mouse drag starts (usually some threshold—3 pixels).

Drag Leaves Original Location
> After the drag object is pulled from its location or object that contains it.

Drag Re-Enters Original Location
> When the object re-enters the original location.

Drag Enters Valid Target
> Dragging over a valid drop target.

Drag Exits Valid Target
> Dragging back out of a valid drop target.

Drag Enters Specific Invalid Target
> Dragging over an invalid drop target.

Drag Is Over No Specific Target
> Dragging over neither a valid or invalid target. Do you treat all areas outside of valid targets as invalid?

Drag Hovers Over Valid Target
> User pauses over the valid target without dropping the object. This is usually when a spring loaded drop target can open up. For example, drag over a folder and pause, the folder opens revealing a new area to drag into.

Drag Hovers Over Invalid Target

User pauses over an invalid target without dropping the object. Do you care? Will you want additional feedback as to why it is not a valid target?

Drop Accepted

Drop occurs over a valid target and drop has been accepted.

Drop Rejected

Drop occurs over an invalid target and drop has been rejected. Do you zoom back the dropped object?

Drop on Parent Container

Is the place where the object was dragged from special? Usually this is not the case, but it may carry special meaning in some contexts.

The Actors

During each event you can visually manipulate a number of *actors*. The page elements available include:

- Page (e.g., static messaging on the page)
- Cursor
- Tool Tip
- Drag Object (or some portion of the drag object, e.g., title area of a module)
- Drag Object's Parent Container
- Drop Target

Interesting Moments Grid

That's 15 events times 6 actors. That means there are 90 possible interesting moments—each requiring a decision involving an almost unlimited number of style and timing choices.

You can pull all this together into a simple interesting moments grid for **Drag and Drop**. Figure 2-2 shows an interesting moments grid for My Yahoo!.

----- **Tip** ---

You can use an interesting moments grid to capture any complex interaction.

The grid is a handy tool for planning out interesting moments during a drag and drop interaction. It serves as a checklist to make sure there are no "holes" in the interaction. Just place the actors along the lefthand side and the moments along the top. In the grid intersections, place the desired behaviors.

	Page Generation	Mouse Hover	Drag Initiated	Drag over Valid	Drag over Invalid	Drag over Original	Drop Accepted	Drop Rejected	Drop on Original
Page Content	Hint	N/A	N/A	N/A	N/A	N/A	N/A	N/A	N/A
Cursor	Normal	Move Cursor	Move Cursor	Move Cursor	Move Cursor	Move Cursor	Normal	Normal	Normal
Drag Object	Normal	Normal	Reduced Opacity & Tracking	Reduced Opacity & Tracking	Reduced Opacity & Tracking + Invalid Badge	Reduced Opacity & Tracking	2. Modules animates into the area just below insertion bar 3. Module comes to rest in new area 4. Modules slide up in a self-healing transition to close hole	Normal Opacity + Zoom Back to Original	Normal Opacity + Zoom Back to Original
Orig Location	Normal	Normal	Hole Opens	Hole Remains	Hole Remains	Hole Remains	Hole Remains	Hole refilled with drag object	Hole refilled with drag object
Drop Target	Normal	Normal	Normal	Insertion Bar	N/A	N/A	1. Insertion Bar Removed	N/A	N/A

Figure 2-2. *A simplified interesting moments grid for the original My Yahoo! drag and drop design;* it *provided a way to capture the complexities of drag and drop into a single page*

Purpose of Drag and Drop

Drag and drop can be a powerful idiom if used correctly. Specifically it is useful for:

Drag and Drop Module
Rearranging modules on a page.

Drag and Drop List
Rearranging lists.

Drag and Drop Object
Changing relationships between objects.

Drag and Drop Action
Invoking actions on a dropped object.

Drag and Drop Collection
Maintaining collections through drag and drop.

---

* A template for the interesting moments grid can be found at *http://designingwebinterfaces.com/resources/ interestingmomentsgrid.xls.*

Drag and Drop Module

One of the most useful purposes of drag and drop is to allow the user to directly place objects where she wants them on the page. A typical pattern is **Drag and Drop Modules** on a page. Netvibes provides a good example of this interaction pattern (Figure 2-3).

Normal display style

Modules are displayed without an explicit cue for drag and drop.

Invitation to drag

Moving the mouse to a module's header changes the cursor to indicate that the item is draggable.

Dragging

The module being moved is dragged directly. A ripped-out "hole" is exposed where the module was dragged from.

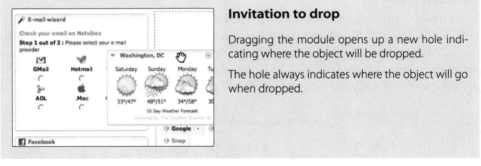

Invitation to drop

Dragging the module opens up a new hole indicating where the object will be dropped.

The hole always indicates where the object will go when dropped.

Figure 2-3. *Netvibes allows modules to be arranged directly via drag and drop; the hole cues what will happen when a module is dropped*

Considerations

Netvibes allows its modules to be rearranged with drag and drop. A number of interesting moments decide the specific interaction style for this site. Figure 2-4 shows the interesting moments grid for Netvibes.

	Mouse Hover	Mouse Down	Drag Initiated	Drag Hovers over Valid Target*	Drop Accepted
Cursor	Change to a hand with finger pointing.*	Change to a hand/move cursor.	No change.*		Cursor returns to normal style.
Dragged Module			Module is dragged with full opacity.		Dragged version is removed.
Dragged Modules Original Location			Hole is shown as a red dashed outline.		Hole is removed.
Drop Target				Hole (red dashed outline) is moved to the new drop spot. Other modules shift to close prior hole.	Module is placed in the new location.
Notes	* A better approach might be to signal draggability with the hand/move cursor.		* On drag initiated, it would be better to switch to a hand that looks like a grab.	* Triggers when the dragged module's title bar has moved past the midpoint of the dragged over module's header.	

Figure 2-4. *Interesting moments grid for Netvibes: there are 20 possible moments of interaction; Netvibes specifically handles 9 of these moments*

While dragging, it is important to make it clear what will happen when the user drops the dragged object. There are two common approaches to targeting a drop:

- Placeholder target
- Insertion target

Placeholder target

Netvibes uses a placeholder (hole with dashed outline) as the drop target. The idea (illustrated in Figure 2-5) is to always position a hole in the spot where the drop would occur. When module ① starts dragging, it gets "ripped" out of the spot. In its place is the placeholder target (dashed outline). As ① gets dragged to the spot between ③ and ④, the placeholder target jumps to fill in this spot as ④ moves out of the way.

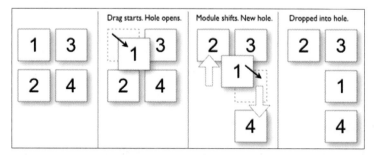

Figure 2-5. *A placeholder target always shows where the dragged module will end after the drop; module 1 is being dragged from the upper right to the position between modules 3 and 4*

The hole serves as a placeholder and always marks the spot that the dragged module will land when dropped. It also previews what the page will look like (in relation to the other modules) if the drop occurs there. For module drag and drop, the other modules only slide up or down within a vertical column to make room for the dragged module.

One complaint with using placeholder targets is that the page content jumps around a lot during the drag. This makes the interaction noisier and can make it harder to understand what is actually happening. This issue is compounded when modules look similar. The user starts dragging the modules around and quickly gets confused about what just got moved. One way to resolve this is to provide a quick animated transition as the modules move. It is important, however, that any animated transitions not get in the way of the normal interaction. In Chapter 11, we will discuss timing of transitions in detail.

There is a point in Figure 2-5 where the placeholder shifts to a new location. What determines placeholder targeting? In other words, what determines where the user is intending to place the dragged object? The position of the mouse, the boundary of the dragged object, and the boundary of the dragged-over object can all be used to choose the module's new location.

Boundary-based placement. Since most sites that use placeholder targeting drag the module in its original size, targeting is determined by the boundaries of the dragged object and the boundaries of the dragged-over object. The mouse position is usually ignored because modules are only draggable in the title (a small region). Both Netvibes and iGoogle take the boundary-based approach. But, interestingly, they calculate the position of their placeholders differently.

In Netvibes, the placeholder changes position only after the dragged module's title bar has moved beyond the dragged-over module's title bar. In practice, this means if you are moving a small module to be positioned above a large module, you have to move it to the very top of the large module. In Figure 2-6 you have to drag the small "To Do List" module all the way to the top of the "Blog Directory" module before the placeholder changes position.

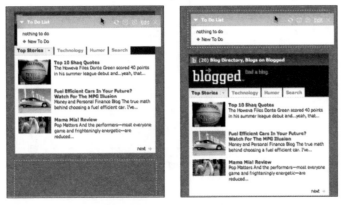

Figure 2-6. *In Netvibes, dragging a small module to be placed above a large module requires dragging a large distance; the "To Do List" has to be dragged to the top of the "Blog Directory" module*

In contrast, moving the small module below the large module actually requires less drag distance since you only have to get the title bar of the small module below the title bar of the large module (Figure 2-7).

Figure 2-7. *Dragging a small module below a large module requires a smaller drag distance; since the targeting is based on the header of the dragged-over module, the drag distance in this scenario is less than in the previous figure*

This approach to boundary-based drop targeting is non-symmetrical in the drag distance when dragging modules up versus dragging modules down (Figure 2-8).

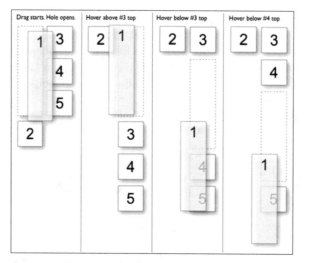

Figure 2-8. *The Netvibes approach requires the dragged object's title to be placed above or below a module before the placement position changes; this results in inconsistent drag distances*

A more desirable approach is that taken by iGoogle. Instead of basing the drag on the *title bar*, iGoogle calculates the placeholder targeting on the dragged-over object's *midpoint*. In Figure 2-9, the stock market module is very large (the module just above the moon phase module).

Figure 2-9. *When dragging a module downward, iGoogle moves the placeholder when the bottom of the dragged module crosses the midpoint of the object being dragged over; the distance to accomplish a move is less than in the Netvibes approach*

With the Netvibes approach, you would have to drag the stock module's title below the moon phase module's title. iGoogle instead moves the placeholder when the *bottom* of the dragged module (stock module) crosses the midpoint of the dragged over module (moon phase module).

What happens when we head the other way? When we drag the stock module up to place it above the moon phase module, iGoogle moves the placeholder when the *top* of the stock module crosses the midpoint of the moon phase module (Figure 2-10).

Figure 2-10. *When dragging a module upward, iGoogle moves the placeholder when the top of the dragged module crosses the midpoint of the object being dragged over; dragging modules up or down requires the same effort, unlike in the Netvibes example*

As Figure 2-11 illustrates, module ① is dragged from the first column to the second column, the placeholder moves above module ③. As module ① is dragged downward, the placeholder moves below ③ and ④ as the bottom of module ① crosses their midpoints.

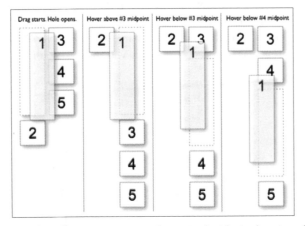

Figure 2-11. *To create the best drag experience, use the original midpoint location of the module being dragged over to determine where to drop the dragged module: module 1 is being dragged into the position just below module 4*

The net result is that the iGoogle approach feels more responsive and requires less mouse movement to position modules. Figure 2-12 shows the interesting moments grid for the iGoogle drag and drop interaction.

	Mouse Hover	Mouse Down	Drag Initiated	Drag Hovers over Valid Target*	Drop Accepted
Cursor	Change to a hand pointer.	Change to normal style.*			
Dragged Module			Slightly transparent.		Dragged module removed.
Dragged Modules Original Location			Hole is shown as a gray, thick, dashed outline.		Hole is removed.
Drop Target				Hole (gray, thick, dashed outline) is moved to the new drop spot. Other modules shift to close prior hole.	Module is placed in the new location.
Notes		* A better approach is to switch to a hand that looks like it grabbed the module.	* Drag initiaties instantly on mouse down.	* Triggers when the mid-point of the dragged object enters a valid drop target.	

Figure 2-12. *Interesting moments grid for iGoogle: as in the Netvibes grid, there are 20 possible moments of interaction; iGoogle specifically handles 8 of these moments*

Insertion target

Placeholder positioning is a common approach, but it is not the only way to indicate drop targeting. An alternate approach is to keep the page as stable as possible and only move around an insertion target (usually an insertion bar). A previous version of My Yahoo! used the insertion bar approach as the dragged module was moved around (see Figure 2-13).

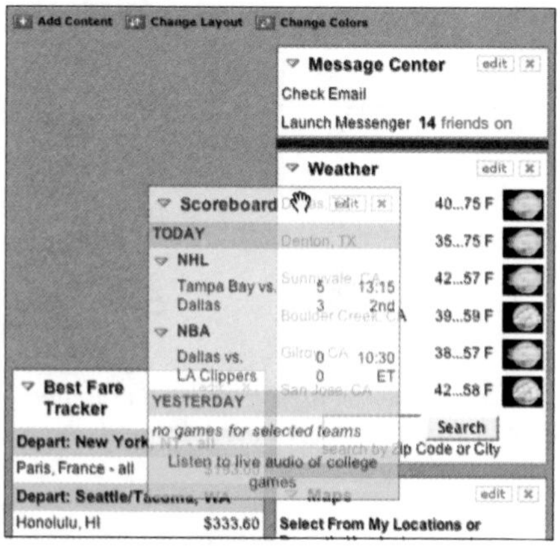

Figure 2-13. *My Yahoo! uses the insertion bar approach*

While the module is dragged, the page remains stable. No modules move around. Instead an insertion bar marks where the module will be placed when dropped.

This technique is illustrated in Figure 2-14. When module ① is dragged to the position between ③ and ④, an insertion bar is placed there. This indicates that if ① is dropped, then ④ will slide down to open up the drop spot.

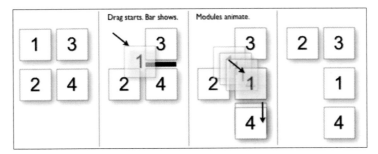

Figure 2-14. *Using an insertion bar keeps the page stable during dragging and makes it clear how things get rearranged when the module is dropped*

Unlike with the placeholder target, the dragged module ① is usually represented with a slightly transparent version of the module (also known as *ghosting*). This is the approach shown in Figure 2-13 in an earlier version of My Yahoo!. In the most current version, full-size module dragging has been replaced with a thumbnail representation (the small gray outline being dragged in Figure 2-15). This is somewhat unfortunate since the small gray outline is not very visible.

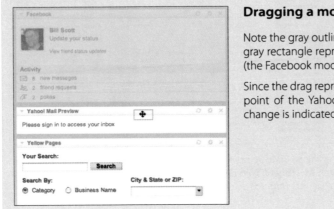

Dragging a module down

Note the gray outline being dragged. The small gray rectangle represents the dragged module (the Facebook module).

Since the drag representation is above the midpoint of the Yahoo! Mail Preview module, no change is indicated for a drop.

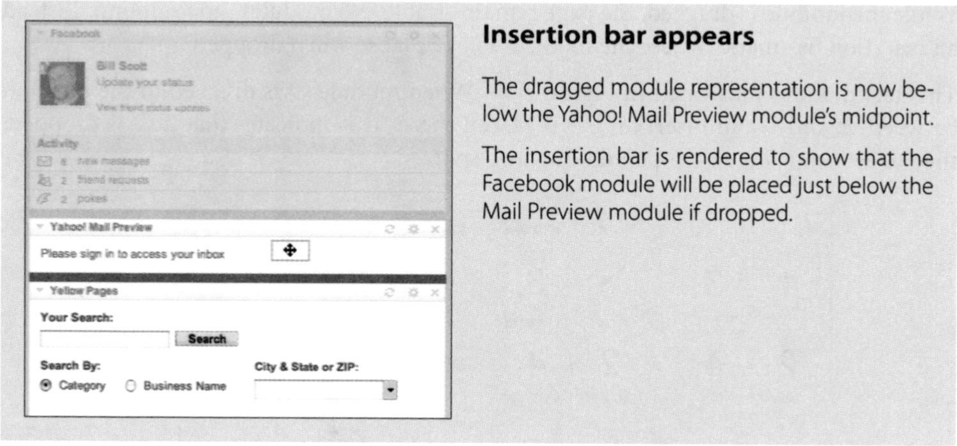

Insertion bar appears

The dragged module representation is now below the Yahoo! Mail Preview module's midpoint.

The insertion bar is rendered to show that the Facebook module will be placed just below the Mail Preview module if dropped.

Figure 2-15. *My Yahoo! uses a small gray rectangle to represent the dragged module*

As you can see in Figure 2-16, the My Yahoo! page makes different decisions about how drag and drop modules are implemented as compared to Netvibes (Figure 2-4) and iGoogle (Figure 2-12).

	Mouse Hover	Mouse Down*	Drag Initiated	Drag Hovers over Valid Target	Drag Hovers over Invalid Target	Drop Accepted	Drop Rejected	Drop On Parent Container
Cursor	Change to a hand pointer.					Change back to normal style cursor.	Change back to normal style cursor.	Change back to normal style cursor.
Dragged Module			Thumbnail represents dragged module. (small, gray outline.)			Thumbnail removed.	Thumbnail removed by zooming back to original location.	Thumbnail removed by zooming back to original location.
Dragged Module's Original Location			Original module shown dimmed at original location.			Modules get rearranged.	Original module is brightened back to original opacity.	
Drop Target (Insertion Bar)			No insertion bar shown until valid drop target available.	Insertion bar shown where module can be dropped.	Insertion bar removed.	Module is placed in the new location, modules re-arrange.	No insertion bar was visible.	No insertion bar was visible.
Notes		* If mouse is held down for more than one second, Drag is initiated.	* Drag is also initiated if the mouse is moved more than 3 pixels after the mouse down.	Triggers when the mid-point of the dragged object enters a valid drop target.				

Figure 2-16. *My Yahoo! uses 15 of the possible 32 moments to interact with the user during drag and drop; the biggest difference between My Yahoo!, Netvibes, and iGoogle is the insertion bar placement—another subtle difference is how drag gets initiated*

Drag distance

Dragging the thumbnail around does have other issues. Since the object being dragged is small, it does not intersect a large area. It requires moving the small thumbnail directly to the place it will be dropped. With iGoogle, the complete module is dragged. Since the module will always be larger than the thumbnail, it intersects a drop target with much less movement. The result is a shorter drag distance to accomplish a move.

> —— **Tip** ——————————————————————————————
>
> Keep in mind that **Drag and Drop** takes additional mouse dexterity. If possible, shorten the necessary drag distance to target a drop.

Drag rendering

How should the dragged object be represented? Should it be rendered with a slight transparency (ghost)? Or should it be shown fully opaque? Should a thumbnail representation be used instead?

As shown earlier, My Yahoo! uses a small gray rectangle to represent a module (Figure 2-15). Netvibes represents the dragged module in full size as opaque (shown back in Figure 2-3), while iGoogle uses partial transparency (Figure 2-17). The transparency (ghosting) effect communicates that the object being dragged is actually a representation of the dragged object. It also keeps more of the page visible, thus giving a clearer picture of the final result of a drop.

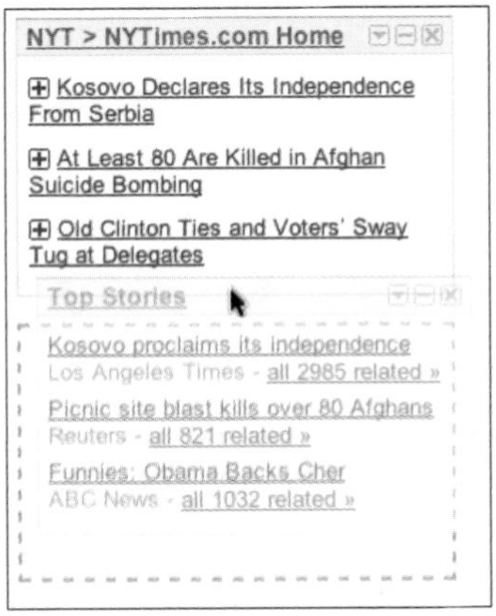

Figure 2-17. *On iGoogle the dragged module Top Stories is given transparency to make it easier to see the page and to indicate that we are in a placement mode*

Ghosting the module also indicates that the module is in a special mode. It signals that the module has not been positioned; instead, it is in a transitional state.

Tip ——————————————————————————

For **Drag and Drop Modules**, use the module's midpoint to control the drop targeting.

Of the various approaches for **Drag and Drop Modules**, iGoogle combines the best approaches into a single interface:

Placeholder targeting
> Most explicit way to preview the effect.

Midpoint boundary
> Requires the least drag effort to move modules around.

Full-size module dragging
> Coupled with placeholder targeting and midpoint boundary detection, it means drag distances to complete a move are shorter.

Ghost rendering
> Emphasizes the page rather than the dragged object. Keeps the preview clear.

Best Practices for Drag and Drop Module

Here are some best practices to keep in mind:

- Use the placeholder approach when showing a clear preview during drag is important.
- Use the insertion bar approach when you want to avoid page jitter.
- Use the midpoint of the dragged object to determine drag position.
- Use a slightly transparent version of the object being dragged (ghost) instead of an opaque version.
- If you drag thumbnail representations, use the insertion bar targeting approach.

Drag and Drop List

Rearranging lists is very similar to rearranging modules on the page but with the added constraint of being in a single dimension (up/down or left/right). The **Drag and Drop List** pattern defines interactions for rearranging items in a list.

37 Signal's Backpackit allows to-do items to be rearranged with **Drag and Drop List** (Figure 2-18).

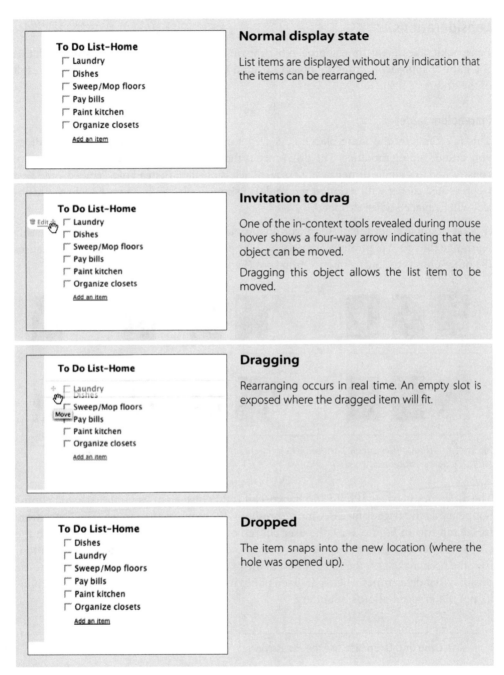

Normal display state

List items are displayed without any indication that the items can be rearranged.

Invitation to drag

One of the in-context tools revealed during mouse hover shows a four-way arrow indicating that the object can be moved.

Dragging this object allows the list item to be moved.

Dragging

Rearranging occurs in real time. An empty slot is exposed where the dragged item will fit.

Dropped

The item snaps into the new location (where the hole was opened up).

Figure 2-18. *Backpackit allows to-do lists to be rearranged directly via drag and drop*

Considerations

Backpackit takes a real-time approach to dragging items. Since the list is constrained, this is a natural approach to moving objects around in a list. You immediately see the result of the drag.

Placeholder target

This is essentially the same placeholder target approach we discussed earlier for dragging and dropping modules. The difference is that when moving an item in a list, we are constrained to a single dimension. Less feedback is needed. Instead of a "ripped-out" area (represented earlier with a dotted rectangle), a simple hole can be exposed where the object will be placed when dropped.

A good example from the desktop world is Apple's iPhoto. In a slideshow, you can easily rearrange the order of photos with drag and drop. Dragging the photo left or right causes the other photos to shuffle open a drop spot (Figure 2-19).

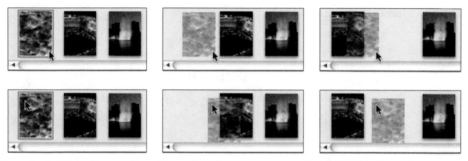

Figure 2-19. *iPhoto uses cursor position: when the cursor crosses a threshold (the edge of the next photo), a new position is opened up*

The difference between iPhoto and Backpackit is that instead of using the dragged photo's boundary as the trigger for crossing a threshold, iPhoto uses the mouse cursor position. In the top row of Figure 2-19, the user clicked on the right side of the photo. When the cursor crosses into the left edge of the next photo, a new space is opened. In the bottom row, the user clicked on the top left side of the photo. Notice in both cases it is the mouse position that determines when a dragged photo has moved into the space of another photo, not the dragged photo's boundary.

> ── **Tip** ────────────────────────────────
> In a **Drag and Drop List**, use the mouse position to control where the item will be dropped.

Insertion target

Just as with **Drag and Drop Modules**, placeholder targeting is not the only game in town. You can also use an insertion bar within a list to indicate where a dropped item will land. Netflix uses an *insertion target* when movies are dragged to a new location in a user's movie queue (Figure 2-20).

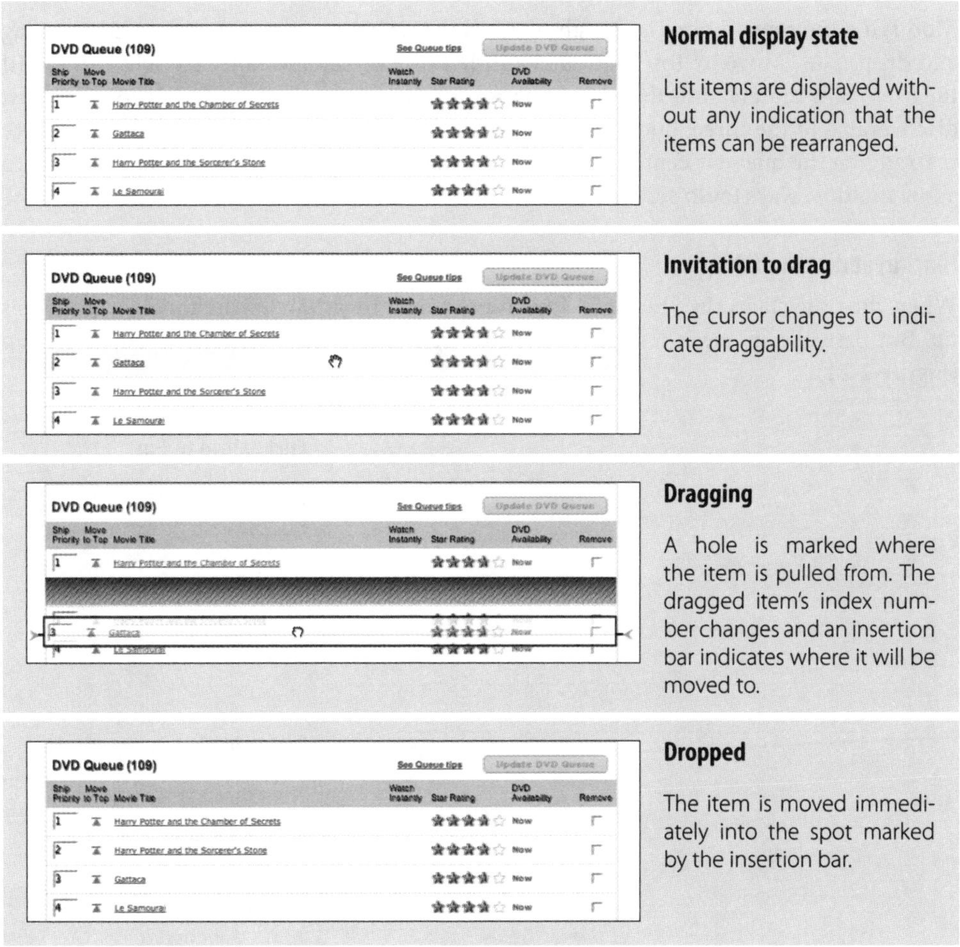

Normal display state

List items are displayed without any indication that the items can be rearranged.

Invitation to drag

The cursor changes to indicate draggability.

Dragging

A hole is marked where the item is pulled from. The dragged item's index number changes and an insertion bar indicates where it will be moved to.

Dropped

The item is moved immediately into the spot marked by the insertion bar.

Figure 2-20. *A Netflix queue can be rearranged via drag and drop*

The upside to this approach is that the list doesn't have to shuffle around during drag. The resulting experience is smoother than the Backpackit approach. The downside is that it is not as obvious where the movie is being positioned. The insertion bar appears under the ghosted item. The addition of the brackets on the left and right of the insertion bar is an attempt to make the targeting clearer.

Non–drag and drop alternative

Besides drag and drop, the Netflix queue actually supports two other ways to move objects around:

- Edit the row number and then press the "Update DVD Queue" button.
- Click the "Move to Top" icon to pop a movie to the top.

Modifying the row number is straightforward. It's a way to rearrange items without drag and drop. The "Move to Top" button is a little more direct and fairly straightforward (if the user really understands that this icon means "move to top"). Drag and drop is the least discoverable of the three, but it is the most direct, visual way to rearrange the list. Since rearranging the queue is central to the Netflix customer's satisfaction, it is appropriate to allow multiple ways to do so.

Hinting at drag and drop

When the user clicks the "Move to Top" button, Netflix animates the movie as it moves up. But first, the movie is jerked downward slightly and then spring-loaded to the top (Figure 2-21).

Click "Move to Top"

Clicking the "Move to Top" button starts the movie moving to the top.

Spring loaded

The movie does not immediately start moving up. Instead, it drops down and to the right slightly. This gives the feeling that the movie is being launched to the top.

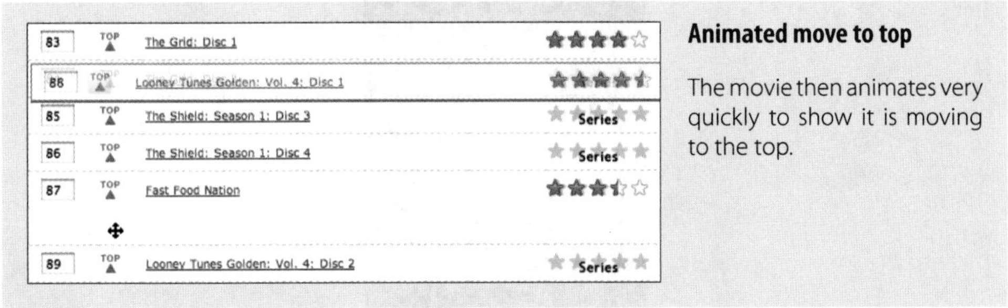

Animated move to top

The movie then animates very quickly to show it is moving to the top.

Figure 2-21. *When a movie is moved to the top with the "Move to Top" button, the movie jerks down slightly, then springs to the top*

The combination of the downward jerk and then the quick animation to the top gives a subtle clue that the object is draggable. This is also an interesting moment to advertise drag and drop. After the move to top completes, a simple tip could appear to invite users to drag and drop. The tip should probably be shown only once, or there should be a way to turn it off. Providing an invitation within a familiar idiom is a good way to lead users to the new idiom.

Tip

If drag and drop is a secondary way to perform a task, use the completion of the familiar task as an opportunity invite the user to drag and drop the next time.

Drag lens

Drag and drop works well when a list is short or the items are all visible on the page. But when the list is long, drag and drop becomes painful. Providing alternative ways to rearrange is one way to get around this issue. Another is to provide a *drag lens* while dragging.

A drag lens provides a view into a different part of the list that can serve as a shortcut target. It could be a fixed area that is always visible, or it could be a miniature view of the list that provides more rows for targeting. The lens will be made visible only during dragging. A good example of this is dragging the insertion bar while editing text on the iPhone (Figure 2-22).

Figure 2-22. *The iPhone provides a drag magnifier lens that makes it easier to position the cursor*

Best Practices for Drag and Drop List

Here are some best practices to keep in mind:

- If possible, drag the items in a list in real time using the placeholder target approach.
- Use the mouse position for drag target positioning.
- If the goal is speed of dragging or if dragged items are large, consider using the insertion target approach, as rendering an insertion bar is inexpensive compared to dynamically rearranging the list.
- Since drag and drop in lists is not easily discoverable, consider providing an alternate way to rearrange the list.
- When the user rearranges the list with an alternate method, use that moment for a one-time advertisement for drag and drop.

Drag and Drop Object

Another common use for drag and drop is to change relationships between objects. This is appropriate when the relationships can be represented visually. Drag and drop as a means of visually manipulating relationships is a powerful tool.

Cogmap is a wiki for organizational charts. **Drag and Drop Object** is used to rearrange members of the organization (Figure 2-23).

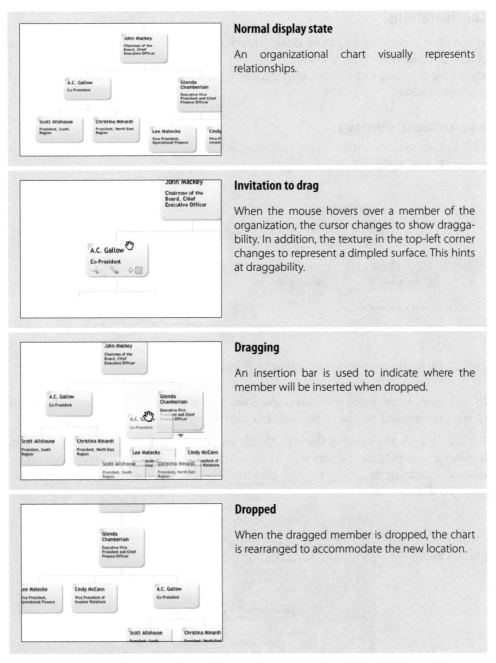

Normal display state

An organizational chart visually represents relationships.

Invitation to drag

When the mouse hovers over a member of the organization, the cursor changes to show draggability. In addition, the texture in the top-left corner changes to represent a dimpled surface. This hints at draggability.

Dragging

An insertion bar is used to indicate where the member will be inserted when dropped.

Dropped

When the dragged member is dropped, the chart is rearranged to accommodate the new location.

Figure 2-23. *Cogmap allows organizational charts to be rearranged on the fly with drag and drop*

Considerations

When object relationships can be clearly represented visually, drag and drop is a natural choice to make these type of changes. Cogmap uses the target insertion approach. This allows the dragging to be nondistracting, since the chart does not have to be disturbed during targeting.

Drag feedback: Highlighting

Bubbl.us, an online mind-mapping tool, simply highlights the node that will be the new parent (Figure 2-24).

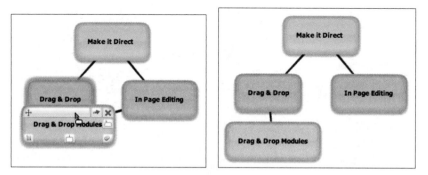

Figure 2-24. Bubbl.us provides a visual indication of which node the dropped node will attach itself to

In both cases, immediate preview is avoided since it is difficult to render the relationships in real time without becoming unnecessarily distracting.

Looking outside the world of the Web, the desktop application Mind Manager also uses highlighting to indicate the parent in which insertion will occur. In addition, it provides insertion targeting to give a preview of where the employee will be positioned once dropped (Figure 2-25).

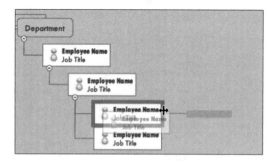

Figure 2-25. Mind Manager is a desktop tool that uses a combination of insertion targeting plus a clear preview of the drop

Drag feedback: Dragged object versus drop target

As we mentioned at the beginning of this chapter, one of the first serious uses for drag and drop was in the Oddpost web mail application. Oddpost was eventually acquired by Yahoo! and is now the Yahoo! Mail application.

Yahoo! Mail uses drag and drop objects for organizing email messages into folders (Figure 2-26).

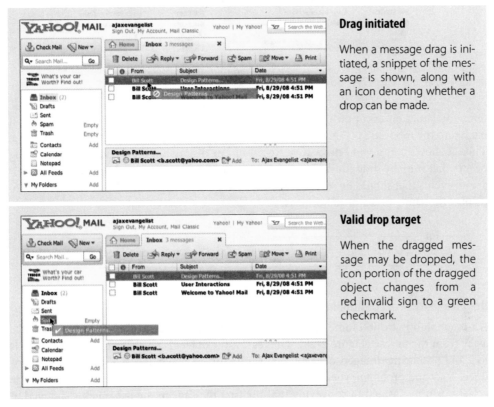

Drag initiated

When a message drag is initiated, a snippet of the message is shown, along with an icon denoting whether a drop can be made.

Valid drop target

When the dragged message may be dropped, the icon portion of the dragged object changes from a red invalid sign to a green checkmark.

Figure 2-26. *Yahoo! Mail allows messages to be dragged to folders*

Instead of signaling that a drop is valid or invalid by changing the visual appearance of the area dragged over, Yahoo! Mail shows validity through the dragged object. When a drop will be invalid (Figure 2-27, left):

- The dragged object's icon becomes a red invalid sign.
- If over an invalid folder, the folder is highlighted as well.

When a drop will be valid (Figure 2-27, right):

- The dragged object's icon changes to a green checkmark.
- The drop target highlights.

Another approach is to signal *both* validity and location in the drop target itself. In this case you would highlight the valid drop target when it is dragged over and *not* highlight the drop target if it is invalid. In Yahoo! Mail's interaction, the signaling of validity and where it can be dropped are kept separate. This allows a drag to indicate that a target is a drop target, just not valid for the current object being dragged.*

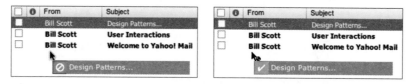

Figure 2-27. *Yahoo! Mail mistakenly shows a valid indicator instead of an invalid indicator for a message when it is dragged back over the inbox*

One odd situation occurs when you first start dragging a message and then later drag it back into the inbox area (Figure 2-27). At first it shows the inbox as an invalid drop area. Then it shows it as a valid drop area. Recall in our discussion on the various interesting events that initially dragging over your "home area" and then later dragging back into it are all events that should be considered during drag and drop. Here the interface needs to display the same indicator in both cases.

Tip ──

Feedback during dragging is key to providing a clear **Drag and Drop Object** interaction.

Drag feedback: Drag positioning

Another slightly troublesome approach is positioning the dragged object some distance away from the mouse (Figure 2-28). The reason the object is positioned in this manner is to avoid obscuring dragged-over folders. While this may alleviate that problem, it introduces a second problem: when you initiate the drag, the dragged message jumps into the offset position. Instead of conveying that the first message in the list is being dragged, it feels like the second message in the list is being dragged (Figure 2-28, bottom).

Before drag initiated

The user is about to drag the first message in the list.

---

* For example, while a contact may be dragged into the Contacts folder, a message may not. In either situation, the Contacts folder will highlight. However, the dragged contact will show a green checkmark, while the dragged message will show a red invalid sign.

Offset drop object

The dragged object appears below the midpoint of the second message after drag is initiated. Targeting is confusing—is it the mouse or the object that determines targeting?

Figure 2-28. *By offsetting the drag object a large distance from the cursor, the message feels disjointed from the actual object being dragged; in fact, it looks like it is closer to the second message in the list instead of the first message actually being dragged*

Drag feedback: Drag start

In Yahoo! Mail, message dragging is initiated when the mouse is dragged about four or five pixels (Figure 2-29).

Figure 2-29. *Yahoo! Mail requires the user to drag four or five pixels to initiate a drag (notice the cursor is at the top of the "B" and has to be dragged 2/3 of the way down to start the drag); this gives the impression that the message is stuck and not easy to drag. Reducing this value will make messages feel easier to drag*

A good rule of thumb on drag initiation comes from the Apple Human Interface Guidelines:

> *Your application should provide drag feedback as soon as the user drags an item at least three pixels. If a user holds the mouse button down on an object or selected text, it should become draggable immediately and stay draggable as long as the mouse remains down.*[*]

It might seem like a small nit, but there is quite a difference between starting a drag after three pixels of movement versus four or five pixels. The larger value makes the object feel hard to pull out of its slot to start dragging. On the flip side, starting a drag with too small a value can cause drag to initiate accidentally, usually resulting in the interface feeling too finicky.

―― **Tip** ――
Start a drag when the object is dragged three pixels or the mouse is held down for half a second.

―――――――――――――――――――――――――――――――――――

* See *http://tinyurl.com/5aqd4k* for the Apple Human Interface Guideline on drag feedback.

The only part of the Apple guideline that could be quibbled with is whether to start drag mode immediately on mouse down or wait about a half-second to start. Why not initiate the drag immediately? Certain devices, like pen input, are not as precise as mouse input. If you allow an object to be dragged and that object has other controls (like hyperlinks), you will want to allow the user to start a drag even if he clicks down over some element within the object (like a hyperlink). You will also want to allow him to just click the hyperlink and not have a drag accidentally initiate. Moving into drag mode immediately will preclude the ability to disambiguate between a click on an item within the object versus a drag start on the object itself.

Best Practices for Drag and Drop Object

Here are some best practices to keep in mind:

- If objects are represented in a complex visual relationship, use insertion targeting to indicate drop location (minimizes disturbing the page during drag).
- For parent/child relationships, highlight the parent as well to indicate drop location.
- If possible, reveal drag affordances on mouse hover to indicate draggability.
- Initiate drag when the mouse is dragged three pixels or if the mouse is held down for at least half a second.
- Position dragged objects directly in sync with the cursor. Offsetting will make the drag feel disjointed.
- When hovering over a draggable object, change the cursor to indicate draggability.

Drag and Drop Action

Drag and drop is also useful for invoking an action or actions on a dropped object. The **Drag and Drop Action** is a common pattern. Its most familiar example is dropping an item in the trash to perform the delete action.

Normally uploading files to a web application includes pressing the upload button and browsing for a photo. This process is repeated for each photo.

When Yahoo! Photos was relaunched in 2006, it included a drag and drop upload feature. It allowed the user to drag photos directly into the upload page. The drop signified the upload action (Figure 2-30).

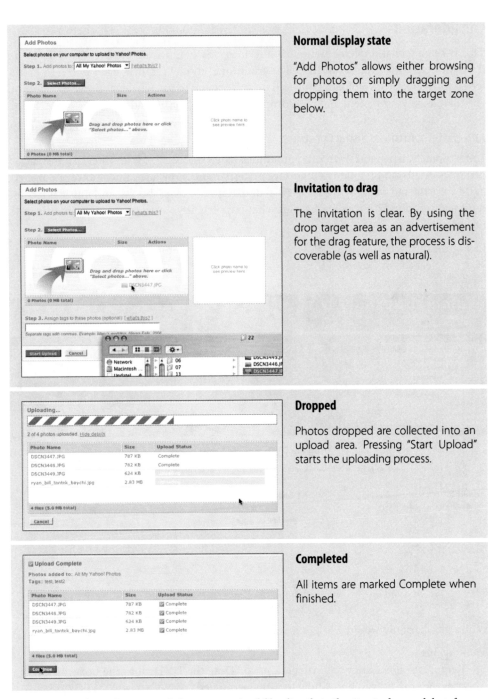

Normal display state

"Add Photos" allows either browsing for photos or simply dragging and dropping them into the target zone below.

Invitation to drag

The invitation is clear. By using the drop target area as an advertisement for the drag feature, the process is discoverable (as well as natural).

Dropped

Photos dropped are collected into an upload area. Pressing "Start Upload" starts the uploading process.

Completed

All items are marked Complete when finished.

Figure 2-30. *Yahoo! Photos provided a way to upload files directly to the site via drag and drop from the user's filesystem into the web page*

Considerations

This is not a trivial implementation. But it does clearly illustrate the benefit of drag and drop for operating on a set of files. The traditional model requires each photo to be selected individually for upload. Drag and drop frees you to use whatever browsing method is available on your system and then drop those photos for upload.

Anti-pattern: Artificial Visual Construct

Unfortunately, drag and drop can sometimes drive the design of an interface instead of being an extension of a natural interface. These interactions are almost always doomed, as they are the tail wagging the proverbial dog. Rating movies, books, and music is a common feature found on many sites. But what happens if you try to use drag and drop to rate movies?

In Figure 2-31 you can rate movies by dragging them into three buckets: "Loved It", "Haven't Seen It", or "Loathed It".

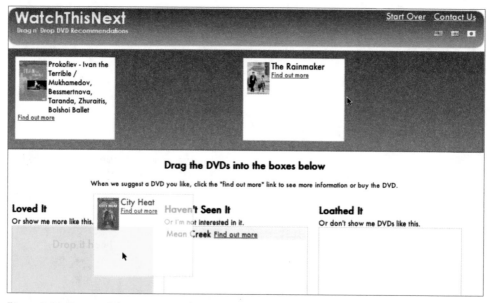

Figure 2-31. *Drag and drop recommendations: the hard way to do ratings*

While this certainly would work, it is wrong for several reasons:

Non-obvious

> Requires some additional instructions to "Drag the DVDs into the boxes below" in order for the user to know how to rate the movies.

Too much effort

Requires too much user effort for a simple task. The user needs to employ mouse gymnastics to simply rate a movie. Drag and drop involves these discrete steps: target, then drag, then target, and then drop. The user has to carefully pick the movie, drag it to the right bucket, and release.

Too much space

Requires a lot of visual space on the page to support the idiom. Is it worth this amount of screen real estate?

Direct rating systems (thumbs up/down, star ratings, etc.) are a much simpler way to rate a movie than using an **Artificial Visual Construct**. A set of stars is an intuitive, compact, and simple way to rate a movie (Figure 2-32).

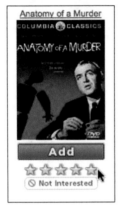

Figure 2-32. *Instead of drag and drop, Netflix uses a simple set of stars to rate a movie*

You might still be tempted to take this approach if you have a lot of objects that you want to add as favorites or set an attribute on. Don't give in. This method still falls way short since the amount of space needed for this far outweighs simpler approaches such as providing an action button for the selected objects.

— Tip —

Drag and drop should never be forced. Don't create an artificial visual construct to support it.

Natural Visual Construct

Another example of **Drag and Drop Action** is demonstrated in Google Maps. A route is visually represented on the map with a dark purple line. Dragging an arbitrary route point to a new location changes the route in real time (Figure 2-33).

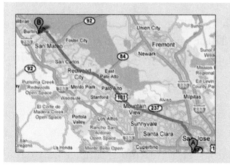

Normal display state

Route is shown in dark purple.

Invitation to drag

Hovering over any part of the route provides a draggable circle (route point) with a tool tip saying "Drag to change route".

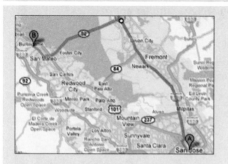

Dragging

We want to stay on the east side of the bay and cross the San Mateo bridge. Dragging the route bubble back over the bridge will reroute our trip.

Dropped

The route changes as we drag. Dropping completes the rerouting action.

Figure 2-33. *Rerouting in Google Maps is as simple as drag and drop*

This is the opposite of the **Artificial Visual Construct** anti-pattern. The route is a **Natural Visual Construct**. Since anywhere along the route is draggable, there are a lot of opportunities to discover the rerouting bubble. When the route is being dragged, Google dynamically updates it. The constant feedback forms the basis of a **Live Preview** (which we will discuss in Chapter 13).

Best Practices for Drag and Drop Action

Here are some best practices to keep in mind:

- Use **Drag and Drop Actions** sparingly in web interfaces, as they are not as discoverable or expected.
- Provide alternate ways to accomplish the action. Use the **Drag and Drop Action** as a shortcut mechanism.
- Don't use drag and drop for setting simple attributes. Instead use a more direct approach to setting attributes on the object.
- Don't construct an artificial visual representation for the sole purpose of implementing drag and drop. Drag and drop should follow the natural representation of the objects in the interface.
- Provide clear invitations on hover to indicate the associated action.

Drag and Drop Collection

A variation on dragging objects is collecting objects for purchase, bookmarking, or saving into a temporary area. This type of interaction is called **Drag and Drop Collection**. Drag and drop is a nice way to grab items of interest and save them to a list. The Laszlo shopping cart example illustrates this nicely (Figure 2-34).

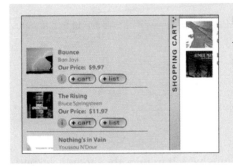

Normal display state

The shopping cart is docked on the right part of the screen.

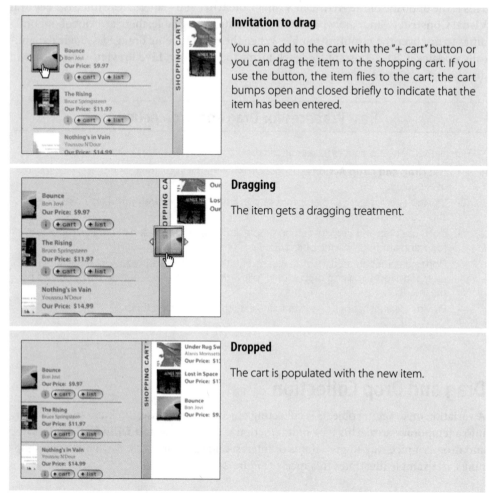

Invitation to drag

You can add to the cart with the "+ cart" button or you can drag the item to the shopping cart. If you use the button, the item flies to the cart; the cart bumps open and closed briefly to indicate that the item has been entered.

Dragging

The item gets a dragging treatment.

Dropped

The cart is populated with the new item.

Figure 2-34. *This Laszlo shopping cart demo uses both drag and drop and a button action to add items to its shopping cart*

Considerations

There are a few issues to consider in this example.

Discoverability

Drag and drop is a natural way collect items for purchase. It mimics the shopping experience in the real world. Grab an item. Drop it in your basket. This is fast and convenient once you know about the feature. However, as a general rule, you should never rely solely on drag and drop for remembering items.

Parallel, more explicit ways to do the same action should be provided. In this example, Laszlo provides an alternative to dragging items in the cart. Notice the "+ cart" button in Figure 2-34. Clicking this button adds the item to the shopping cart.

Best Practices for Drag and Drop Collection
Here are some best practices to keep in mind: • Use as an alternate way to collect items (e.g., a shopping cart). • When a drag gets initiated, highlight the valid drop area to hint where drop is available. • Provide alternate cues that drag and drop into collections as available.

Teachable moment

When providing alternates to drag and drop, it is a good idea to hint that dragging is an option. In the Laszlo example, clicking the "+ cart" button causes the shopping cart tray to bump slightly open and then closed again. This points to the physicality of the cart. Using another interaction as a teachable moment to guide the user to richer interactions is a good way to solve discoverability issues.

> **Tip**
> Look for opportunities for teachable moments in the interface leading users to advanced features.

The Challenges of Drag and Drop

As you can see from the discussion in this chapter, Drag and Drop is complex. There are four broad areas where Drag and Drop may be employed: **Drag and Drop Module, Drag and Drop List, Drag and Drop Object,** and **Drag and Drop Action.** And in each area, there are a large number of interesting moments that may be handled in numerous ways. Being consistent in visual and interaction styles across all of these moments for all of these types of interactions is a challenge in itself. And keeping the user informed throughout the process with just the right amount of hints requires design finesse. In Chapter 10, we explore some ways to bring this finesse into Drag and Drop.

General Best Practices for Drag and Drop

- Keep page jitter to a minimum while dragging objects.
- Initiate dragging if the user presses the mouse down and moves the mouse three pixels, or if she holds the mouse down for at least half a second.
- Use drag and drop for performing direct actions as an alternate method to more direct mechanisms in the interface.
- Hint at the availability of drag and drop when using alternatives to drag and drop.
- Pay attention to all of the interesting moments during drag and drop. Remember, you must keep the user informed throughout the process.
- Use **Invitations** (discussed more in Chapters 9 and 10) to cue the user that drag and drop is available.

Chapter 3

Direct Selection

When the Macintosh was introduced, it ushered into the popular mainstream the ability to directly select objects and apply actions to them. Folders and files became first-class citizens. Instead of a command line to delete a file, you simply dragged a file to the trash-can (Figure 3-1).

Figure 3-1. *DOS command line for deleting a file versus dragging a file to the trash on the Macintosh*

Treating elements in the interface as directly selectable is a clear application of the *Make It Direct* principle. On the desktop, the most common approach is to initiate a selection by directly clicking on the object itself. We call this selection pattern **Object Selection** (Figure 3-2).

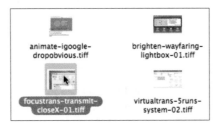

Figure 3-2. *Files can be selected directly on the Macintosh; Object Selection is the most common pattern used in desktop applications*

In this chapter we will look at the following types of selection patterns:

Toggle Selection
  Checkbox or control-based selection.

Collected Selection
  Selection that spans multiple pages.

Object Selection
  Direct object selection.

Hybrid Selection
  Combination of **Toggle Selection** and **Object Selection**.

Toggle Selection

The most common form of selection on the Web is **Toggle Selection**. Checkboxes and toggle buttons are the familiar interface for selecting elements on most web pages. An example of this can be seen in Figure 3-3 with Yahoo! Mail Classic.

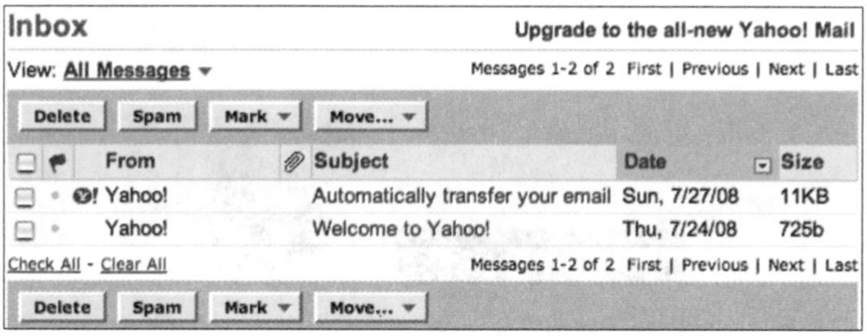

Figure 3-3. *In Yahoo! Mail Classic a mail message can be selected by clicking on the corresponding row's checkbox*

The way to select an individual mail message is through the row's checkbox. Clicking on the row itself does not select the message. We call this pattern of selection **Toggle Selection** since toggle-style controls are typically used for selecting items.

—— **Tip** ——
Toggle Selection is the easiest way to allow discontinuous selection.

Once items have been check-selected, actions can be performed on them. Usually these actions are performed on the selection by clicking on a separate button (e.g., the Delete button). Gmail is a good example of actions in concert with **Toggle Selection** (Figure 3-4).

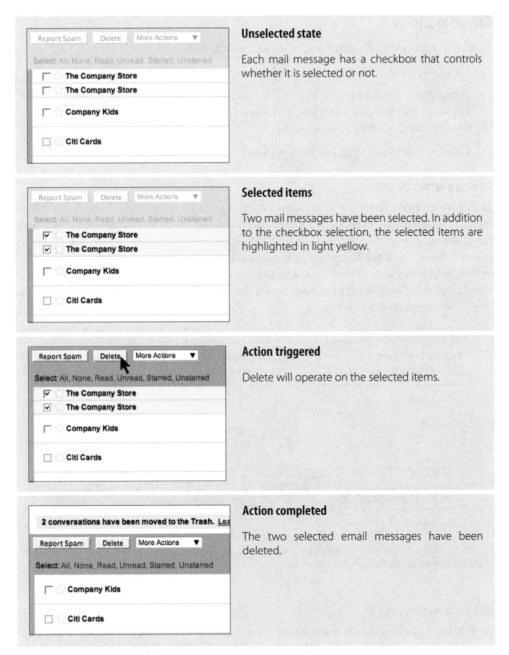

Unselected state

Each mail message has a checkbox that controls whether it is selected or not.

Selected items

Two mail messages have been selected. In addition to the checkbox selection, the selected items are highlighted in light yellow.

Action triggered

Delete will operate on the selected items.

Action completed

The two selected email messages have been deleted.

Figure 3-4. *Gmail uses checkbox selection to operate on messages*

Considerations

Toggle Selection with checkboxes has some nice attributes:

- Clear targeting, with no ambiguity about how to select the item or deselect it.

- Straightforward discontinuous selection, and no need to know about Shift or Control-key ways to extend a selection. Just click the checkboxes in any order, either in a continuous or discontinuous manner.

- Clear indication of what has been selected.

Scrolling versus paging

The previous examples were with paged lists. But what about a scrolled list? Yahoo! Mail uses a scrolled list to show all of its mail messages (Figure 3-5). While not all messages are visible at a time, the user knows that scrolling through the list retains the currently selected items. Since the user understands that all the messages not visible are still on the same continuous pane, there is no confusion about what an action will operate on—it will affect all selected items in the list. Sometimes the need for clarity of selection will drive the choice between scrolling and paging.

---- Tip ----

Toggle Selection is the normal pattern used when content is paged. Actions normally apply only to the selected items on the visible page.

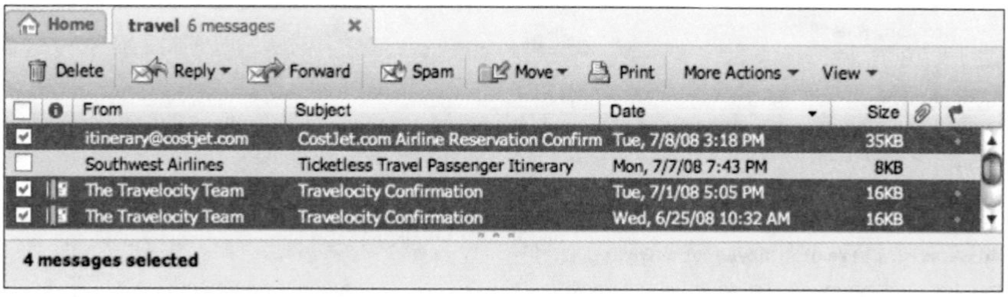

Figure 3-5. *Yahoo! Mail uses a scrolled list for its messages; selection includes what is in the visible part of the list as well as what is scrolled out of view*

Making selection explicit

With Yahoo! Bookmarks you can manage your bookmarks by selecting bookmarked pages and then acting on them. The selection model is visually explicit (Figure 3-6).

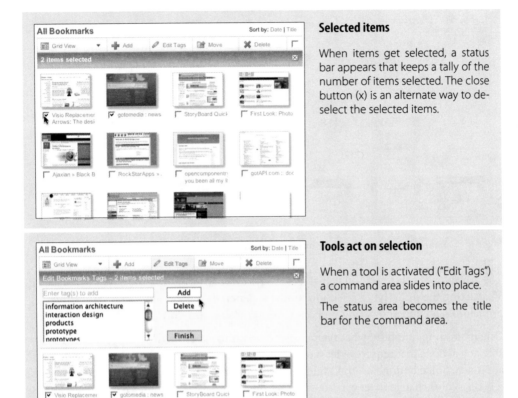

Selected items

When items get selected, a status bar appears that keeps a tally of the number of items selected. The close button (x) is an alternate way to de-select the selected items.

Tools act on selection

When a tool is activated ("Edit Tags") a command area slides into place.

The status area becomes the title bar for the command area.

Select all

A "select all" checkbox selects all items on the page. The selection status then shows the current number of items selected.

Figure 3-6. *Yahoo! Bookmarks explicitly displays the state of the selection*

The advantage of this method is that it is always clear how many items have been selected. Visualizing the underlying selection model is generally a good approach. This direct approach to selection and acting on bookmarks creates a straightforward interface.

One interesting question: what happens when nothing is selected? One approach is to disable any actions that require at least one selected item. Yahoo! Bookmarks takes a different approach. Since buttons on the Web do not follow a standard convention, you often can't rely on a color change to let you know something is not clickable. Yahoo! Bookmarks chose to make selection very explicit and make it clear when a command is invalid because nothing is selected ("No selection" in Figure 3-6). This is not normally the optimal way to handle errors. Generally, the earlier you can prevent errors, the better the user experience.

Netflix disables the "Update DVD Queue" button when nothing is selected and enables it when a movie gets selected (Figure 3-7).

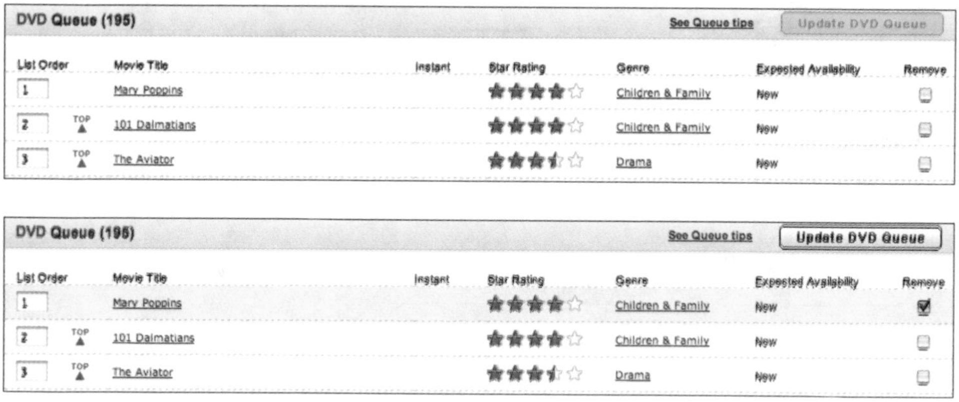

Figure 3-7. *When nothing is selected, Netflix disables the "Update DVD Queue" button to prevent errors early*

Best Practices for Toggle Selection

Here are some best practices to keep in mind:

- Use **Toggle Selection** for selecting elements in a row.
- Use **Toggle Selection** to make it easy to select discontinuous elements.
- In a list, highlight the row in addition to the checkbox to make the selection explicit.
- When moving from page to page, actions should only operate on the items selected on that page.
- If offering a "select all" option, consider providing a way to select all elements across all pages.
- Provide clear feedback for the number of elements selected.
- If possible, disable unavailable actions when nothing is selected. If you keep the action enabled, you will need additional interface elements to signal that it can't be completed.

Collected Selection

Toggle Selection is great for showing a list of items on a single page. But what happens if you want to collect selected items across multiple pages? **Collected Selection** is a pattern for keeping track of selection as it spans multiple pages.

In Gmail, you can select items as you move from page to page. The selections are remembered for each page. If you select two items on page one, then move to page two and select three items, there are only three items selected. This is because actions only operate on a single page. This makes sense, as users do not normally expect selected items to be remembered across different pages.

Considerations

Gmail does provide a way to select all items across different pages. When selecting all items on a individual page (with the "All" link), a prompt appears inviting the user to "Select all 2785 conversations in Spam". Clicking that will select all items across all pages (Figure 3-8). The "Delete Forever" action will operate on all 2785 conversations, not just the 25 selected on the page.

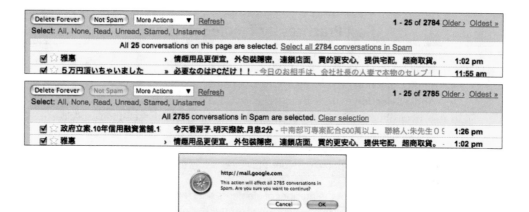

Figure 3-8. *Gmail provides a way to select all items across all pages, allowing the user to delete all items in a folder without having to delete all items on each page individually*

Keeping the selection visible

The real challenge for multi-page selection is finding a way to show selections gathered across multiple pages. You need a way to collect and show the selection as it is being created. Here is one way that **Collected Selection** comes into play.

LinkedIn uses **Collected Selection** to add potential contacts to an invite list (Figure 3-9).

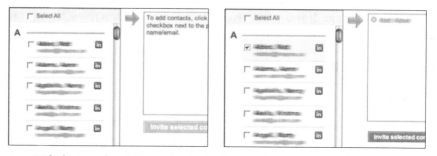

Figure 3-9. *LinkedIn provides a holding place for saving selections across multiple pages*

The list of potential invitees is shown in a paginated list on the lefthand side. Clicking the checkbox adds them to the invite list. The invite list becomes the place where selected contacts across multiple pages are remembered.

Any name in the invite list can be removed by clicking the "X" button beside it. Once the complete list of invitees is selected, clicking the "Invite selected contacts" sends each selected contact a LinkedIn invitation.

Collected Selection and actions

When Yahoo! Photos was working its way through an early design of its Photo Gallery (see Figure 3-13, later in this chapter), the plan was to show all photos in a single, continuous scrolling page (we discuss virtual scrolling in Chapter 7). In a long virtual list, the selection model is simple. Photos are shown in a single page and selection is easily understood in the context of this single page.

However, due to performance issues, the design was changed. Instead of a virtual page, photos had to be chunked into pages. In order to support **Collected Selection**, Yahoo! Photos introduced the concept of a "tray" into the interface (Figure 3-10). On any page, photos can be dragged into the tray. The tray keeps its contents as the user moves from page to page. So, adding a photo from page one and three more from page four would yield four items in the tray. As a nice touch, the tray would make itself visible (by sliding into view) even when the user was scrolled down below the fold.

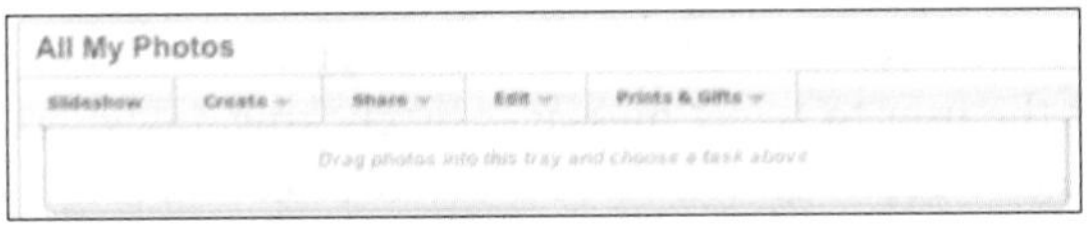

Figure 3-10. *Yahoo! Photos used a "tray" to implement a form of Collected Selection; the confusing aspect was which actions in the menu operated on the tray versus the photos selected on the page*

There was a problem with the design, however. In the menu system it was hard to discern whether the user meant to operate on the selection (photos on the page could be selected through an **Object Selection** model) or on the collected items in the tray. To resolve this ambiguity, the drop-down menus contained two identical sets of commands. The first group of commands in the menu operated on the collected items in the tray. The second set of commands operated on the selected objects. Needless to say, this was confusing since it required the user to be fully aware of these two selection models when initiating a command.

One way to remove this ambiguity would have been to have a single set of commands that operated on either the tray or the photos—depending on which had the focus. This would require a way to select the tray and a way to deselect it (by clicking outside the tray). A possible approach would be to slightly dim the photo gallery when the tray is selected (causing it to clearly have the focus), and do the opposite when the tray is not the focus.

Best Practices for Collected Selection

Here are some best practices to keep in mind:

- If you allow selection across page boundaries, accumulate the selected items (from each page) into a separate area. This makes the selection explicit even when moving from page to page.
- Use **Collected Selection** to blend **Toggle Selection** and **Object Selection** in the same interface.
- Watch out for ambiguity between items selected with **Collected Selection** and any items or objects that can be normally selected on the page.

Object Selection

As we mentioned earlier, **Toggle Selection** is the most common type of selection on the Web. The other type of selection, **Object Selection,** is when selection is made directly on objects within the interface.

Sometimes using a checkbox does not fit in with the style of interaction desired. Laszlo's WebTop mail allows the user to select messages by clicking anywhere in the row. The result is that the whole row gets highlighted to indicate selection (Figure 3-11).

Nothing selected

Normal view when nothing is selected and the mouse is not over a message.

Hovered state

When the mouse hovers over a row, the row is subtly highlighted to indicate focus and what will be selected if the user clicks.

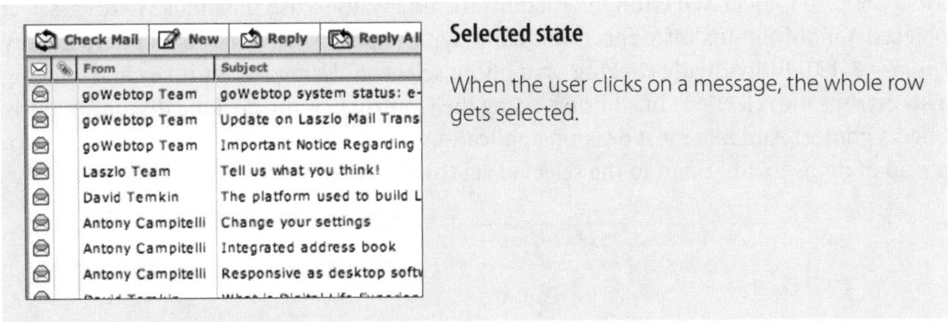

Selected state

When the user clicks on a message, the whole row gets selected.

Figure 3-11. *Laszlo WebTop Mail uses highlighting to indicate row selection*

Considerations

Desktop applications tend to use **Object Selection**. It is also natural that web-based mail applications that mimic desktop interactions employ this same style of selection. Instead of showing a control (like a checkbox), the object itself can be selected and acted on directly.

Object Selection can be extended by holding down the Shift key while clicking on a different item. The Command key (Macintosh) or Control key (Windows) can be used to individually add items in a discontinuous manner. The downside to this approach is that it is not obvious to use the modifier keys for extending the selection. **Toggle Selection**'s use of toggle buttons makes the selection extension model completely obvious.

Flickr is a simple example of the keyboard being used to extend the selection in a web application. In the Organizr tool, multiple photos can be selected by using modifier keys to extend the selection (Figure 3-12).

Figure 3-12. *Flickr allows for discontinuous selection by using the Command/Control key to extend selection*

Desktop-style selection

For now **Object Selection** is not as common on the Web. Given that most sites have been content-oriented, there have been few objects to select. Also, with the Web's simple event model, **Object Selection** was not easy to implement. In typical web pages, keyboard events have rarely made sense since they are also shared with the browser. However, all of this is changing as the capabilities of web technologies continue to improve.

Most desktop **Object Selection** interactions include ways to use the mouse to drag-select objects. Yahoo! Photos introduced this same type of object selection to its photo gallery (Figure 3-13). Individually clicking on a photo selects it. Using the Shift key and clicking also extends the selection. In addition, using the Control key and clicking discontinuously selects photos. And like most desktop applications, you can drag a selection box around a group of items to add them to the selected set (in this case, photos).

Figure 3-13. *Yahoo! Photos 3.0 created a rich drag selection mechanism for selecting photos*

Best Practices for Object Selection

Here are some best practices to keep in mind:

- Use **Object Selection** when selectable elements can be dragged.
- Use **Object Selection** when the application will simulate desktop style interactions.
- Allow standard modifier key extensions (Shift to extend selection; Ctrl for discontinuous selection).
- If possible, degrade **Object Selection** to **Toggle Selection** when browser capabilities are limited.

Hybrid Selection

Mixing **Toggle Selection** and **Object Selection** in the same interface can lead to a confusing interface. Referring back to Yahoo! Bookmarks, you'll see an odd situation arise during drag and drop (Figure 3-14).

Figure 3-14. *In Yahoo! Bookmarks, one item is selected, but two items can be dragged by dragging on the unselected item*

Considerations

There are a few important issues to consider when using **Hybrid Selection**.

Confusing two models

In the left panel of Figure 3-14, one bookmark element is selected (notice the checkbox **Toggle Selection**). The second bookmark element ("Dr. Dobb's") is unselected (the checkbox is clear). In the right panel of Figure 3-14, clicking and dragging on the unselected bookmark element initiates a drag. The drag includes both the selected element and the unselected element. Since only one is shown as selected, this creates a confusing situation.

This occurs because three things are happening in the same space:

- **Toggle Selection** is used for selecting bookmarks for editing, deleting, etc.
- **Object Selection** is used for initiating a drag drop.
- Mouse click is used to open the bookmark on a separate page.

The problem is that more than one interaction idiom is applied to the same place on the same page. In this case, if you happen to try to drag, but instead click, you will be taken to a new page. And if you drag an unselected item, you now have two items selected for drag but only one shown as selected for other operations (Figure 3-14, right). This is definitely confusing. Simply selecting the item (automatically checking the box) when the drag starts would keep the selection model consistent in the interface. However, it might lead the user to expect a single click to also do the same (which it cannot since it opens the bookmark).

So, mixing the two selection models together can be problematic. However, there is a way to integrate the **Toggle Selection** and **Object Selection** and have them coexist peacefully as well as create an improved user experience.

Blending two models

Yahoo! Mail originally started with the **Toggle Selection** model (Figure 3-15). When the new Yahoo! Mail Beta was released, it used **Object Selection** exclusively (Figure 3-16). But since there are advantages to both approaches, the most recent version of Yahoo! Mail incorporates both approaches in a **Hybrid Selection** (Figure 3-17).

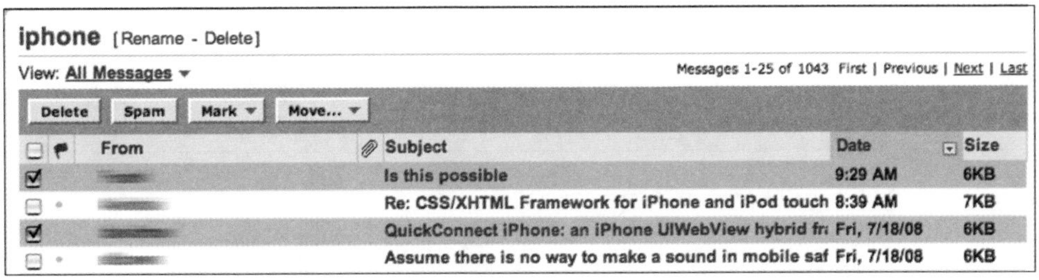

Figure 3-15. *Yahoo! Mail Classic uses Toggle Selection; it also highlights selected rows, but rows can only be selected by clicking the message's checkbox*

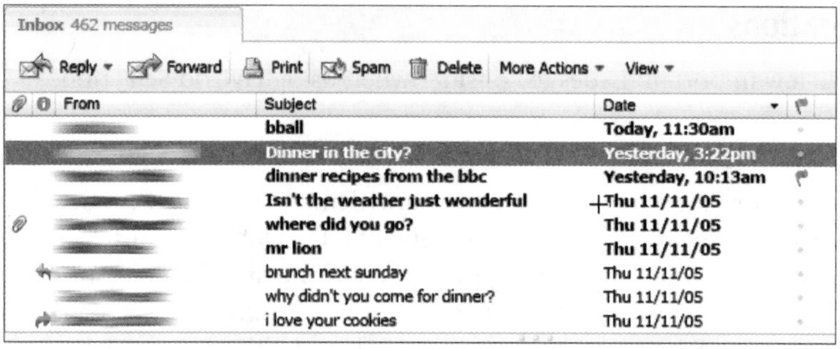

Figure 3-16. *Yahoo! Mail Beta launched with Object Selection: no checkboxes were provided, and discontiguous selection could only be done by using keyboard modifiers*

Figure 3-17. *Yahoo! Mail now uses a hybrid approach: it incorporates both the Toggle Selection and the Object Selection patterns (messages can be selected with checkboxes or by clicking on the row); Toggle Selection selects the message without loading the message in the viewing pane*

Hybrid Selection brings with it the best of both worlds. You can use the checkbox selection model as well as normal row selection. You get the benefit of explicit selection and simplified multiple selection that **Toggle Selection** brings. And you get the benefit of interacting with the message itself and direct object highlighting.

---- **Tip** ----

Combining **Toggle Selection** and **Object Selection** is a nice way to bridge a common web idiom with a common desktop idiom.

There is an additional meaning applied to **Toggle Selection** versus **Object Selection**. Clicking on a row with the checkbox has the benefit of selecting the message without loading its contents in the message pane (think spam!). Clicking on a message itself will load the contents in the message pane.

Best Practices for Hybrid Selection

Here are some best practices to keep in mind:

- Use checkbox selection to select an object without opening it.
- Use object selection to select and open an object.

Principle Two

Keep It Lightweight

Digg is a popular news site where the community votes on its favorite stories. If you see a story on Digg that you like you can vote your approval with a simple click action on the "digg it" button (Figure P2-1).

Figure P2-1. *Digg makes it easy to vote to digg articles with the "digg it" button next to each article*

It wasn't always this simple. Kevin Rose founded Digg to democratize the finding of tech articles. In the earliest versions of Digg, the user had to complete a two-step process to digg a story (Figure P2-2).

> sorting by: [newest | oldest | most digs | least digs]
>
> **IBM, AMD, Sony boost chip speeds by 24%**
> "IBM and AMD have found a way to improve transistor performance by up to 24% without increasing the power draw - using a tweaked implementation of Big Blue's 'strained silicon' process."
> [dig this story | comment | by: anonymous]

> **+1 digs added story**
> Begin to earn credit for your digs - more info

Figure P2-2. *The first version of Digg required a two-page process to "digg" a story*

In the current version of Digg it's much simpler—just click the "digg it" button, and the vote is immediately recorded (Figure P2-3).

Figure P2-3. *Digg now uses a "digg it" button to immediately record a "digg" within the same page*

Kevin Rose has noted that changing to a one-step process had a huge impact on the number of stories being dug and thus on the success of his site. Here is his view on what transpired:

> There was a huge shift in activity on Digg when we made the move to the one-click digg in November 2005. Once we added Ajax, activity went through the roof on [the number of] diggs. It was just insane. Just the ease of the "one-click and you're done" made all the difference in the world. Once the users grasped that the content is syndicated to friends, friends' activities then went through the roof. These small incremental steps in feature additions drove the growth.[*]

Did you get that? Changing to a one-click digg was not technically difficult. Yet it made a significant impact on Digg's success. It not only increased the ease of digging stories, but it also had an impact on other site activities. This is the power of making interactions lightweight.

Next, in Chapter 4, we look at a set of patterns that can make our interactions lightweight:

Contextual Tools
Tools placed in context within the page content.

---

[*] From Rose's talk at the San Francisco Bay Area Chapter of ACM SIGCHI (BayCHI), April 11, 2006. See *http:// www.baychi.org/calendar/20060411/*.

Contextual Tools

Interaction in Context

Most desktop applications separate functionality from data. Menu bars, toolbars, and palettes form islands of application functionality. Either the user chooses a tool to use on the data or makes a selection and then applies the tool.

Early websites were just the opposite. They were completely content-oriented. Rich tool sets were not needed for simply viewing and linking to content pages. Even in e-commerce sites like Amazon or eBay, the most functionality needed was the hyperlink and "Submit" button.

However, this simplistic approach no longer exists in the current web application landscape. As the Web has matured, a wide variety of application styles has emerged.

On one end of the spectrum there are simple sites that need no more functionality than the hyperlink and a "Submit" button. On the other end of the spectrum there are full applications hosted as a website. Google Search and Yahoo! Mail are two typical applications that illustrate this variation (Figure 4-1).

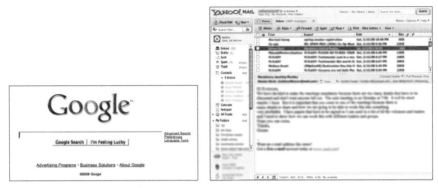

Figure 4-1. *Google Search needs only hyperlinks and a search button; Yahoo! Mail, on the other hand, is a full-featured application with toolbars and menus*

Between these two opposites are a lot of sites that need to mix content and functionality. It is to this intersection that we turn our attention in this chapter.

Think for a moment where user interfaces are headed.

Touch-based interfaces were the stuff of research labs and, more recently, interesting You-Tube videos. But now they're as close as our phones. Most notably, the Apple iPhone brought touch to the masses (Figure 4-2). Gesture-based interfaces seemed even further out. Yet these became reality with the Nintendo Wii.

Figure 4-2. *The Apple iPhone introduced touch-based interfaces to the consumer market*

With both gesture and touch-based interfaces, interaction happens directly with the content.

Tip

The *content is the interface.* Instead of being contained in separate areas of functionality, the actions feel close to the objects being interacted with.

This concept also informs our current challenge. How do we bring tools nearer to the content to make the interaction as lightweight as possible?

Fitts's Law

Fitts's Law is an ergonomic principle that ties the size of a target and its contextual proximity to ease of use. Bruce Tognazzini restates it simply as:

The time to acquire a target is a function of the distance to and size of the target.

In other words, if a tool is close at hand and large enough to target, then we can improve the user's interaction. Putting tools in context makes for lightweight interaction.

Contextual Tools

We could simply isolate our functionality into islands of tools (toolbars and menus). But this would work against Fitts's Law by requiring more effort from the user. It would also add more visual weight to the page. Instead of interacting with the functionality separately, we can bring the functionality into the content with **Contextual Tools**.

Contextual Tools are the Web's version of the desktop's right-click menus. Instead of having to right-click to reveal a menu, we can reveal tools in context with the content. We can do this in a number of ways:

Always-Visible Tools
> Place **Contextual Tools** directly in the content.

Hover-Reveal Tools
> Show **Contextual Tools** on mouse hover.

Toggle-Reveal Tools
> A master switch to toggle on/off **Contextual Tools** for the page.

Multi-Level Tools
> Progressively reveal actions based on user interaction.

Secondary Menus
> Show a secondary menu (usually by right-clicking on an object).

Always-Visible Tools

The simplest version of **Contextual Tools** is to use **Always-Visible Tools**. Digg is an example of making Contextual Tools always visible (Figure 4-3).

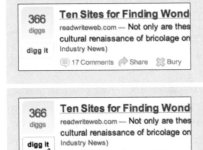

Visible tool

Beside each story is a digg scorecard. Just below is the "digg it" button. The digg button shows for all stories.

Other actions are represented less prominently.

Invitation

On mouse hover, the digg button border changes to a darker color and the text label changes to black. Highlighting is an effective way to signal interactivity.

Completion

Once the user clicks the "digg it" button, the vote is counted. The current vote fades out and then the new digg count (including your vote) appears instantly. The digg button changes to "dugg" and is no longer clickable (indicated by the gray text).

Figure 4-3. *Digg's "digg it" button is a simple Contextual Tool that is always visible*

Considerations

The "digg it" button and Digg scorecard provide **Always-Visible Tools** next to each story.

Clear call to action

Why not hide the tools and only reveal them when the mouse is over the story? Since digging stories is central to the business of Digg, always showing the tool provides a *clear call to action*. There are other actions associated with news stories (comments, share, bury, etc.) but they are represented less prominently. In the case of Digg, the designers chose to show these at all times. An alternate approach would be to hide them and show them on mouse hover (we will discuss this approach in the next section).

It turns out that voting and rating systems are the most common places to make tools always visible. Netflix was the earliest to use a one-click rating system (Figure 4-4).

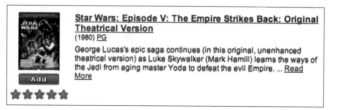

Figure 4-4. *Netflix star ratings are always visible*

Just as with Digg, rating movies is central to the health of Netflix. The Cinematch™ recommendation engine is driven largely by the user's ratings. So a clear call to action (to rate) is important. Not only do the stars serve as a strong call to action to rate movies, but they also provide important information for the other in-context tool: the "Add" button. Adding movies to your movie-shipping queue is key to having a good experience with the Netflix service.

Relative importance

One way to clarify this process is to decide on the relative importance of each exposed action. Is the "digg it" action as important as the "bury it" action? In the case of Digg, the answer is no. The "digg it" action is represented as a button and placed prominently in the context of the story. The "bury it" action is represented as a hyperlink along with other "minor" actions just below the story. The contrast of a button and a hyperlink as well as its placement gives a strong indication as to the relative importance of each action.

Tip ——
If an action is critical, expose it directly in the interface.

Discoverability

Discoverability is a primary reason to choose **Always-Visible Tools**. On the flip side, it can lead to more visual clutter. In the case of Digg and Netflix, there is a good deal of visual space given to each item (story, movie). But what happens when the items you want to act on are in a list or table?

Generally **Contextual Tools** in a list work well when the number of actions is kept to a minimum. Gmail provides a single **Always-Visible Tool** in its list of messages—the star rating—for flagging emails (Figure 4-5).

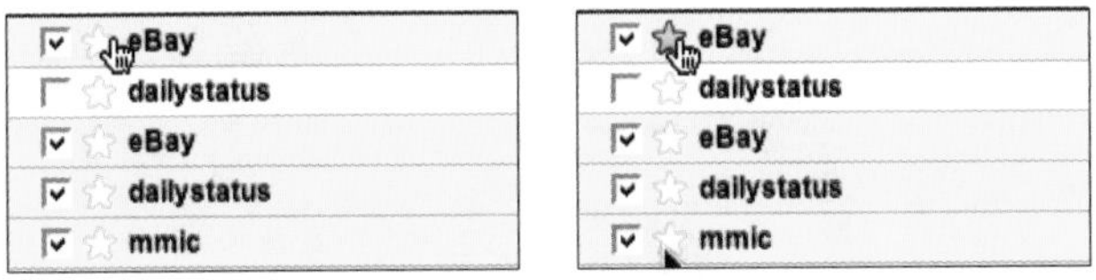

Figure 4-5. *Google Mail uses Contextual tools to flag favorites*

Simply clicking the star flags the message as important. The unstarred state is rendered in a visually light manner, which minimizes the visual noise in the list.

The following list, from Google Reader, takes a different approach. It shows several tools for managing subscriptions: rename, delete, and change folders for each subscription in the list. This is convenient but is definitely heavier visually (Figure 4-6).

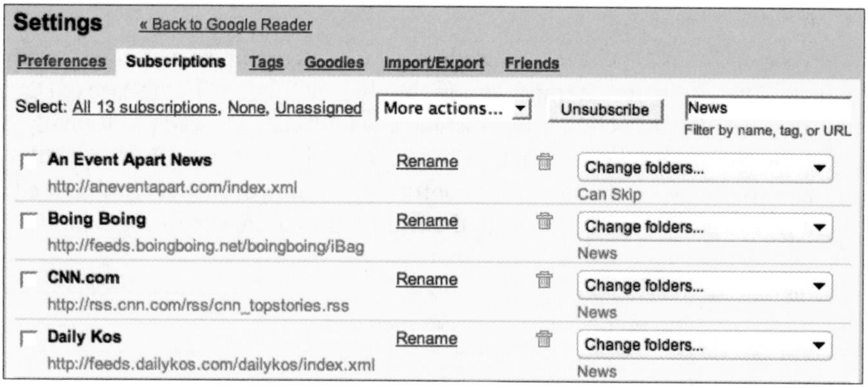

Figure 4-6. *Google Reader's Manage Subscriptions page displays lots of actions for each subscription, leading to a visually heavier display*

Sometimes concerns over visual noise must take a back seat to discoverability. The Yahoo! India Our City team struggled with a design early on. They wanted to hide the "email this" icon and only show it on hover. However, since the site was specifically for India, they were concerned with how much exposure the population had with simple web interactions like mouse rollover. So instead of hiding the icon, they chose to show it for every story (Figure 4-7).

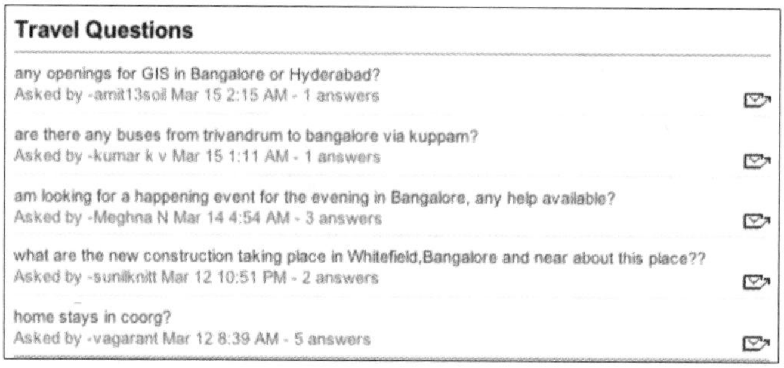

Figure 4-7. *Yahoo! India Our City was designed for users who were not familiar with mouse rollover; the email icon is shown at all times*

Best Practices for Always-Visible Tools

Here are some best practices to keep in mind:

- Make your **Contextual Tools** always visible if it is important to make a prominent call to action.
- Keep visual clutter to a minimum.
- Keep the number of visual items to a minimum.

Hover-Reveal Tools

Instead of making **Contextual Tools** always visible, we can show them on demand. One way to do this is to reveal the tools when the user pauses the mouse over an object. The **Hover-Reveal Tools** pattern is most clearly illustrated by 37 Signal's Backpackit (Figure 4-8). To-do items may be deleted or edited directly in the interface. The tools to accomplish this are revealed on mouse hover.

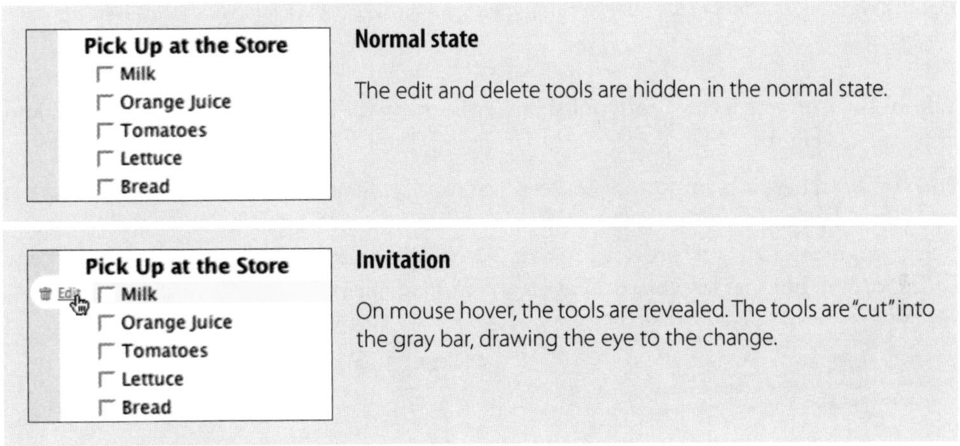

Pick Up at the Store ⬜ Milk ⬜ Orange Juice ⬜ Tomatoes ⬜ Lettuce ⬜ Bread	**Normal state** The edit and delete tools are hidden in the normal state.
Pick Up at the Store 🗑 Edit ⬜ Milk ⬜ Orange Juice ⬜ Tomatoes ⬜ Lettuce ⬜ Bread	**Invitation** On mouse hover, the tools are revealed. The tools are "cut" into the gray bar, drawing the eye to the change.

Figure 4-8. *Backpackit reveals its additional tools on mouse hover*

Considerations

The gray bar on the left is a nice visual reinforcement for the interaction. By allowing the tools to "cut" into the sidebar, the designers draw your eye to the available tools. The light yellow background draws attention to the to-do item being acted on. These two simple treatments make it clear which line has the focus and that additional tools have been revealed.

Tip

To reduce visual clutter, hide non-primary actions until they are needed.

Visual noise

Showing the items on hover decreases the visual noise in the interface. Imagine if instead the delete and edit actions were always shown for all to-do items. Figure 4-9 shows just how visually noisy that approach would have been.

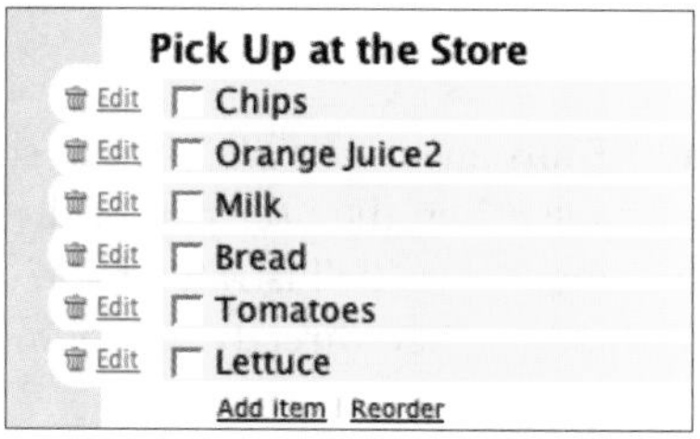

Pick Up at the Store

🗑 Edit ☐ Chips
🗑 Edit ☐ Orange Juice2
🗑 Edit ☐ Milk
🗑 Edit ☐ Bread
🗑 Edit ☐ Tomatoes
🗑 Edit ☐ Lettuce
                Add item Reorder

Figure 4-9. *What the Backpackit interface would have looked like if the Contextual Tools were always visible*

Yahoo! Buzz reveals its tools on mouse hover for both its Top Searches (Figure 4-10) and Top Stories (Figure 4-11).

For Top Searches, it is important to keep the top-ten list as simple as possible. Showing tools would compete with the list itself. Since the actions "Search Results" and "Top Articles" (Figure 4-10, right) are less important, they are revealed on hover. The actions may be important, but making the content clear and readable is a higher priority.

Figure 4-10. *Yahoo! Buzz reveals additional tools for the top searches when the user hovers over each item*

Similarly, for Top Stories, Yahoo! Buzz shows only "Share", "Post", and "Buzz Down" tools on hover. "Buzz Up" is shown at all times, but gets extra visual treatment on mouse hover (Figure 4-11, right). "Buzz Up" is important enough to show at all times, but can be toned down when not the focus.

Figure 4-11. *Yahoo! Buzz highlights the row and brings in additional tools*

Discoverability

A serious design consideration for **Hover-Reveal Tools** is just how discoverable the additional functionality will be. In the earlier Backpackit example (Figure 4-8), while the **Contextual Tools** are revealed on hover, the checkbox is always visible for each to-do item. To check off an item, users have to move the mouse over it. When they do, they will discover the additional functionality.

Flickr provides a set of tools for contacts. To avoid clutter, contact profile photos are shown without any tool adornment. When the mouse hovers over the contact's photo, a drop-down arrow is revealed (Figure 4-12). Clicking reveals a menu with a set of actions for the contact. This works because users often know to click on an image to get more information. Being drawn to the content is a good way to get the user to move the mouse over the area and discover the additional functionality.

Figure 4-12. *Flickr reveals the drop-down menu on hover*

Tip
Help users understand revealed tools by using familiar idioms (such as hyperlinks for actions or drop-down arrows to expose additional functionality).

Yahoo! Mail's flagging feature is revealed when the user hovers over the flagged column on a mail message (Figure 4-13). Contrast this to Google's always-revealed star approach we discussed earlier (Figure 4-5).

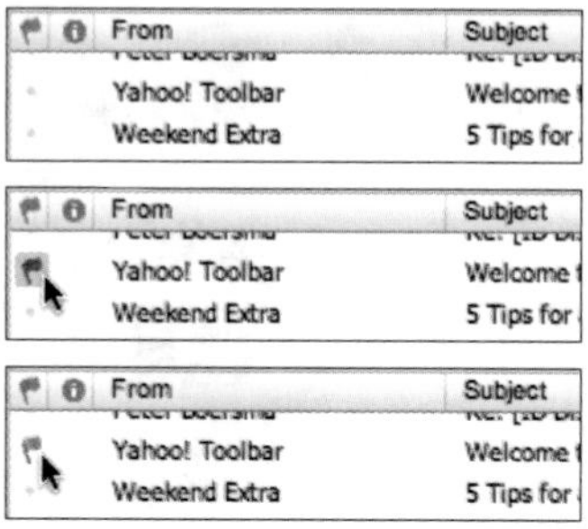

Figure 4-13. *Yahoo! Mail reveals the flag button when the user's mouse hovers over the flag column of a message*

The Yahoo! approach is visually cleaner, but less discoverable. We will have more to say about making tools discoverable in Chapter 10 when we discuss **Dynamic Invitations**.

Contextual Tools in an overlay

Sometimes there are several actions available for a focused object. Instead of placing tools beside the object being acted on, the revealed tools can be placed in an overlay. However, there can be issues with showing contextual tools in an overlay:

1. Providing an overlay feels heavier. An overlay creates a slight contextual switch for the user's attention.

2. The overlay will usually cover other information—information that often provides context for the tools being offered.

3. Most implementations shift the content slightly between the normal view and the overlay view, causing the users to take a moment to adjust to the change.

4. The overlay may get in the way of navigation. Because an overlay hides at least part of the next item, it becomes harder to move the mouse through the content without stepping into a "landmine."

Anti-pattern: Hover and Cover

Figure 4-14 illustrates all four of these situations. In an early version of Yahoo! for Teachers,* hovering over a clipped item brought in three tools: copy, delete, and preview. However, when these tools were placed in an overlay, it covered the item to the right, making it hard to see that content and even navigate to it. In addition, since the overlay had some additional padding (as well as rounded corners), the image shown in the overlay was about two pixels off from the non-overlay version. This slight jiggle was distracting. To add insult to injury, the overlay was sluggish to bring into view.

---

* Yahoo! for Teachers was only released in beta and never widely publicized. It was recently closed down, and another company (edtuit.com) will be launching a similar site.

Figure 4-14. *An early version of the Yahoo! for Teachers beta revealed Contextual Tools in an overlay; the overlay covered more than half of the item to its right*

The final straw was if users wanted to delete several items, they would hover over the image, wait for the overlay, click Delete, then be forced to move out and back in again to activate the next image's **Contextual Tools** (Figure 4-15). **Hover and Cover** is a common anti-pattern that occurs when exposing an overlay on hover and hiding important context or further navigation.

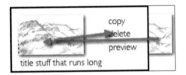

Figure 4-15. *Navigating required a zigzag approach to get around the tool overlay*

Hover and Cover was resolved by no longer using an overlay. Instead, additional margin space was added to each image, and the **Contextual Tools** were hidden. On mouse hover, the tools were simply revealed, along with a border defining the image being acted on (Figure 4-16).

Figure 4-16. *In the redesigned version, tools were shown on hover directly surrounding the image instead of in an overlay*

The difference (Figure 4-14 versus Figure 4-16) is dramatic. Not only is the experience improved, but overall page performance is improved as well. On mouse hover, the image no longer shifts in a distracting manner. In redesign, the delete always shows up in the same place relative to the image; this means the user "remembers spatially" where the command is, making it easier to target (Figure 4-17).

Figure 4-17. *Since the Delete action appears in the same spot relative to the image, the user can easily anticipate where the action will appear*

Tip ———————————————————————————————
Be careful when using overlays to expose additional information or tools. The overlay can get in the way of normal navigation or hide important information.

Anti-pattern: Mystery Meat

Have you ever found a can in the back of the pantry whose label has long since fallen off? The only way to identify this *mystery meat* is to open it. Unidentifiable icons are pretty much the same as a row of unlabeled cans. You have to hover over each icon and hope for a tool tip to label it. Even worse is when no tool tip is available. The easiest way to avoid this predicament is to use either a text label or combine an icon with a text label. **Mystery Meat** is a common anti-pattern that occurs when you have to hover over an item to understand how to use it.

Tip ———————————————————————————————
Don't make users hover over your tools in order to figure out what they mean.

Figure 4-18 illustrates this in an early version of Zooomr. The only recourse for the user was to pause over each icon and wait a second or so to read a tool tip about the purpose of the icon. This does not create a lightweight interaction!

Figure 4-18. *A very early version of Zooomr revealed a number of unidentifiable icons when the mouse hovered over a photo*

Activation

Tool overlays should activate immediately. The tools are an extension of the interface, and any delay creates too much of a delay between the activation and invocation of the action. In Chapter 5, we will discuss **Dialog Overlays**. In that discussion we suggest a delay before showing informational overlays. Why the difference? Since information may not be needed to understand the object, and given the fact that activation might be accidental, it is best to place a small delay when showing the additional information (usually a half-second delay is sufficient). But actions are different. Following the suggestions just mentioned (avoid **Hover and Cover** anti-pattern), the actions can be revealed without a lot of disruption. And if they show immediately, the user can access the additional commands almost as quickly as with **Always-Visible Tools**.

Best Practices for Hover-Reveal Tools

Here are some best practices to keep in mind:

- Hide **Contextual Tools** behind a mouse hover if the actions are secondary and you want to make the content more important (or other visible commands more important).
- Avoid using overlays when revealing additional tools. They will lead to the **Hover and Cover** anti-pattern, as well as require the user to perform mouse gymnastics to accomplish the most basic tasks.
- When additional tools are revealed, make sure that all parts of the page remain stable.
- Avoid any element shifting by a few pixels or page elements moving around. These cause the user to be directed away from what is really happening.
- Make sure revealed icons are clear and understandable. When possible, just use text labels.
- Activate tool overlays instantly. Unlike informational overlays, the user needs the additional tools to be available for immediate interaction.

Toggle-Reveal Tools

A variation on the two previous approaches is to not show any **Contextual Tools** until a special mode is set on the page. A good example of **Toggle-Reveal Tools** is in Basecamp's category editing, which we discussed in Chapter 1 (Figure 4-19).

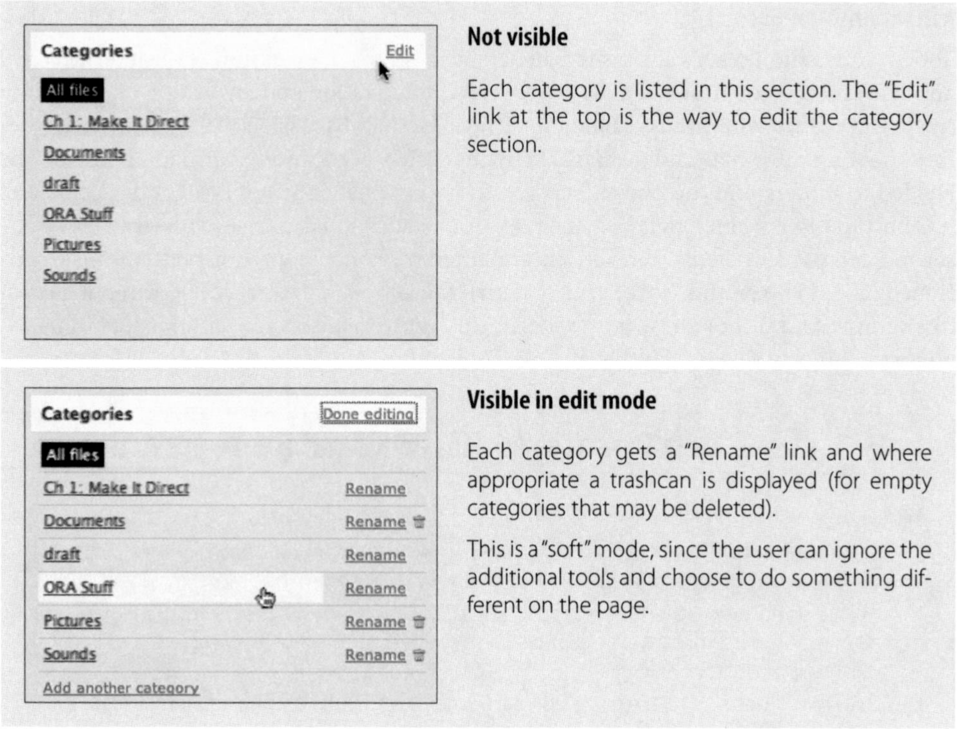

Categories   Edit

All files
Ch 1: Make It Direct
Documents
draft
ORA Stuff
Pictures
Sounds

Not visible

Each category is listed in this section. The "Edit" link at the top is the way to edit the category section.

Categories   Done editing

All files
Ch 1: Make It Direct   Rename
Documents   Rename 🗑
draft   Rename
ORA Stuff   Rename
Pictures   Rename 🗑
Sounds   Rename 🗑
Add another category

Visible in edit mode

Each category gets a "Rename" link and where appropriate a trashcan is displayed (for empty categories that may be deleted).

This is a "soft" mode, since the user can ignore the additional tools and choose to do something different on the page.

Figure 4-19. *Basecamp reveals category-editing tools only when the edit mode is turned on for the area*

Considerations

Here are a few considerations to keep in mind when using **Toggle-Reveal Tools**.

Soft mode

Generally, it is a good thing to avoid specific modes in an interface. However, if a mode is *soft* it is usually acceptable. By "soft" we mean the user is not trapped in the mode. With Basecamp, the user can choose to ignore the tools turned on. It just adds visual noise and does not restrict the user from doing other actions. This is a nice way to keep the interaction lightweight.

—— **Tip** ——————————————————————————————
Interfaces should strive to be modeless. Often, though, a "soft mode" can be employed to provide context for an action that is easy to activate and easy to remove.

When would you use this technique? When the actions are not the main thing and you want to reduce visual noise. This fits the category example perfectly. Items are renamed or deleted occasionally. It is common, however, to want to click through and see the contents of a category (the category is always hyperlinked). Hence, make it readable and easily navigable in the normal case—but still give the user a way to manage the items in context.

Google Reader could potentially be improved in this manner. In the current interface, clicking "Manage Subscriptions" takes the user to another page to edit subscriptions. One possible change is the addition of an "edit" button that toggles in a set of context tools for each subscription (Figure 4-20). This would allow the user to rename and unsubscribe without leaving the context of the reading pane.

Figure 4-20. *Adding an "edit" link to Google Reader's feed list and toggling in common actions could potentially make it easier to manage subscriptions*

Best Practices for Toggle-Reveal Tools

Here are some best practices to keep in mind:

- Toggle a tool mode for an area or page when the actions are not the main flow, but you want to provide the most direct way to act on these objects when the need arises.
- Make the activation and deactivation of the edit mode as symmetrical as possible.
- Keep the transition between display and edit as seamless as possible to provide a "soft mode" for editing.

Multi-Level Tools

Contextual Tools can be revealed progressively with **Multi-Level Tools**. Songza* provides a set of tools that get revealed after a user clicks on a song. Additional tools are revealed when hovering over the newly visible tools (Figure 4-21).

---

* Aza Raskin is the designer of Songza, founder of Humanized. He is the son of the late human-computer interface expert Jef Raskin.

Normal state

The tools are not visible normally. Mouse hover just highlights the song—it does not reveal the **Contextual Tools**.

Click activation

On mouse click, a cloverleaf-style menu is shown with the four basic functions: play, rate, add, and share.

Hover expose

Second-level actions are exposed while hovering over share or rate.

Figure 4-21. *Songza uses a multi-level contextual tool menu*

Considerations

Songza reveals the four options "play", "rate", "share", and "add to playlist" after the user clicks on a song title. Hovering over "share" or "rate" reveals a secondary set of menu items (Figure 14-21, center).

Radial menus

Radial menus[*] such as in Songza have been shown to have some advantages over more traditional menus. First, experienced users can rely on muscle memory rather than having to look directly at the menu items. Second, the proximity and targeting size make the menu easy to navigate since the revealed menu items are all equally close at hand (recall Fitts's Law).

The one potential downside to this approach is that rating a song requires several steps: an initial click on the song, moving the mouse over the "rate" menu item, then clicking either the thumbs up or thumbs down option. If rating songs was an important activity, the extra effort might prevent some users from doing so. An alternate approach would be to replace "rate" directly with the thumbs up and the thumbs down options.

Activation

Another interesting decision Songza made was to not activate the radial menu on hover. Instead, the user must click on a song to reveal the menu. Activating on click makes the user intent more explicit.

Making activation more explicit avoids the issues described earlier in the **Hover and Cover** anti-pattern. The user has chosen to interact with the song. Conversely, with a mouse hover, it's never quite clear if the user meant to activate the menu or just happened to pause over a song title.

Default action

However, this does mean there is no way to start a song playing with just a simple click. Playing a song requires moving to the top leaf. One possible solution would be to place the "play" option in the middle of the menu (at the stem) instead of in one of the leaves. Clicking once would activate the menu. Clicking a second time (without moving the mouse) would start playing the song. This interaction is very similar to one commonly used in desktop applications: allowing a double-click to activate the first item (default action) in a right-click menu.

> **Tip**
>
> Keep the most common actions as near to the activation point as possible.

---

[*] Also known as *pie menus*. See Jack Callahan et al. (1988), "An empirical comparison of pie vs. linear menus." *Proceedings of ACM CHI Conference on Human Factors in Computing Systems*: 95–100.

Contextual toolbar

Picnik is an online photo-editing tool that integrates with services like Flickr. In all, there are six sets of tools, each with a wide range of palette choices. Picnik uses **Multiple-Level Tools** to expose additional functionality. By wrapping the photo with tools in context and progressively revealing the levels of each tool, Picnik makes editing straightforward (Figure 4-22).

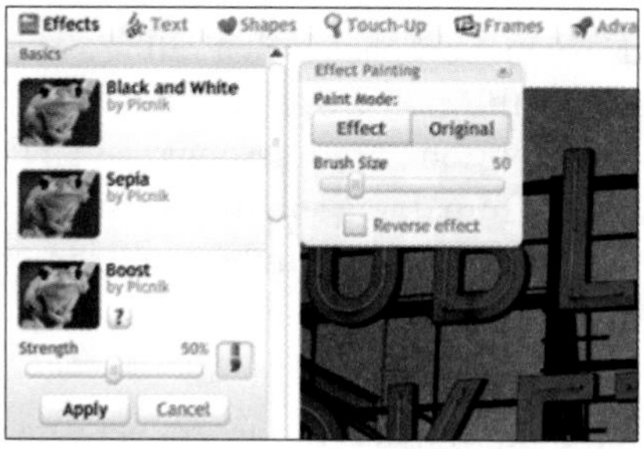

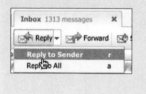

Figure 4-22. Picnik wraps layers of Contextual Tools around the image being edited

Muttons

Another variation on **Multi-Level Tools** is the "mutton" (menu + button = mutton). Muttons are useful when there are multiple actions and we want one of the actions to be the default. Yahoo! Mail uses a mutton for its "Reply" button (Figure 4-23).

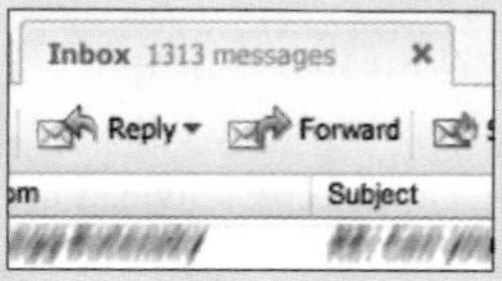

	Normal state
	Yahoo! Mail displays the "Reply" mutton in its toolbar as a button with a drop-down arrow control.
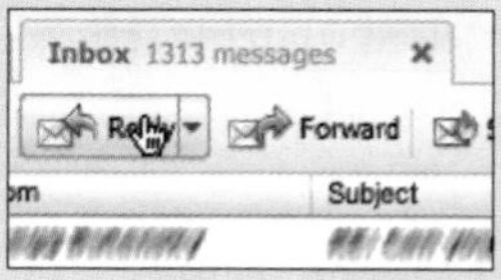	**As a button**
	On mouse hover, the button gets a 3D treatment and color highlight. The drop-down arrow gets the same treatment to call out its functionality.
	Clicking the "Reply" button at this point will trigger a reply without activating the menu.
	As a menu
	Clicking on the drop-down arrow reveals two commands: "Reply to Sender" is the same as the default "Reply" button action; "Reply to All" is an additional action that was hidden until the menu was revealed.

Figure 4-23. Yahoo! Mail's "Reply" button looks like a drop-down when hovered over; clicking "Reply" replies to sender, and clicking the drop-down offers the default action as well as "Reply to All"

Clicking "Reply" performs the individual reply. To reply to all, the menu has to be activated by clicking on the drop-down arrow to show the menu.

Muttons are used to:

- Provide a default button action ("Reply to Sender")
- Provide a clue that there are additional actions
- Provide additional actions in the drop-down

If muttons are not implemented correctly, they can be problematic for those using accessibility technologies. Because an earlier version of Yahoo! Mail did not make the mutton keyboard accessible, Yahoo!'s accessibility guru, Victor Tsaran, was convinced that there was no "Reply to All" command in the Yahoo! Mail interface. Only after the mutton was made more accessible could he find the "Reply" command.

Anti-pattern: Tiny Targets

At the beginning of this chapter, we discussed Fitts's Law. Recall that the time it takes to acquire a target is a function of both distance and size. Even if tools are placed close by in context, don't forget to make them large enough to target.

Both Flickr and Yahoo! Mail provide a reasonable-size target for the drop-down arrow. Compare this with the expand/collapse arrow used in an early version of Yahoo! for Teachers (Figure 4-24).

Figure 4-24. *The Yahoo! for Teachers Profile Card info is hidden unnecessarily*

Tip

Never use small targets. Make targets large enough to notice and interact with.

The arrow is tiny (8×8 pixels). It is exposed only on hover. Providing **Tiny Targets** makes interaction much more difficult. An alternate approach would be to always show a "more info" link. Clicking it could toggle the additional profile information. Alternatively, providing a larger target for the arrow would improve its findability and targeting.

Best Practices for Multi-Level Tools

Here are some best practices to keep in mind:

- Use **Multi-Level Tools** when you want to avoid revealing **Contextual Tools** on a mouse hover.
- Use **Multi-Level Tools** to make activation explicit.
- Use muttons when you have a default action that the user normally takes but alternate actions are still fairly frequent.
- Avoid cascades where possible. Users have a hard time maneuvering the various mouse turns that are required to get to these secondary menus.
- Keep actions as close to the activation point as possible.

Secondary Menu

Desktop applications have provided **Contextual Tools** for a long time in the form of **Secondary Menus**. These menus have been rare on the Web. Google Maps uses a secondary menu that is activated by a right-click on a route. It shows additional route commands (Figure 4-25).

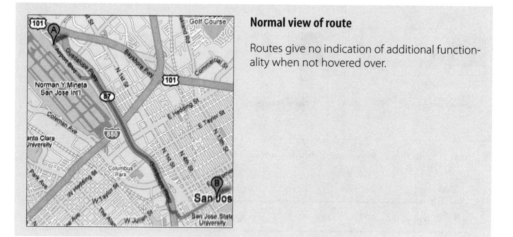

Normal view of route

Routes give no indication of additional functionality when not hovered over.

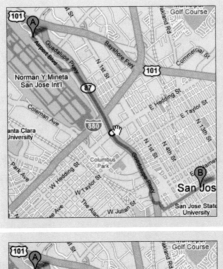

Invitation

When the mouse is over the route, potential stops are marked with a white circle.

Menu

Right-clicking on the item exposes four commands that act on the point selected: "Add a destination", "Zoom in", "Zoom out", and "Center map here".

Figure 4-25. *Google Maps uses a right-click menu to add new route stops or to adjust the map around the current point on the route*

Considerations

Secondary Menus have not been common in web applications.

Conflict with browser menu

One problem is the browser inserts its own right-click menu. Replacing the menu in normal content areas can confuse users, as they may not know if the standard browser menu or the application-specific menu will be shown. It will depend on whether it is clear that an object exists in the interface (as in the route line above), and if the menu is styled differently enough to disambiguate the menus.

Discoverability

As a general rule, never put anything in the **Secondary Menu** that can't be accomplished elsewhere. **Secondary Menus** are generally less discoverable. More advanced items or shortcuts, however, can be placed in the **Secondary Menu** as an alternate way to accomplish the same task.

Accessibility

Right-click is not the only way to activate a **Secondary Menu**. You can activate the menu by holding down the mouse for about one second. This provides a more accessible approach to popping up a **Secondary Menu**. This technique is used in the Macintosh Dock. Clicking and holding down on an application in the dock will reveal the **Secondary Menu** without requiring a right-click activation.

Acting on multiple objects

Keep in mind that all of the other **Contextual Tools** presented in this chapter have a limitation on the number of items they can operate on. **Always-Visible Tools, Hover-Reveal Tools, Toggle-Reveal Tools,** and **Multi-Level Tools** all operate on a single item at a time (even **Toggle-Reveal Tools** just shows a tool per item). **Secondary Menus** are different. They can be combined with a selection model (as described in Chapter 3) to perform actions on selected set of items.

Best Practices for Secondary Menus

Here are some best practices to keep in mind:

- Place alternate or shortcut commands in **Secondary Menus**.
- Consider activating **Secondary Menus** by holding down the mouse for one second as an alternative to right-clicking to show the menu.
- Style **Secondary Menus** differently than the Browser's standard secondary menu.
- Avoid **Secondary Menus** for all but redundant commands
- Avoid **Secondary Menus** in places where there is little resemblance to a traditional web page.
- Use **Secondary Menus** for operating on a selected set of objects.

General Practices for Contextual Tools

To sum up, here are some overall best practices to keep in mind:

- **Contextual Tools** are useful for reducing the user's path to completing a task. By placing tools near the point of focus and making these tools easy to activate, you can create a lightweight interaction.
- Use **Contextual Tools** when you have no way to select elements and operate on them as a whole.
- Use **Contextual Tools** when you want to shorten the path the user must take to complete a task for an item shown on the page.
- Use **Contextual Tools** when you want to provide a clear call to action at the point of focus.
- Always make your actions as immediate as possible, avoiding additional steps where you can.
- Where possible use familiar techniques (hyperlinks, drop-down arrows, buttons) when providing actions in unexpected places (hover-revealed **Contextual Tools**).
- Make the actions clear and direct. Avoid using icons for all but the most obvious (an [x] or a trashcan for delete, for instance).
- Use buttons for strong calls to action and links for minor actions.
- Make sure that targets used to open menus or expand information are suitably sized. Never use 8×8 pixel targets.
- Make tools easy to understand, easy to target, and quick to execute. This will make them feel lightweight.

Principle Three
Stay on the Page

Flow

In the book, *Flow: The Psychology of Optimal Experience*, published by Harper Perennial, Mihaly Csikszentmihalyi describes the state of "optimal experience" as *the times when people enter a state of concentration so focused it creates a state of effortless control*. Athletes may enter into flow and report the feeling of unself-consciousness as well as rising to the peak of their abilities. Flow, however, can be broken by a sudden awareness of the surroundings or by some interruption that happens to come along.

Unfortunately, users of our web applications rarely experience this level of happiness. In fact, the traditional web experience is punctuated with a page refresh each time the user chooses an action. It's like watching a play where the curtain comes down between each line of dialogue. The page refresh creates an artificial break in the action—or a break in the user's flow.

Change Blindness

The break can cause visual consequences as well. I recently took some of my children to the Exploratorium in San Francisco (a wonderful hands-on science museum for all ages). An exhibit that caught my eye was the one demonstrating *change blindness*.[*] A large screen displayed an image of a store-front typical of those seen in most urban areas, complete with awning, windows, doors—all of a distinctive style. Then suddenly a new updated image of the store-front replaced the original one. The new image had a slight change from the original. However, try as I might I could not detect the change. Why? The transition was punctuated by a very brief (less than a fourth of a second) delay. Showing the original image, going blank, then showing the second image made it really hard to detect the change between the two.

Wikipedia describes *change blindness* as:

> In visual perception, change blindness is the phenomenon where a person viewing a visual scene apparently fails to detect large changes in the scene.[†]

---

[*] You can see a demonstration of this at *http://www.usd.edu/psyc301/ChangeBlindness.htm*.
[†] See *http://en.wikipedia.org/wiki/Change_blindness*.

Fortunately the exhibit included a button to press that removed the "page refresh." When I held down this button, the change was obvious.

Including the page refresh in web applications was not the desire of web designers but rather an artifact of the technology underlying the Web. Each action generated a request for a new page, which included the refresh break. With this limitation, the ability to provide a seamless flow-based experience with continuous visual perception to the user was almost impossible.

However, this is no longer the case. We now have a button we can hold down! With the rise of Ajax, Flash, and other new technologies, it is possible to perform actions and bring back results for those actions while remaining on the same page and disturbing none of the surrounding context.

The principle *Stay on the Page* gets at the idea of creating a continuous visual perception that enhances flow nirvana. Given the history of the Web, it is important to always ask ourselves, "Can we create this experience in context, within the current page?" Sometimes, though, we may answer these questions with a "No." That can be OK. It is important to realize that there are times when switching the page makes more sense than staying within the page. We will explore these situations in the next few chapters.

In Chapters 5 through 8, we look at four ways to keep the user on the page:

Overlays
> Instead of going to a new page, a mini-page can be displayed in a lightweight layer over the page.

Inlays
> Instead of going to a new page, information or actions can be inlaid within the page.

Virtual Pages
> By revealing dynamic content and using animation, we can extend the virtual space of the page.

Process Flow
> Instead of moving from page to page, sometimes we can create a flow within a page itself.

Overlays

Overlays are really just lightweight pop ups. We use the term *lightweight* to make a clear distinction between it and the normal idea of a *browser pop up*. Browser pop ups are created as a new browser window (Figure 5-1). *Lightweight overlays* are shown within the browser page as an overlay (Figure 5-2). Older style browser pop ups are undesirable because:

- Browser pop ups display a new browser window. As a result these windows often take time and a sizeable chunk of system resources to create.

- Browser pop ups often display browser interface controls (e.g., a URL bar). Due to security concerns, in Internet Explorer 7 the URL bar is a permanent fixture on any browser pop-up window.

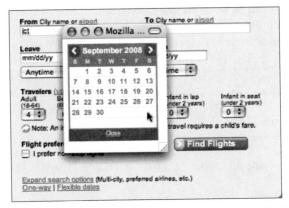

Figure 5-1. *If Orbitz used a browser pop-up window for its calendar chooser (it does not), this is how it might look*

By using either Flash or Ajax-style techniques (Dynamic HTML), a web application can present a pop up in a lightweight overlay within the page itself. This has distinct advantages:

- Lightweight overlays are just a lightweight in-page object. They are inexpensive to create and fast to display.

- The interface for lightweight overlays is controlled by the web application and not the browser.

- There is complete control over the visual style for the overlay. This allows the overlay to be more visually integrated into the application's interface (compare Figures 5-1 and 5-2).

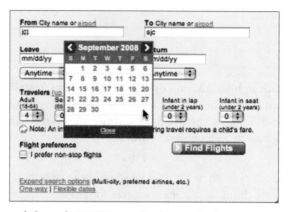

Figure 5-2. Orbitz uses a lightweight DHTML overlay for its calendar chooser; since it does not require the overhead of a separate browser window, it can pop up quickly and is better integrated into the page visually

Lightweight overlays can be used for asking questions, obtaining input, introducing features, indicating progress, giving instructions, or revealing information. They can be activated directly by user events (e.g., clicking on an action, hovering over objects) or be provided by the web application at various stages in the completion of an action.

Tip ───

Never use browser overlays. They are expensive to create, hard to control, slower than lightweight overlays, and visually unappealing.

We will look at three specific types of overlays: **Dialog Overlays**, **Detail Overlays**, and **Input Overlays**.

Dialog Overlay

Dialog Overlays replace the old style browser pop ups. Netflix provides a clear example of a very simple **Dialog Overlay**. In the "previously viewed movies for sale" section, a user can click on a "Buy" button to purchase a DVD. Since the customer purchasing the DVD is a member of Netflix, all the pertinent shipping and purchasing information is already on record. The complete checkout experience can be provided in a single overlay (Figure 5-3).

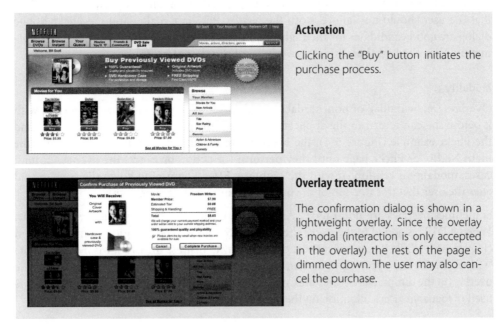

Activation

Clicking the "Buy" button initiates the purchase process.

Overlay treatment

The confirmation dialog is shown in a lightweight overlay. Since the overlay is modal (interaction is only accepted in the overlay) the rest of the page is dimmed down. The user may also cancel the purchase.

Figure 5-3. Netflix uses a lightweight pop up to confirm a previously viewed DVD purchase; in addition, it uses the Lightbox Effect to indicate modality

Considerations

Because the overlay is a lightweight pop up, the confirmation can be displayed more rapidly and the application has complete control over its look and placement.

Lightbox Effect

One technique employed here is the use of a **Lightbox Effect**. In photography a lightbox provides a backlit area to view slides. On the Web, this technique has come to mean bringing something into view by making it brighter than the background. In practice, this is done by dimming down the background.

You can see the **Lightbox Effect** pattern used by Flickr when rotating images (Figure 5-4).

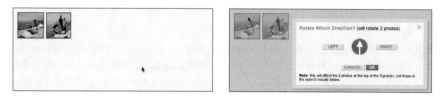

Figure 5-4. *Flickr also uses a Lightbox Effect to focus attention on the overlay*

The **Lightbox Effect** is useful when the **Dialog Overlay** contains important information that the user should not ignore. Both the Netflix Purchase dialog and the Flickr Rotate dialog are good candidates for the **Lightbox Effect**. If the overlay contains optional information, then the **Lightbox Effect** is overkill and should not be used.

Modality

Overlays can be modal* or non-modal. A modal overlay requires the user to interact with it before she can return to the application. In both the Netflix example (Figure 5-3) and the Flickr example (Figure 5-4), the overlays are *modal*: users cannot interact with the main Netflix or Flickr page until they perform the action or cancel the overlay. In both cases, modality is reinforced with the **Lightbox Effect**. Dimming down the background cues the user that this portion of the interface cannot be interacted with.

Sometimes overlays are non-modal. An example of this can be found in the Netflix site. When a DVD is added to the user's shipping list (queue), a confirmation overlay is shown (Figure 5-5). While it may appear that the only way to dismiss the overlay is by clicking the "Close" box in the upper-right corner, in reality the user can click anywhere outside the overlay (in the dimmed area) and the overlay will dismiss. In this case the **Lightbox Effect** is used to focus the user's attention on the confirmation and recommendations available.

---

* For a discussion on modality, see Jef Raskin's "The Humane Interface" (2000), 100, 141.

Figure 5-5. *Netflix uses a non-modal overlay with the Lightbox Effect to focus attention on the confirmation and recommendation*

The **Lightbox Effect** emphasizes that we are in a separate mode. As a consequence, it is not needed for most non-modal overlays. As an example, refer back to Figure 5-2, the Orbitz calendar pop up. Since the overlay is really more like an in-page widget, it would not be appropriate to make the chooser feel heavier by using a **Lightbox Effect**.

—— **Tip** ——————————————————————————————————
Use the **Lightbox Effect** to emphasize modality or call attention to special information in an overlay.
——

Staying in the flow

Overlays are a good way to avoid sending a user to a new page. This allows the user to stay within the context of the original page. However, since overlays are quick to display and inexpensive to produce, sometimes they can be tempting to use too freely, and in the process, may actually break the user's flow.

Anti-pattern: Idiot Boxes

Alan Cooper states a simple principle:

> *Don't stop the proceedings with idiocy.*[*]

————————————————————

[*] Cooper, Alan and Robert Reimann. *About Face 2.0: The Essentials of Interaction Design* (Wiley, 1995), 178.

In the context of flow he describes how egregious it is to interrupt the user needlessly:

> *One form of excise is so prevalent that it deserves special attention. … Flow is a natural state, and people will enter it without much prodding. It takes some effort to break into flow after someone has achieved it. Interruptions like a ringing telephone will do it, as will an error message box. Some interruptions are unavoidable, but most others are easily dispensable. … Interrupting a user's flow for no good reason is **stopping the proceedings with idiocy** and is one of the most disruptive forms of excise.*[*]

This is a clear anti-pattern that should be avoided. We call these types of overlays **Idiot Boxes**.

One of the clearest examples of **Idiot Boxes** is the way certain confirmation overlays were used in Yahoo! Photos. When users selected a set of photos and dragged and then dropped them onto an album, they were treated with not just one confirmation, but with two (Figure 5-6).

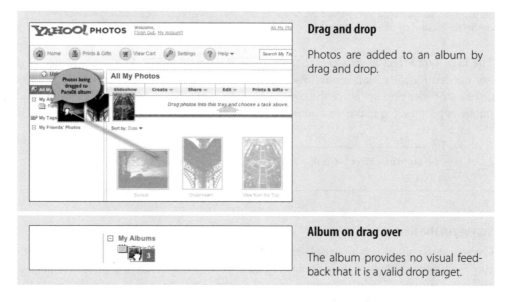

Drag and drop

Photos are added to an album by drag and drop.

Album on drag over

The album provides no visual feedback that it is a valid drop target.

---

* Cooper, Alan et al. *About Face 3: The Essentials of Interaction Design* (Wiley, 2007), 228.

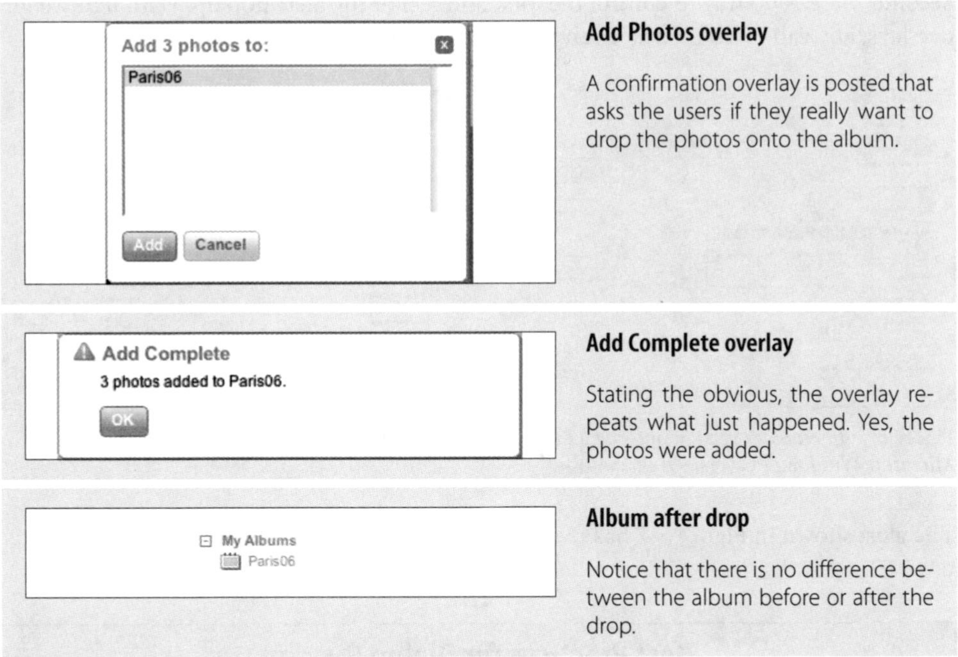

Add 3 photos to: [x] Paris06 [Add] [Cancel]	**Add Photos overlay** A confirmation overlay is posted that asks the users if they really want to drop the photos onto the album.
⚠ Add Complete 3 photos added to Paris06. [OK]	**Add Complete overlay** Stating the obvious, the overlay repeats what just happened. Yes, the photos were added.
⊟ My Albums 🗓 Paris06	**Album after drop** Notice that there is no difference between the album before or after the drop.

Figure 5-6. *Yahoo! Photos uses unnecessary overlay pop ups to communicate what happens when the user drops photos into an album*

A fundamental problem in this interaction is the lack of clear invitations and feedback at just the right moment. Lacking feedback when the user drags over the album (to signal you will be dropping it on the "Paris06" album) and after it has been dropped is often "remedied" by the heavy-handed use of pop-up overlays to state the obvious. We will discuss these concepts in more detail in later chapters.

Tip
Mind the interesting moments in an interaction. They can remove the need for **Idiot Boxes**.

Using JavaScript alerts

It is tempting to use the alert mechanism built into the browser for some confirmations. The problem with using this type of alerts is two-fold.

First, they do not present themselves consistently across different operating systems. Under Microsoft Windows they will appear centered in the browser window, but with the Macintosh they will slide out from under the title bar. Depending on where the action takes place, users may have to move their mouse a lot further each time they need to dismiss the alert (Figure 5-7).

Second, there is no way to control the look and feel of the alert pop up. With lightweight overlays, any valid web interface can be created to interact with the user.

Figure 5-7. *In an older version of Google Reader, the JavaScript alert box displays differently on a Microsoft Windows PC versus a Macintosh*

The alert shown in Figure 5-7 has recently been replaced with a lightweight overlay (Figure 5-2).

Best Practices for Dialog Overlay

Here are some best practices to keep in mind:

- Always use **Dialog Overlays** instead of browser pop ups.
- Use the **Lightbox Effect** when the overlay contains important information, if the user should not ignore it, or if the interaction with the dialog should be modal.
- Avoid unnecessary **Dialog Overlays** (**Idiot Boxes**), as they interrupt the user's flow.
- Don't use an overlay when a simpler, in-page interaction would suffice (see discussion in the next chapter on **Inlays**).
- Avoid JavaScript alert boxes, as they don't provide a consistent user experience between operating systems.

Detail Overlay

The second type of overlay is somewhat new to web applications. The **Detail Overlay** allows an overlay to present additional information when the user clicks or hovers over a link or section of content. Toolkits now make it easier to create overlays across different browsers and to request additional information from the server without refreshing the page.

Taking another example from Netflix, information about a specific movie is displayed as the user hovers over the movie's box shot (Figure 5-8).

Box shots

In the more recent versions of the Netflix site, large box shots are employed without synopsis text. Box shots convey a lot of information.

Detail overlay activation

However, often more information is needed to decide whether a movie should be played or added to a movie queue.

By providing a synopsis along with personalized recommendation information, the user can quickly make a determination.

The movie detail information is displayed after a slight delay.

Detail overlay deactivation

Moving the mouse outside the box shot immediately removes the movie detail information.

Figure 5-8. *Netflix shows "back of the box" information in an overlay as the user hovers over a movie's box shot*

Considerations

The overlay provides a nice way to reveal a synopsis for a movie. In a sense it is like flipping over the DVD box and reading what is on the back.

Activation

The overlay is displayed when the mouse hovers over a box shot. There is about a half-second delay after the user pauses over a movie. The delay on activation prevents users from accidentally activating the overlay as they move the cursor around the screen. Once the user moves the cursor outside the box shot, the overlay is removed immediately. Removing it quickly gives the user a fast way to dismiss it without having to look for a "Close" box.

Tip

For **Detail Overlays** activated by a mouse hover, provide a slight delay before displaying.

You can find the same interaction style employed on Yahoo! News. When the user hovers over news story links in various areas (like Most Popular), a sneak peek shows the news photo and lead of the story (Figure 5-9).

Figure 5-9. *Yahoo! News reveals more about a story without a user having to click to another page*

In both cases the user is given the additional context to make a decision about what to do next. In the case of Netflix, a movie's description or rating prediction may lead to the user renting the movie. With Yahoo! News, since click-throughs to news stories are more intentional, the user will be taken to stories that interest him. This creates a sense of user satisfaction and control, both of which are ingredients to a good user experience.

Anti-pattern: Mouse Traps

It is important to avoid activating the **Detail Overlay** too easily. We have seen usability studies that removed the delay in activation, and users reported that the interface was "too noisy" and "felt like a trap". We label this anti-pattern the **Mouse Trap.**

The reasoning for this is not clear, but Amazon uses the **Mouse Trap** anti-pattern in one of its "associate widgets". In Figure 5-10 the link "Ray! Original Motion Picture Soundtrack" activates an overlay providing information on the soundtrack and a purchase option. Presumably, this approach is intended to drive purchases—but it also presents an annoying experience.

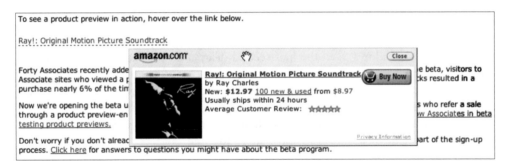

Figure 5-10. *Amazon shows a book-buying widget on simple hover—but requires clicking the "Close" box to dismiss it*

Anti-pattern: Non-Symmetrical Activation/Deactivation

When the user moves her mouse over the link, the overlay springs up immediately. The only way she can remove the overlay is by clicking the small close button in the upper right. Using **Non-Symmetrical Activation/Deactivation** is also a general anti-pattern that should be avoided. It should take the same amount of effort to dismiss an overlay as it took to open it.

Compare the Amazon approach to both the Netflix and Yahoo! News approaches. The activation is slightly harder (pause, slight delay) than the deactivation (immediate when mouse is moved away).

―――― **Tip** ――――――――――――――――――――――――――――――――――――
Make activation and deactivation symmetrical interactions.
――

Another example of **Non-Symmetrical Activation/Deactivation** turns up in a previous version of Yahoo! Foods (Figure 5-11). To see all main ingredients for a recipe, the user clicked a red arrow. This activated an overlay with the ingredients. However, clicking on the arrow again did not collapse the overlay. Instead, the user had to click on the close button (red X).

Figure 5-11. *Yahoo! Foods All Main Ingredients drop-down is activated by clicking on the arrow and can only be deactivated by clicking the close button (X)*

Anti-pattern: Needless Fanfare

One of the advantages of a lightweight overlay is the ability to pop it up quickly. After a slight delay in activation (recall the half-second delay used by Netflix), you would not want or need the overlay to come up slowly. But in the case of Borders online, this is precisely the approach taken (Figure 5-12). First the activation is immediate (no delay). This creates the noisy, mouse-trap interface just discussed. Second, there's a needless animation that zooms the box up into place and then back down when the mouse moves away from a book. **Needless Fanfare** is an anti-pattern to avoid.

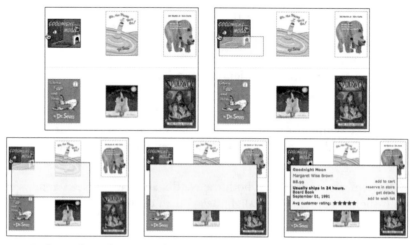

Figure 5-12. *Each Detail Overlay is preceded by the Needless Fanfare of a one-second animation that zooms the information into place*

The animation takes a full second to complete. Instead of delaying before activation, it delays after activation. Perhaps the design team thought that the animation tied the details to the item it zoomed out from. However, the Netflix approach simply creates a bubble effect that points back to the item it is revealing information for (Figure 5-7, right).

—— **Tip** ——
Once activated, show **Detail Overlays** immediately without fanfare.

Anti-pattern: Hover and Cover

We discussed the anti-pattern **Hover and Cover** in Chapter 2, and it's important to keep this anti-pattern in mind when providing a **Detail Overlay**. In the Netflix example (Figure 5-7), the overlay does not get in the way of moving to the next box shot. Even though it covers the neighboring box shot, moving the mouse outside the original one removes the overlay immediately, providing a clear path to get an overlay on the next box shot.

Compare this to the **Detail Overlay** provided by barnesandnoble.com (Figure 5-13).

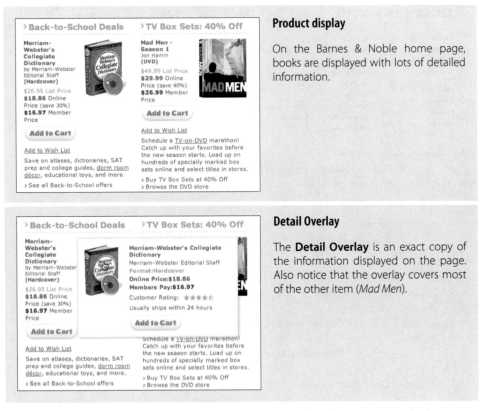

Product display

On the Barnes & Noble home page, books are displayed with lots of detailed information.

Detail Overlay

The **Detail Overlay** is an exact copy of the information displayed on the page. Also notice that the overlay covers most of the other item (*Mad Men*).

Figure 5-13. *Barnes & Noble does not need Detail Overlay since the information is exactly the same as displayed on the page*

Barnes & Noble uses a **Detail Overlay** in a completely useless manner. The overlay contains exactly the same information that the page already contained! Not only that, but the overlay almost completely obscures the other item displayed on the page. It also creates another common problem—the book image (dictionary) in the overlay is not positioned the same as the book image on the page (about 12 pixels difference). The shift causes the annoying illusion that the book is wiggling back and forth, which detracts from the experience.

On the other hand, AOL Finance provides a very nice example of pulling detailed stock information into an overlay that fits in a seamless manner, provides additional information, and does not cover up the navigation to the next item that might be of interest (Figure 5-14).

185.50 5.69 ↑ 3.16%
as of 04:00 PM EST on 12/05/2007 in USD (NASDAQ Delay: 15 mins.)

Day Low	182.41	52-Wk Low	76.77
Day High	186.00	52-Wk High	192.68
Volume	31.87 M	Prev. Close	179.81
30-Day Avg. Vol.	40.51 M	Today's Open	182.89
Market Cap.	182.41 B	Dividend	0.00
Shares Out.	875.54 M	Dividend Yield	0.00
Revenue	24 B	Beta	1.86
Earnings	3.49 B	P/E Ratio (TTM)	47.20
EPS (TTM)	3.93	P/E Ratio (Fwd.)	37.17

More Details

185.50 5.69 ↑ 3.16%   **Extended Hours** 186.75 1.25 ↑ 0.67%
as of 04:00 PM EST on 12/05/2007 in USD (NASDAQ Delay: 15 mins.)   as of 07:50 PM EST on 12/05/2007

Day Low 9:35 AM EST	182.41	
Day High 12:04 PM EST	186.00	
30-Day Avg. Vol.	40.51 M	
Market Cap.	182.41 B	
Shares Out.	875.54 M	
Revenue	24 B	
Earnings	3.49 B	
EPS (TTM)	3.93	

Today's Range
Day Trading Range and Last Price for AAPL

Range 3.59 — Day High 186.00 12:04 PM EST — Day Low 182.41 9:35 AM EST

Last Price 185.50 as of 04:00 PM EST on 12/05/2007 in USD

Top Competitors

Name	Last Price	Day Low	Day High
Microsoft (MSFT)	34.15	33.03	34.52
Hewlett-Packard (HPQ)	51.86	51.04	51.76
Dell (DELL)	24.31	23.75	24.35
APPLE INC (AAPL)	185.50	182.41	186.00
Industry: Computer Hardware	68.82	67.57	69.00
Sector: Technology	30.34	29.74	30.58

Set and Manage Alerts

Figure 5-14. *AOL Finance provides additional information without preventing other navigation; the detail is activated by clicking on the blue arrow button*

Best Practices for Detail Overlay

Here are some best practices to keep in mind:

- Use **Detail Overlays** to give a sneak peek at detailed information. This will avoid unnecessary page transitions.
- For hover-activated **Detail Overlays**, provide a slight delay for activation (about half a second). This will avoid the interface behaving like a **Mouse Trap**.
- For hover-activated **Detail Overlays**, provide a simple deactivation (e.g., simple mouse out).
- For **Detail Overlays**, make activation and deactivation symmetrical (don't make it harder to get out of the overlay than it was to activate it).
- Once activated, avoid lengthy animations or effects that delay showing a **Detail Overlay**. Use hover when clicking the object is reserved for a different action. In Yahoo! News, clicking on the link takes you to the news story page. Hovering gives you a sneak peek.
- Use hover when it is not obvious how to get more information. If you use hover to activate the details, you don't need additional user interface controls for activation.
- Use click if you prefer to make getting details more explicit. Usually you will couple this with a "see more" or a button that exposes more detail. Yahoo! Foods (Figure 5-11) uses a red arrow to indicate drop-down information. AOL Finance uses a blue arrow button to indicate more information (Figure 3-10).
- Use click if you will be providing additional links inside the overlay. Trying to keep an overlay in place (that was activated by hover) and click a link inside it is difficult.

Input Overlay

Input Overlay is a lightweight overlay that brings additional input information for each field tabbed into. American Express uses this technique in its registration for premium cards such as its gold card (Figure 5-15).

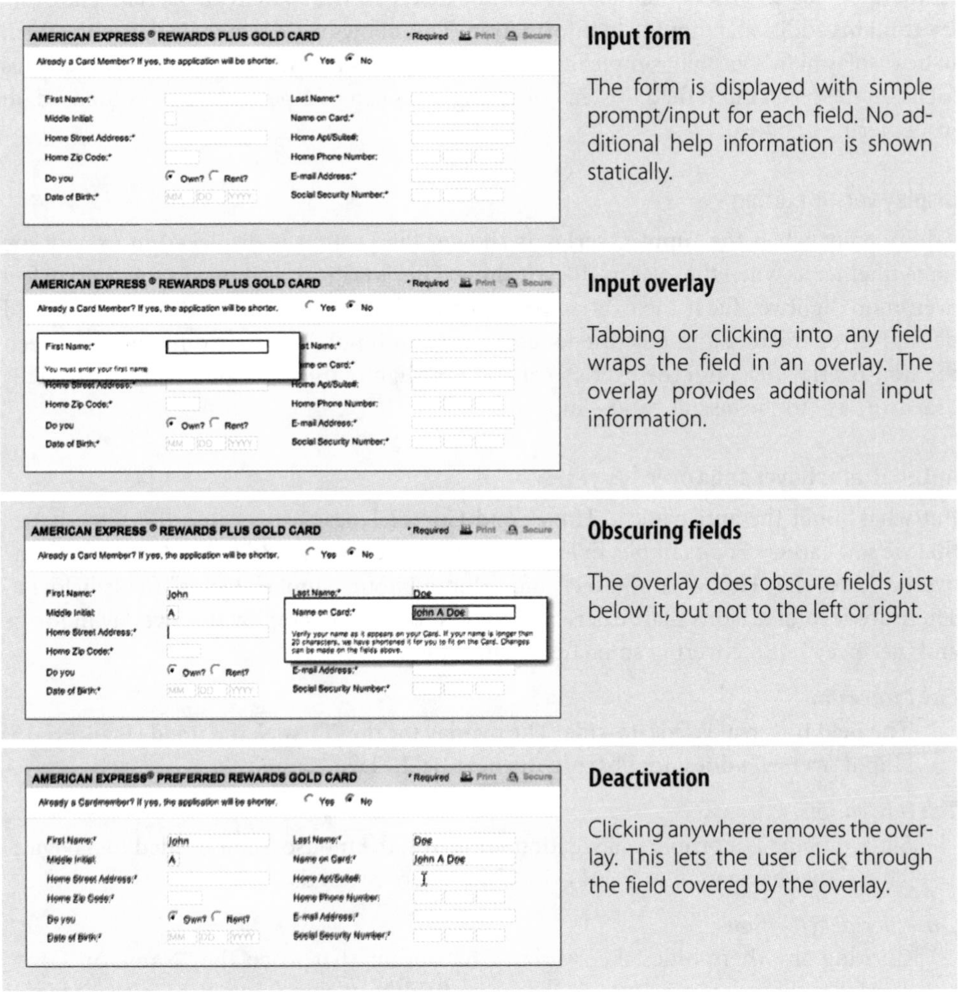

Input form

The form is displayed with simple prompt/input for each field. No additional help information is shown statically.

Input overlay

Tabbing or clicking into any field wraps the field in an overlay. The overlay provides additional input information.

Obscuring fields

The overlay does obscure fields just below it, but not to the left or right.

Deactivation

Clicking anywhere removes the overlay. This lets the user click through the field covered by the overlay.

Figure 5-15. *American Express provides Input Overlays to guide the user through the signup process*

Considerations

There are a few things to keep in mind when using **Input Overlays**.

Clear focus

As the user tabs or clicks from field to field, the field gets wrapped in an overlay. The overlay contains additional input help information. This allows the normal display of the form to be displayed in a visually simple manner (just prompts and inputs). The overlay creates focus on the given input field. Instead of seeing an ocean of inputs, the user is focused on just entering one field.

Display versus editing

Additionally, when the **Input Overlay** is shown, the prompt is displayed in exactly the same manner as when the overlay doesn't show. This is critical, as it makes the overlay feel even more lightweight. If the overlay prompt were bold, for example, the change would be slightly distracting and take the focus away from input. The only difference between the non-overlay field and the overlay version is a slightly thicker input field border. This draws the eye to the task at hand—input.

Anti-pattern: Hover and Cover

But what about the anti-pattern, **Hover and Cover**? Doesn't this cause the same issues that we saw earlier? For example, in Figure 5-15 ("Obscuring fields"), the "Name on Card" overlay hides the "Home Apt/Suite#" and "Home Phone Number Fields" fields below it. There are several reasons that American Express was able to employ this overlay in forms and "get away" with covering some fields during input:

Field traversal
> The field traversal is side-to-side. The overlay for the "First Name" field (Figure 5-15, "Input overlay") does not obscure the next field, "Last Name".

Tab navigation
> Since tabbing is a primary navigation for forms, the mouse is not needed to navigate. This allows navigation to fields even if they were covered.

One-click deactivation
> Clicking anywhere hides the overlay. That means that when the "Name on Card" overlay is shown (Figure 5-15, "Obscuring fields"), clicking anywhere in the "Home/ Apt Suite#" field will remove the overlay, allowing the user to click in the previously hidden field (Figure 5-15, "Deactivation").

Two additional touches that would help with field-covering issues include:

- Give the overlay a slight translucency in order to faintly reveal the fields below.

- Allow a click deactivation to not only deactivate the overlay but click through to the field that was clicked over. This allows the user to click into a field shown through the overlay.

Best Practices for Input Overlay

Here are some best practices to keep in mind:

- Use **Input Overlays** to simplify the visual style of a form. Place additional help in the overlay.
- For **Input Overlays**, make sure the only visual change between the field and the overlay field is intentional (e.g., making input field visually bolder).
- For **Input Overlays**, allow clicking anywhere to deactivate the overlay.

Chapter 6

Inlays

Not every bit of additional control, information, or dialog with the user needs to be an overlay. Another approach is to inlay the information directly within the page itself. To distinguish from the pop-up overlay, we call these in-page panels **Inlays**.

Dialog Inlay

A simple technique is to expand a part of the page, revealing a dialog area within the page. The BBC recently began experimenting with using a **Dialog Inlay** as a way to reveal customization controls for its home page (Figure 6-1).

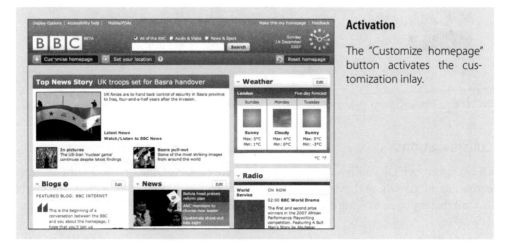

Activation

The "Customize homepage" button activates the customization inlay.

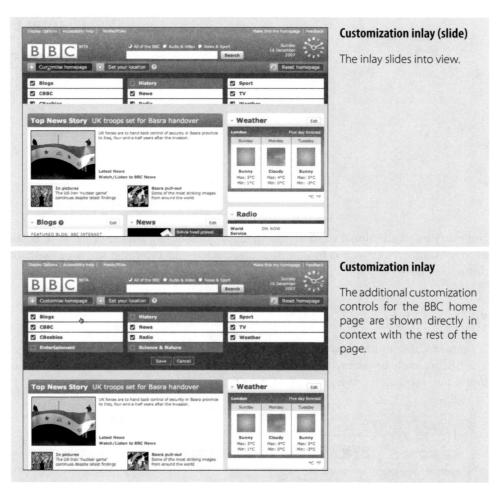

Customization inlay (slide)

The inlay slides into view.

Customization inlay

The additional customization controls for the BBC home page are shown directly in context with the rest of the page.

Figure 6-1. *The BBC home page puts its customization tools in an inlay that slides out when activated*

Considerations

Of course an overlay could have been used instead. However, the problem with overlays is that no matter where they get placed, they will end up hiding information. Inlays get around this problem by inserting themselves directly into the context of the page.

—— **Tip** ——
Inlays provide in-context dialog with the user.

In context

This **Dialog Inlay** is similar to a drawer opening with a tray of tools. Instead of being taken to a separate page to customize the home page appearance, the user can make changes and view the effects directly. The advantage is the ability to tweak the page while viewing the actual page.

My Yahoo! also provides a **Dialog Inlay** for revealing its home page customization tools. The original version of My Yahoo! did not use this approach. Instead, customizations would take the user away to a separate page (Figure 6-2).

Figure 6-2. *In an original version of My Yahoo!, clicking on "Change Colors" takes you to a separate page to customize colors*

Figure 6-3 shows the new My Yahoo!, incorporating an **Dialog Inlay** that slides into place to reveal customization tools for changing the page's appearance.

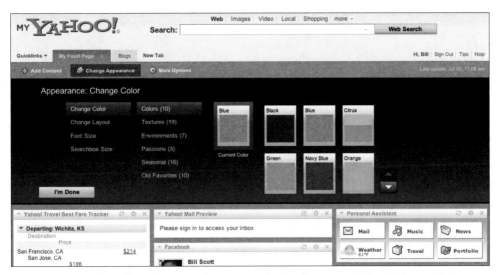

Figure 6-3. *My Yahoo! allows the page to be customized inline by using an Inlay Dialog panel that slides into view*

Here's one more example, which shows how a **Dialog Inlay** can be used to operate on specific objects within an interface. In Yahoo! Bookmarks, selected bookmarks can be edited, deleted, etc. Because a pop up will often hide the items being operated on (the user ends up having to move the dialog pop up out of the way to make sure the right object is being deleted), an inlay can work nicely when tied in with a toolbar (Figure 6-4).

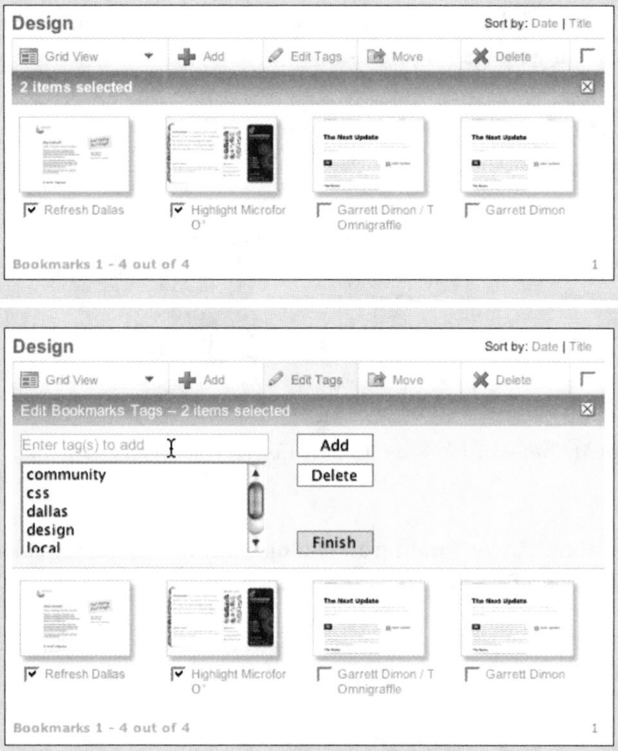

Toolbar + selected items

Two bookmarks are selected. The toolbar at the top operates on the selected bookmarks.

Edit tags

Clicking the "Edit Tags" button slides an "Edit Bookmark Tags" panel into place. The panel provides full editing for the selected bookmarks. The bookmarks gallery is still visible.

Figure 6-4. *In Yahoo! Bookmarks, clicking "Edit Tags" expands a Dialog Inlay for editing the two bookmarks selected*

By being in proximity to the toolbar and keeping the objects visible, the **Dialog Inlay** provides a clear way to expose additional interface elements in context. In all of the previous examples, the panel is revealed with an animated slide in transition. This provides a nice way to smooth out the experience (we will discuss transitions in Chapters 11 and 12).

Best Practices for Dialog Inlay

Here are some best practices to keep in mind:

- Use **Dialog Inlays** for page customization. It is helpful to tweak the page and see the results at the same time.
- To smooth the introduction of the **Dialog Inlay** into the page, use a quick slide in animation.
- Use **Dialog Inlays** to connect the dialog with the element it slides out from.
- Use **Dialog Inlays** for secondary tools that aren't primary to the main flow of the page.

List Inlay

Lists are a great place to use **Inlays**. Instead of requiring the user to navigate to a new page for an item's detail or popping up the information in an **Overlay**, the information can be shown with a **List Inlay** in context. The **List Inlay** works as an effective way to hide detail until needed—while at the same time preserving space on the page for high-level overview information.

Google Reader provides an expanded view and a list view for unread blog articles. In the list view, an individual article can be expanded in place as a **List Inlay** (Figure 6-5).

Google Reader list view

In list view, articles are shown as a list of blog article titles.

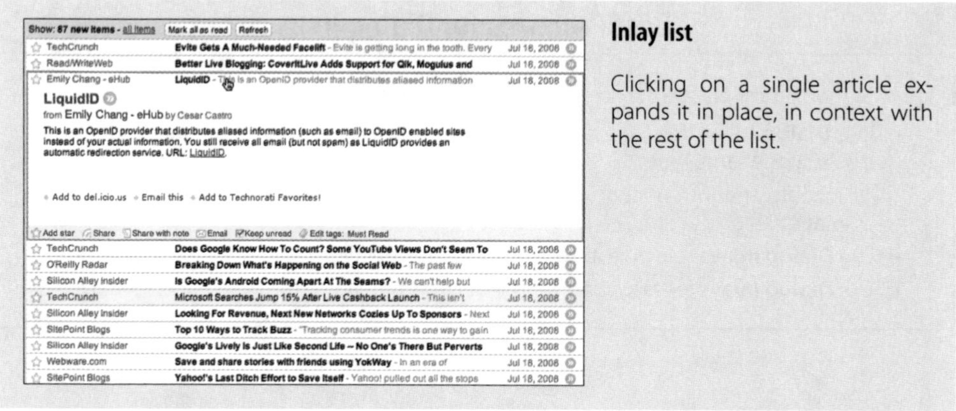

Inlay list

Clicking on a single article expands it in place, in context with the rest of the list.

Figure 6-5. *In list view, Google Reader shows all articles as a collapsed list—except for the one that is currently selected*

Considerations

By allowing the reader to move through a list of article titles (by mouse or keyboard), the articles can be scanned quickly so she can decide which should be looked at in detail. Clicking on an article title expands the article in place. Showing one item at a time focuses the reader on the current content.

Tip

Expanding content in context is a powerful way to help users understand information. It follows the principle of focus+context.*

Accordion: One-at-a-time expand

The **Accordion** is an interface element that employs the **List Inlay** pattern to show only one open panel in a list at a time. The following weather widget demo uses weather.com to display real-time weather information in an accordion (Figure 6-6).

---

* Focus+context enables users to see the object of interest in full detail while at the same time getting a overview of the surrounding context. It is also related to Jenifer Tidwell's design pattern, "Overview Plus Detail," described in her book *Designing Interfaces* (O'Reilly).

One panel at a time

The weather demo uses an accordion to display a single panel of weather-related information at a time.

Opening and closing

Opening a new panel ("Current Conditions") closes the previous panel ("Moon").

The sliding transition makes it clear which panel is being switched to.

One panel at a time

It is important that the accordion control stay the same height throughout the sliding transition.

Figure 6-6. *The weather demo illustrates the way an accordion works: only one panel is revealed at a time*

In this example, the accordion allows only one weather pane to be visible at a time. When a pane is activated it slides open, simultaneously closing the previously open panel.

Accordions work best when:

- Each pane of content is independent
- Only one pane is visible at a time
- Each pane can be logically titled

Accordion: More than one pane visible at a time

You may want to allow multiple panes to be visible at a time if:

- Detail panes provide context for one another
- The vertical height of the accordion area is not fixed
- Different panels of content may be different heights

Parallel content

The Yahoo! Autos Car Finder tool (Figure 6-7) uses an accordion-style interaction for search filters that allows more than one pane to be open at a time. This choice makes sense because the decisions needed for one detail pane may be affected by the details of another pane. However, one problem with this specific implementation is the lack of information when a pane is closed. For example, no summary information is given for the "Price" tab. Looking at that button, it is not clear whether search criteria has been set or what it might be set to without first opening the pane.

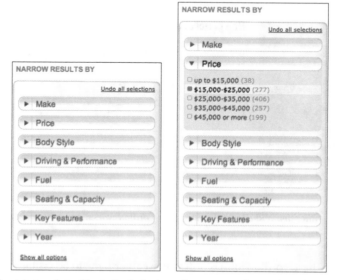

Figure 6-7. *Yahoo! Autos places filter criteria in Accordion panes; when panes are hidden, no summary information is provided*

Wine.com takes the opposite approach (Figure 6-8). Each area is initially open. All filters are displayed. As the user selects filters, the area collapses partially to show the results of filtering. This strategy accomplishes a few things. First, it gets rid of detail progressively—unnecessary information is hidden. Second, it invites the user to interact with the hidden content (with the "view all" link). Third, it provides summary information for panels that do not need to be opened as often.

Figure 6-8. *Wine.com never closes a pane completely; as filters are selected, it partially closes and summarizes the choices*

Accordions can also be horizontally oriented. This is usually best done in nontraditional interfaces. A good example is the Xbox 360 interface (Figure 6-9).

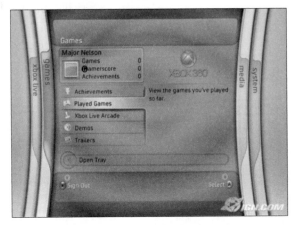

Figure 6-9. *The Xbox 360 provides a novel menu interface by using a horizontal accordion*

Even though the previous examples vary in visual and interaction styles, they all share the **List Inlay** pattern as a basic approach to revealing additional content in the context of the existing page.

Best Practices for List Inlay

Here are some best practices to keep in mind:

- Use **List Inlay** when the context of the other items in the list help the user understand the visible inlay.
- Use **List Inlay** to avoid having users navigate to a new page or popping up an overlay to see an item's detail.
- Restrict it to show only a single item when you need to preserve space and the hidden content is not critical to the opened content.
- Allow multiple items to be visible for parallel content (like filters in a search).

Detail Inlay

A common idiom is to provide additional detail about items shown on a page. We saw this with the example of the Netflix movie detail pop up in Chapter 5 (Figure 5-8). Hovering over a movie revealed a **Detail Overlay** calling out the back-of-the-box information.

Details can be shown inline as well. Roost allows house photos to be viewed in-context for a real estate listing with a **Detail Inlay** (Figure 6-10).

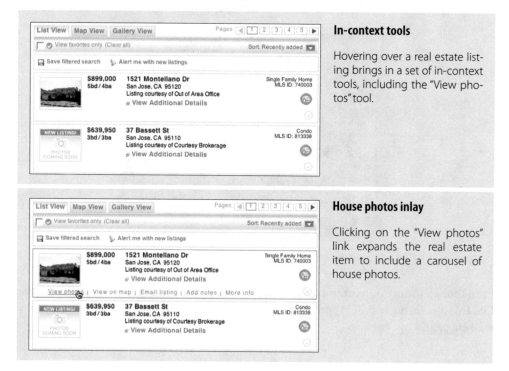

In-context tools

Hovering over a real estate listing brings in a set of in-context tools, including the "View photos" tool.

House photos inlay

Clicking on the "View photos" link expands the real estate item to include a carousel of house photos.

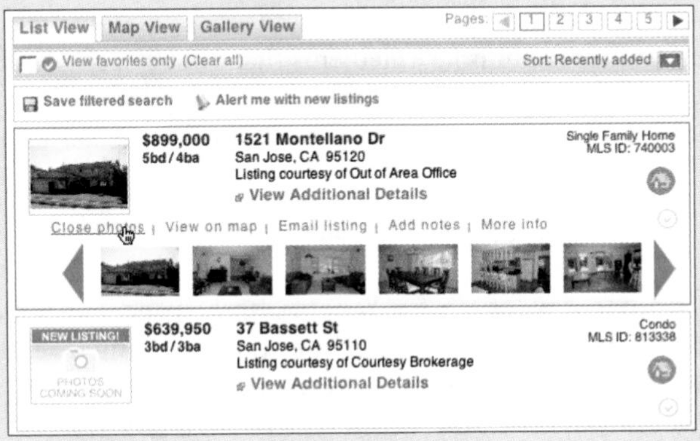

Detail overlay

The **Detail Inlay** contains thumbnails of house photos. Clicking on an individual thumbnail pops up a **Detail Overlay** with a larger photo of the house.

Figure 6-10. *Roost provides both Detail Inlay and Detail Overlay patterns to show home photos*

Considerations

One of the more difficult things to do on most real estate sites is get a view of the house in context without having to navigate from page to page. The curb appeal, inside view, and backyard are all key factors in driving interest for a house. Knowing this, the team at Roost wanted to make it really easy to get to the photos quickly.

Combining inlays and overlays

Roost's solution was to combine several patterns. First, it uses the **Hover Reveal**, a **Contextual Tools** pattern, to reveal a set of tools when the user hovers over a listing. Second, it uses the **Detail Inlay** pattern to show a carousel of photos when the user clicks on the "View photos" link. And finally, it uses a **Detail Overlay** to blow up a thumbnail when clicked on.

Compare this to the traditional approach, one that requires the user to navigate from the listing page to a photo page and back again. The Roost team actually expended a Herculean effort in setting up this convenience, as it is dealing with hundreds of MLS listings with different contractual requirements for displaying real estate photos. The Roost team worked out the difficulties behind the scenes to create a nice user experience.

Best Practices for Detail Inlay

Here are some best practices to keep in mind:

- Use **Detail Inlay** to provide additional information in context without hiding other information.
- Use **Detail Inlay** to avoid the anti-pattern **Hover and Cover**.
- Make it easy to dismiss the **Detail Inlay**.

Tabs

Lest we forget, there are some very traditional interface elements that can be used to inlay details. *Tabs*, for instance, can be used as a **Detail Inlay**. Instead of moving the user from page to page (site navigation), tabs can be used to bring in content within the page, keeping the user in the page.

Considerations

In Figure 6-11 you can see not just one type of tab for Yahoo!'s home page, but three! Three different tab styles and interactions can be confusing. In fact, user-testing revealed this to be the case. However, the design sidestepped some of the problem by giving the three tab areas each a different visual style. Let's look at each type of tab interaction.

Figure 6-11. *Yahoo's home page employs three different Tab styles to encourage exploration of additional content*

Traditional tabs

The Featured, Entertainment, Sports, and Video sections are styled as a traditional tab notebook (Figure 6-11, callout ①). Going from section to section requires the user to click on the corresponding tab. Most studies on tabs find that the first and second tabs get the most activity and the subsequent tabs get clicked less frequently. This is the rationale for placing the "Featured" content first.

Content tabs

Each section has four featured stories. In this example, the "Cute hamster" is tied to the thumbnail and story lead (Figure 6-11, callout ②). Clicking on a story lead switches the content inside the tab. Effectively this is a secondary tab control, but visually it appears as a content story. By switching in the story without leaving the page, the user can get a peek at the top stories.

Personal assistant tabs

On the right side of the page, Yahoo! provides what it calls a *Personal Assistant*. Each tab in this area (Mail, Messenger, etc.) is activated by hovering over the tab. In our example the mouse is hovered over the Mail tab (Figure 6-11, callout ③) and it automatically expands open. Clicking on the link actually takes the user to Yahoo! Mail.

The three types of tabs vary greatly, visually and interactively. However, Yahoo! is able to pull this off because:

- Normal users of Yahoo! will discover these interactions over time.

- Creating the contrast makes a more visually compelling interface, as well as making the interaction feel deeper (inviting exploration).

- It is a great improvement over the old Yahoo! home page, which was completely static. Every link took the user to a different page. Keeping users on the page until they are ready to leave actually creates a happier user experience.

Best Practices for Tabs

Here are some best practices to keep in mind:
- Use tabs to display additional content inline.
- Avoid using multiple tabs on a single page.
- If you do use more than one set of tabs on a page, create a visual contrast to distinguish the tab content areas.
- Put the most important content in the first tab. Many users may not navigate to any of the other tabs.
- Activate tabs with mouse click.
- If revealing the content on other tabs is important, you can activate tabs on hover—but use this sparingly as it can be annoying (e.g., personal assistant tab on the Yahoo! home page).

Inlay Versus Overlay?

In these last two chapters we discussed overlays and inlays. How do we choose which makes sense in our interface? The following guidelines provide some suggestions on which to choose in a given situation:

- Use an overlay when there may be more than one place a dialog can be activated from (the exception may be showing details for items in a list).

- Use an overlay to interrupt the process.

- Use an overlay if there is a multi-step process.

- Use an inlay when you are trying to avoid covering information on the page needed in the dialog.

- Use an inlay for contextual information or details about one of many items (as in a list): a typical example is expanding list items to show detail.

Chapter 7

Virtual Pages

Overlays allow you to bring additional interactions or content in a layer above the current page. Inlays allow you to do this within the page itself. However, another powerful approach to keeping users engaged on the current page is to create a *virtual page*. That is to say, we create the illusion of a larger virtual page.

> —— **Tip** ——
> Think of the interface as a children's pop-up book. Additional real estate can be called on as needed to extend the interface.

Patterns that support virtual pages include:

- **Virtual Scrolling**
- **Inline Paging**
- **Scrolled Paging**
- **Panning**
- **Zoomable User Interface**

Virtual Scrolling

The traditional Web is defined by the "page." In practically every implementation of websites (for about the first 10 years of the Web's existence) pagination was the key way to get to additional content. Of course, websites could preload data and allow the user to scroll through it. However, this process led to long delays in loading the page. So most sites kept it simple: go fetch 10 items and display them as a page and let the user request the next page of content. Each fetch resulted in a page refresh.

The classic example of this is Google Search. Each page shows 10 results. Moving through the content uses the now-famous Google pagination control (Figure 7-1).

Figure 7-1. *The now-famous Google pagination control illustrates the most common way to move through data on the Web*

Another approach is to remove the artificial page boundaries created by paginating the data with **Virtual Scrolling**. In Yahoo! Mail, mail messages are displayed in a scrolled list that loads additional messages on demand as the user scrolls (Figure 7-2).

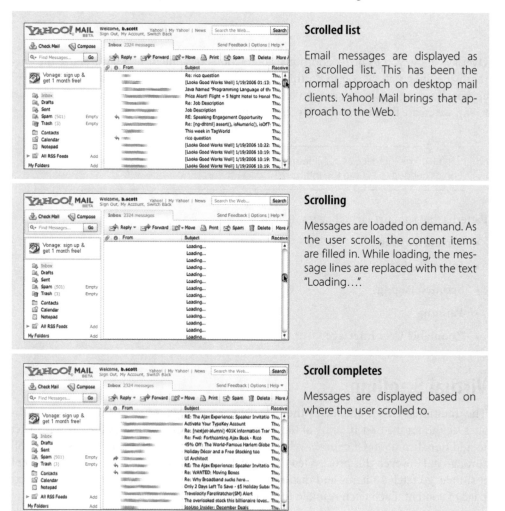

Scrolled list

Email messages are displayed as a scrolled list. This has been the normal approach on desktop mail clients. Yahoo! Mail brings that approach to the Web.

Scrolling

Messages are loaded on demand. As the user scrolls, the content items are filled in. While loading, the message lines are replaced with the text "Loading…".

Scroll completes

Messages are displayed based on where the user scrolled to.

Figure 7-2. *Instead of showing just the messages that can be displayed on a single page, Yahoo! Mail dynamically loads messages as the user scrolls*

Considerations

In some sense **Virtual Scrolling** turns the scrollbar into a "pagination control." But instead of a page refresh, the messages are seamlessly brought into the message-list pane, giving the illusion of a larger virtual space.

Desktop-style applications

In testing **Virtual Scrolling**, Yahoo! found that users naturally understood the scrolling paradigm, most likely because they were already accustomed to this feature on desktop mail clients. Since the Yahoo! Mail Web application looks very similar to desktop web applications, the expectation for scrolling already exists in the user's mind.

Tip

The more the web application looks and behaves like a desktop application, the more intuitive desktop idioms (like **Virtual Scrolling**) are to the user.

Loading status

There are a few downsides to the Yahoo! Mail version of **Virtual Scrolling**. First, if the loading is slow, it spoils the illusion that the data is continuous. Second, since the scrollbar does not give any indication of where users are located in the data, they have to guess how far down to scroll. A remedy would be to apply a constantly updating status while the user is scrolling.

Progressive loading

Microsoft has applied **Virtual Scrolling** to its image search. However, it implements it in a different manner than Yahoo! Mail. Instead of all content being virtually loaded (and the scrollbar reflecting this), the scrollbar reflects what has been loaded. Scrolling to the bottom causes more content to load into the page (Figure 7-3).

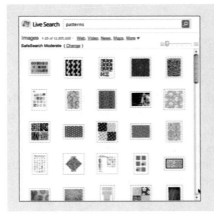

Scrolled list

12,500,000 image results are represented as a scrolled list. Obviously there is no way to accurately represent that many items in a list with a scrollbar. Notice the scrollbar shows size relative to the amount of data that has been loaded.

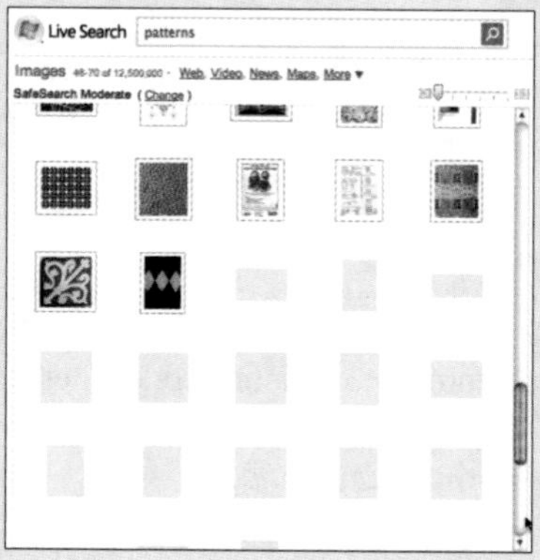

Scrolling

By scrolling into the area where results have not been loaded, images are initially represented as gray squares to indicate that they are currently not loaded.

As each image is loaded it replaces the gray squares.

At the top, the start and end range of the visible images is displayed ("Images 46–70 of 12,500,00").

Scroll completes

Image results are fully loaded, and the scrollbar is updated to reflect where this page is in relation to the previously loaded content.

Figure 7-3. *Microsoft Live Image Search uses Virtual Scrolling to fetch additional search results*

The Live Image Search approach does a nice job of eliminating paging. It gets around the "Where am I?" issue by progressively loading and dynamically adapting the scrollbar to reflect how much has been loaded.

—— Tip ——————————————————————————————
Use progressive loading of content when the data size is large or unknown.

This type of **Virtual Scrolling** (where the scrollbar only reflects what has been directly loaded) works well for search results since relevance starts dropping off the further you move through the data. But with mail messages, this is not the case and would not be a good approach since users need to access messages beyond just those loaded at the top. The Microsoft approach also provides no way to jump to the bottom (although in this case the option is not needed since the end of all results has little or no relevance).

One more example illustrates an endless wall of pictures and uses a novel approach to a scrollbar control for **Virtual Scrolling**. PicLens is a Firefox add-on that allows viewing images from Google Search, Flickr, and other services to be displayed in the browser as a wall of photos that can be scrolled through (Figure 7-4).

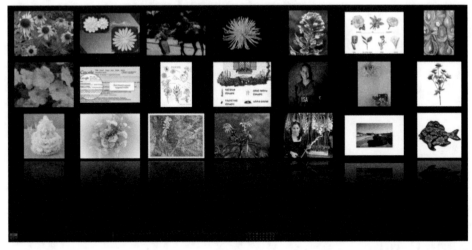

Figure 7-4. *PicLens provides an endless wall of photos; the scroller at the bottom continues to expand with more content*

The scrollbar dynamically resizes and relocates its thumb based on the amount of content loaded and where it is in the data (Figure 7-5). It also cleverly discards the beginning as it gets further and further into the content. The basic idea is to give users good navigation no matter where they are in the gallery of images.

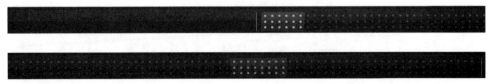

Figure 7-5. *The scroller in PicLens dynamically adapts to show the user's orientation in the data; it indicates how many images are shown and to some degree where the user is in the wall of images*

These examples of **Virtual Scrolling** demonstrate three different ways to manage the virtual space:

- Yahoo! Mail creates the illusion that all data has been loaded up-front by having the scrollbar reflect the total virtual space.

- Microsoft Live Search creates the virtual illusion as the user moves down through the search results.

- And PicLens does the same with the caveat that it shows a virtual window in the larger virtual space (by only providing a scroller control for where the user is and some before and after context).

Best Practices for Virtual Scrolling

Here are some best practices to keep in mind:

- Keep the users informed about where they are. Either use a tool tip or status area to communicate the range of data they are scrolling into.
- Give feedback while waiting on data to load.
- Create the illusion of an entire loaded virtual space for when the data feels like a data set (e.g., Yahoo! Mail's mail messages).
- Extend the virtual space during scroll for search results (e.g., Microsoft Live Search).
- Keep a limited virtual space when the user is moving through search results in order to provide a nice back-and-forth experience (e.g., PicLens).

Inline Paging

What if instead of scrolling through content we just wanted to make pagination feel less like a page switch? By only switching the content in and leaving the rest of the page stable, we can create an **Inline Paging** experience. This is what Amazon's Endless.com site does with its search results (Figure 7-6).

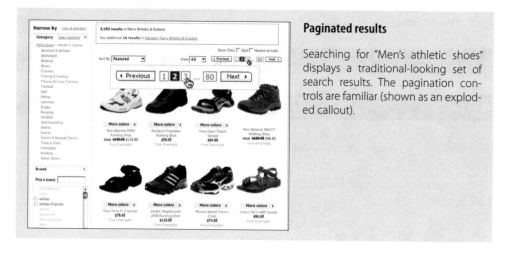

Paginated results

Searching for "Men's athletic shoes" displays a traditional-looking set of search results. The pagination controls are familiar (shown as an exploded callout).

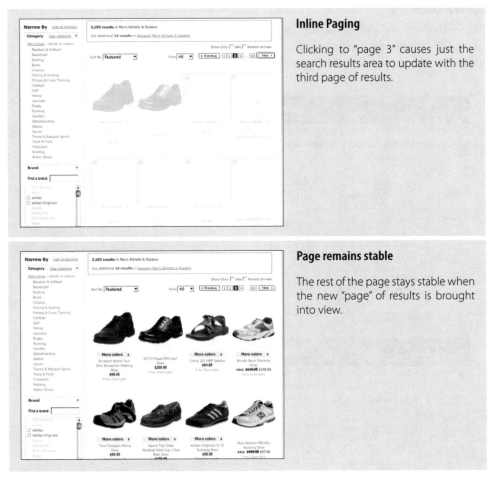

Inline Paging

Clicking to "page 3" causes just the search results area to update with the third page of results.

Page remains stable

The rest of the page stays stable when the new "page" of results is brought into view.

Figure 7-6. *Endless uses Inline Paging to create a seamless experience moving through search results*

Considerations

There are some issues to consider with **Inline Paging**.

In-page update

Endless.com provides the normal pagination controls. But instead of the whole page refreshing, only the results area is updated. Keeping the context stable creates a better flow experience. With **Inline Paging** it feels like the user never leaves the page even though new virtual pages of results are being brought into view.

Tip ───
Paging is sometimes the most convenient and natural way to break up information.

Natural chunking

Inline Paging can also be useful when reading news content online. The *International Herald Tribune* applied this as a way to page through an article while keeping the surrounding context visible at all times (Figure 7-7).

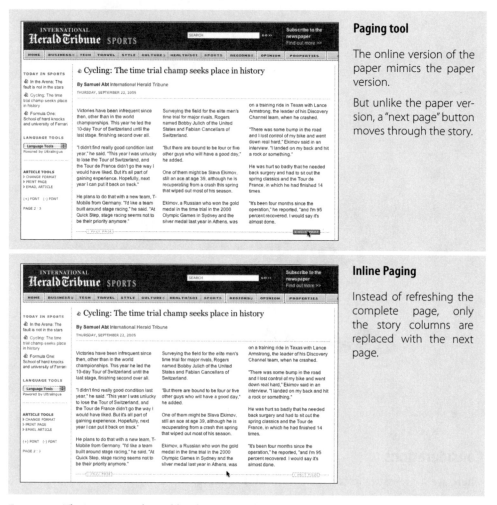

Paging tool

The online version of the paper mimics the paper version.

But unlike the paper version, a "next page" button moves through the story.

Inline Paging

Instead of refreshing the complete page, only the story columns are replaced with the next page.

Figure 7-7. *The International Herald Tribune uses Inline Paging to seamlessly move through a story without losing context*

Gmail also uses **Inline Paging** (Figure 7-8). A set number of messages is displayed on the page. Clicking the "Older" or "Newer" links moves the user to a new set of messages. However, instead of refreshing the complete page, just the message area updates. While there is still some interruption whenever the user switches pages, by making the transition "stay in the page" the interaction feels much lighter, and a virtual space is created through clever use of pagination.

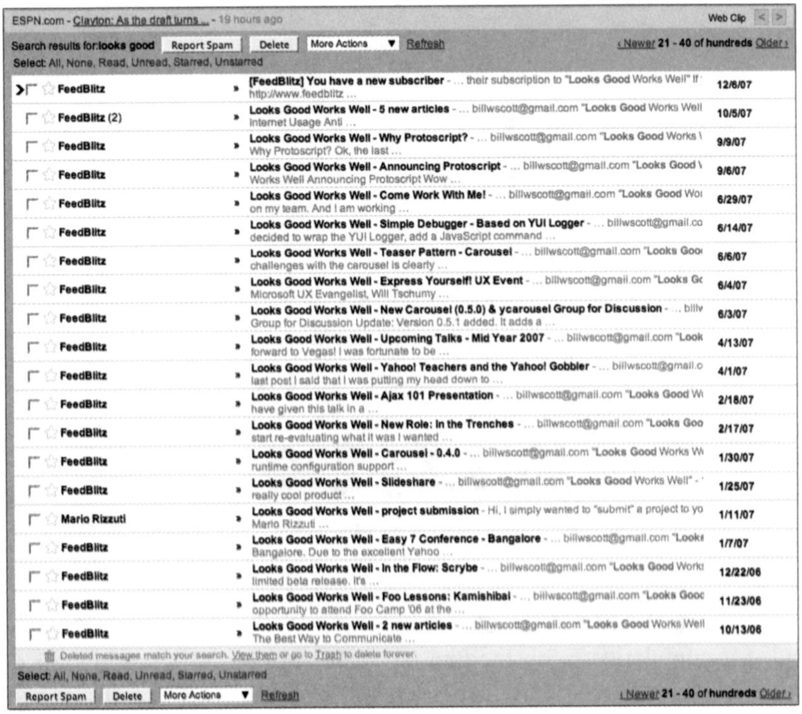

Figure 7-8. *Gmail paginates seamlessly by only updating the message area*

Sometimes **Inline Paging** can be as simple as clicking on a button to load more items into the page on demand. The newly loaded content can be added to the current page. This allows the content to be scrolled, but places the control outside the scrollbar.

Back button

The biggest issue with **Inline Paging** is whether the back button works correctly. One criticism of Endless.com is that if the user pages through search results and then hits the back button, it jumps to the page just before the search. This unexpected result could be fixed by making the back button respect the virtual pages as well. This is the way Gmail handles the back button.* Clicking back moves you through the virtual pages.

Interactive content loading

The iPhone employs inline paging when displaying search results in the iTunes store (Figure 7-9).

---

* This was not always the case. Originally, Gmail did not handle the back button correctly. In the most recent versions, however, it has provided correct handling for the back button.

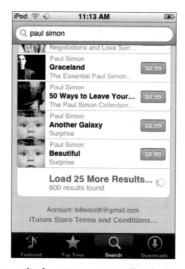

Figure 7-9. *The iPhone iTunes store displays 25 songs initially; the "Load 25 More Results..." button fetches 25 more songs*

Each tap of the "Load 25 More Results..." button loads 25 more songs. The number of songs loaded is cumulative. With the first tap there are now 50 songs; the third tap, 75 songs; and so on. Normally no scrollbar is shown. However, if the user places a finger on the list to move up or down, the scrollbar is displayed (Figure 7-10). Since the finger is the "scroller," the scrollbar becomes just an indicator of how many songs are loaded and where the user is in the list.

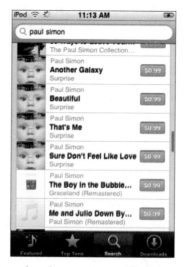

Figure 7-10. *The scrollbar displays when the user starts scrolling through the content; the scrollbar is just a feedback mechanism to indicate scrolling is happening, how much content is loaded, and where the user is in the scroll operation*

Best Practices for Inline Paging

Here are some best practices to keep in mind:

- Use **Inline Paging** for material that is naturally "chunked" but for which you still want to create a smooth viewing experience when moving between pages.
- Respect the back button. Make it work for paging (e.g., Gmail).
- Only update the "virtual page" and not the entire page when inline paging.
- Consider progressive loading as a way to page-in more content in a virtual space.

Scrolled Paging: Carousel

Besides **Virtual Scrolling** and **Virtual Paging**, there is another option. You can combine both scrolling and paging into **Scrolled Paging**. Paging is performed as normal. But instead the content is "scrolled" into view.

The **Carousel** pattern takes this approach. A **Carousel** provides a way to page-in more data by scrolling it into view. On one hand it is a variation on the **Virtual Scrolling** pattern. In other ways it is like **Virtual Paging** since most carousels have paging controls. The additional effect is to animate the scrolled content into view.

Yahoo! Underground uses a **Carousel** (Figure 7-11) to provide a way to page/scroll through articles.

Timeline

The top section provides a navigation control through various Underground articles. "Previously" and "Up Next" indicate where the user can go.

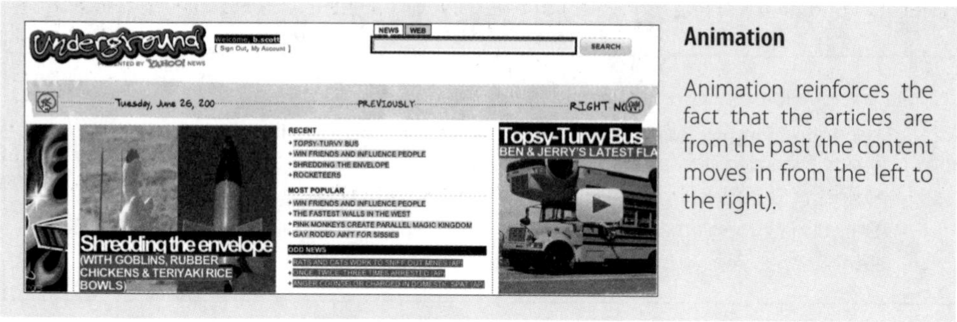

Animation

Animation reinforces the fact that the articles are from the past (the content moves in from the left to the right).

Figure 7-11. *Yahoo! Underground uses a Carousel to communicate a timeline of blog articles*

Considerations

There are some issues to consider when using **Scrolled Paging**.

Time-based

Carousels work well for time-based content. Flickr employs a **Carousel** to let users navigate back and forth through their photo collection (Figure 7-12).

Figure 7-12. *Flickr uses a Carousel to allow the user to get photos in chronological order; this makes it possible to find photos without leaving the current page*

Tip

Carousels are best for featured or recent content. They are also good for small sets of time-based content.

Animation direction

Inexplicably, AMCtheatres.com animates its **Carousel** the opposite way. This leads to a confusing experience, and it's harder to know which control to click (Figure 7-13).

Figure 7-13. AMC animates its carousel backward from the accepted standard: clicking the right arrow should scroll in content from the right (not the left)

Carousel Best Practices

Here are some best practices to keep in mind:

- **Carousels** are best for visually distinct contents. Images, CD covers, and movie box shots are all natural items to place in a carousel.
- If the content is not in a discernible order, users will get frustrated navigating.
- If the content is highly relevant at the beginning and relevancy drops off, a **Carousel** is a good solution, since it spotlights the most relevant items.
- If there is a lot of content to display, carousels provide too small of a window and thus can frustrate users when they actually try to find content.
- If there is limited space available for a set of content, a **Carousel** allows the virtual content to be placed in a row on the page.
- Placing arrows at each end can become tedious if the **Carousel** is not circular or if the user needs to go back and forth through the content.
- Placing back and forth arrows next to each other is simpler to operate but somewhat less discoverable. It solves the back and forth issue but moves the buttons away from their naturally expected position (think scrollbars).
- Make the content big enough to view easily, providing enough whitespace to make each item distinct.
- Allow a portion of the next item to be partially revealed. This invites the user to scroll the content to see the partial content fully.
- Clicking the left arrow should scroll content in from the left (left to right), and clicking the right arrow should scroll content in from the right (right to left).

Virtual Panning

One way to create a virtual canvas is to allow users the freedom to roam in two-dimensional space. A great place for **Virtual Panning** is on a map. Google Maps allows you to pan in any direction by clicking the mouse down and dragging the map around (Figure 7-14).

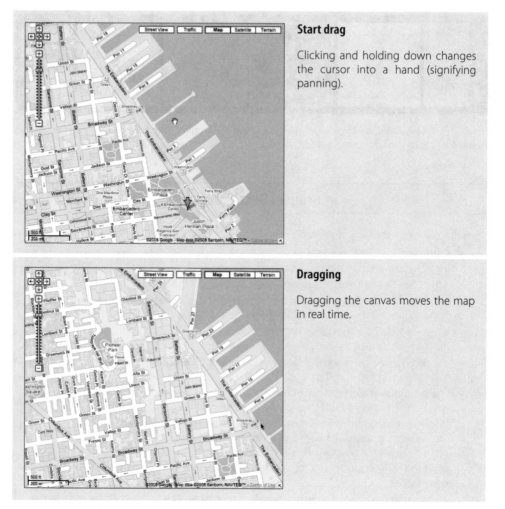

Start drag

Clicking and holding down changes the cursor into a hand (signifying panning).

Dragging

Dragging the canvas moves the map in real time.

Figure 7-14. *Google Maps creates a virtual canvas; one tool that helps with that illusion is the ability to pan from area to area*

Considerations

There are some issues to consider while using **Virtual Panning**.

Natural Visual Construct

When we discussed dragging routes in Google Maps, we pointed out that drag and drop worked well since it fit with the natural visual representation of routes on the map (see Figure 2-26). In the same way, panning around in a map is a natural visual metaphor. Extending the visual space to a larger virtual space is a natural fit.

Gestures

Besides map applications, the idea of **Virtual Panning** has been extended to other devices thanks to gesture-based interfaces.* With the introduction of the iPhone, the user can simply "flick" through weather locations, photos, or an iTunes playlist.

Flicking is similar to panning yet has some differences. With **Virtual Panning** the canvas only moves while the mouse is dragging it around. With flicking, if the user starts the dragging operation and releases, the canvas will continue moving with some momentum. The canvas slows in such a way as to mimic real-world forces.

Best Practices for Virtual Panning

Here are some best practices to keep in mind:

- Use **Virtual Panning** as an alternative to scrolling through an infinite 2D canvas.
- Consider allowing panning to continue with some momentum (think "flicking").

Zoomable User Interface

A **Zoomable User Interface** (**ZUI**) is another way to create a virtual canvas. Unlike panning or flicking through a flat, two-dimensional space, a **ZUI** allows the user to also zoom in to elements on the page. This freedom of motion in both 2D and 3D supports the concept of an infinite interface.

Practically speaking, ZUIs have rarely been available in everyday software applications, much less on the Web. But with more advanced features added to Flash and the advent of Silverlight, this type of interface is starting to emerge and may be commonplace in the not-too-distant future.

Considerations

Hard Rock Café has a large rock and roll memorabilia collection. Recently, it digitized photos of the collection and placed them online for virtual viewing.† The memorabilia application uses a **ZUI** interface to move around from artifact to artifact and zoom in to see details on each item (Figure 7-15).

---

* For a discussion on gestural interfaces, see *Designing Gestural Interfaces* by Dan Saffer (O'Reilly).

† The Hard Rock Memorabilia site is located at *http://memorabilia.hardrock.com/*. It was developed in Silverlight using Deep Zoom (a.k.a. Seadragon) by Vertigo Software in Point Richmond, CA.

Zoomed-out

At the zoomed-out level the user can see thumbnails of the total collection.

Zooming in

By using the mouse thumbwheel, the user can zoom in (it is like flying) on any object.

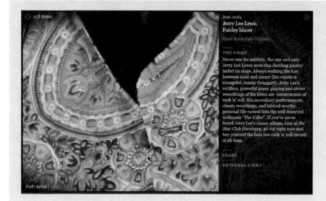

Detail stitched in

As the user gets closer and closer, more detail is stitched in. Detail is only limited by what can be dynamically mapped in as the user zooms.

Figure 7-15. Hard Rock Café uses a zoomable user interface (ZUI) to allow its memorabilia collection to be viewed online

Aza Raskin, son of the late Jef Raskin (who pioneered many of the original ZUI concepts) is continuing to experiment with user interfaces that push the current norms. He demonstrated some potential **ZUI** interactions in a concept demo for Firefox on the mobile (Figure 7-16).[*]

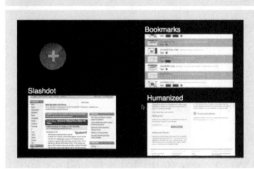

Zoomed-in to content

This browser page lives on a large canvas. This view is zoomed in to the page.

Slide over

Using a panning technique, the page is pulled to the right, revealing a hidden toolbar on the left.

Zoomed-out

The canvas can contain many "Tabs", or windows.

---

[*] You can see Aza's concept video at *http://www.azarask.in/blog/post/firefox-mobile-concept-video/*.

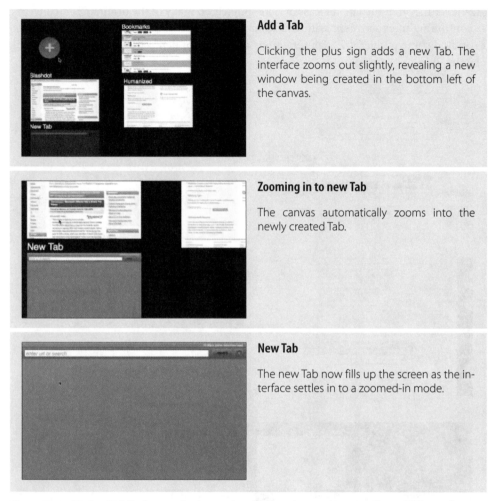

Add a Tab

Clicking the plus sign adds a new Tab. The interface zooms out slightly, revealing a new window being created in the bottom left of the canvas.

Zooming in to new Tab

The canvas automatically zooms into the newly created Tab.

New Tab

The new Tab now fills up the screen as the interface settles in to a zoomed-in mode.

Figure 7-16. *Firefox Mobile Concept Prototype showing panning gestures as well as a ZUI interface*

In this concept prototype, two key ideas are presented:

- Additional interface elements are just off the page to the top, left, bottom, and/or right. Pulling the content to one side or the other reveals these tools.

- Moving between the canvas (desktop) and windows is accomplished with a ZUI interface.

ZUIs provide the ultimate virtual canvas. By extending the concept of the page, the user never actually leaves the virtual page.

Best Practices for Virtual Spaces

Here are some best practices to keep in mind:

- Use a hybrid **Scrolled Paging** for content that is time-based.
- Use **Virtual Panning** for moving around in a canvas (e.g., Google Maps).
- Use **ZUI**s to work on large sets of information that have lots of detail.

Paging Versus Scrolling

Leading web designers and companies have taken different approaches to solving the same problems. Yahoo! Mail chose **Virtual Scrolling**. Gmail chose **Inline Paging**.

How do you choose between paging and scrolling? While there are no hard and fast rules, here are some things to consider when making the decision:

- When the data feels "more owned" by the user—in other words, the data is not transient but something users want to interact with in various ways. If they want to sort it, filter it, and so on, consider **Virtual Scrolling** (as in Yahoo! Mail).

- When the data is more transient (as in search results) and will get less and less relevant the further users go in the data, **Inline Paging** works well (as with the iPhone).

- For transient data, if you don't care about jumping around in the data to specific sections, consider using **Virtual Scrolling** (as in Live Image Search).

- If you are concerned about scalability and performance, paging is usually the best choice. Originally Microsoft's Live Web Search also provided a scrollbar. However, the scrollbar increased server-load considerably since users are more likely to scroll than page.

- If the content is really continuous, scrolling is more natural than paging.

- If you get your revenue by page impressions, scrolling may not be an option for your business model.

- If paging causes actions for the content to become cumbersome, move to a scrolling model. This is an issue in Gmail. The user can only operate on the current page. Changing items across page boundaries is unexpected. Changing items in a continuous scrolled list is intuitive.

Chapter 8

Process Flow

In the last three chapters we've been discussing the principle *Stay on the Page*. Sometimes tasks are unfamiliar or complicated and require leading the user step-by-step through a **Process Flow**. It has long been common practice on the Web to turn each step into a separate page. While this may be the simplest way break down the problem, it may not lead to the best solution. For some **Process Flows** it makes sense to keep the user on the same page throughout the process.

Google Blogger

The popular site Google Blogger generally makes it easy to create and publish blogs. One thing it does not make easy, though, is deleting comments that others may leave on your blog. This is especially difficult when you are the victim of hundreds of spam comments left by nefarious companies hoping to increase their search ranking.

Blogger forces you to delete these comments through a three-step process. Each step is an individual page, all punctuated with a page refresh (Figure 8-1).

Figure 8-1. *Google Blogger forces you through a three-step process for each comment you delete, which is especially tiresome if you have dozens of spam comments to delete*

My (Bill's) blog site was recently spammed. It turns out that my 100 or so articles all had 4 or more spam comments. That means that I had to delete more than 400 spam comments. Given the way Google Blogger implemented comment deleting, I had to follow these steps for each comment on each blog article:

1. Scroll to find the offending comment.

2. Click the trash icon to delete the comment.

3. After page refreshes, click the "Remove Forever" checkbox.

4. Click the "Delete Comment" button.

5. After the page refreshes, click the link to return to my blog article.

6. Repeat steps 1–5 for each article with spam comments.

It took 1,600 clicks, 1,200 page refreshes, 400 scroll operations, and several hours to finally rid myself of all of the spam comments. If the delete action could have been completed in the same page as the comments, that would have eliminated hundreds of clicks and well over a thousand page refreshes, and scrolling would have been all but eliminated. I would not have wasted all the mental energy to reorient myself after each page transition. And I would have been a much happier man.

This is a common interaction flow on the Web. It turns out to be simpler to design and implement a process as a series of pages rather than a single interactive space.

The Magic Principle

Alan Cooper discusses a wonderful technique for getting away from a technology-driven approach and discovering the underlying mental model of the user. He calls it the "magic principle."* Ask the question, "What if when trying to complete a task the user could invoke some magic?" For example, let's look at the problem of taking and sharing photos. The process for this task breaks down like this:

- Take pictures with a digital camera.

- Sometime later, upload the photos to a photo site like Flickr. This involves:

    — Finding the cable.

    — Starting iTunes.

    — Importing all photos.

---

* Discussed in his "Interaction Design Practicum" course, found at *http://www.cooper.com/services/training/ ixd_practicum.html.*

— Using a second program, such as Flickr Uploadr, to upload the photos to Flickr.

— Copying the link for a Flickr set (which involves first locating the page for the uploaded set).

- Send the link in email to appropriate friends.

If some magic were invoked, here is how it might happen:

- The camera would be event-aware. It would know that is your daughter's eighth birthday.

- When finished taking pictures of the event, the camera would upload the pictures to Flickr.

- Flickr would notify family and friends that the pictures of the birthday party are available.

Thinking along these lines gets some of the artifacts out of the way. Of course the magic could be taken to the extreme: just eliminate the camera altogether! But by leaving some elements in the equation, the potentially unnecessary technology pieces can be exposed. How about the cable? What if the camera could talk magically to the computer?

This kind of thinking led to some recent products that allow users to upload photos automatically from their digital camera to their favorite photo site. The camera's memory card actually contains a Wi-Fi connection, giving it direct access to a photo-upload service.[*]

Turning back to our world, when we look at the multiple page **Process Flows** that litter the Web, we find that a little magic could dispense with the artifact of the "page" in many places. Amazon's shopping process illustrates this artifact. It provides a fairly typical multi-page experience when users add items to a cart (Figure 8-2).

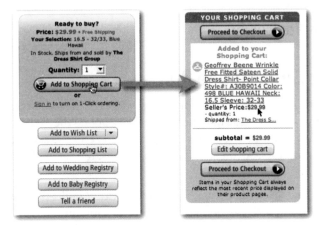

Figure 8-2. *Amazon's multi-page "Add to Shopping Cart" process*

---

[*] Eye-Fi is an example of this. See *http://www.eye.fi/overview/*.

First, the user finds a book. Then when she adds it to her shopping cart, she is taken to a separate page. Getting back happens either through the back button or finding the "Continue Shopping" button elsewhere on the page. Each book add is a heavy context switch to the second page.

But what if we could apply some magic? Could we get away with having fewer page transitions? Could we eliminate the multi-page transition?

Yes. It is possible to take flows like this and present them in a single interactive space. At other times, we can convert a multi-page experience into a single, long page. But sometimes the process is best left broken into individual pages. In those cases we can often encapsulate the multiple pages into a simple **Dialog Overlay**, which effectively maintains the context while preserving distinct page-to-page flow.

John Maeda, author of the book *Laws of Simplicity* (MIT Press), discusses the magic of hiding complexity:

> *Hiding complexity through ingenious mechanical doors or tiny display screens is an overt form of deception. If the deceit feels less like malevolence, more like magic, then hidden complexities become more of a treat than a nuisance.*

In this chapter we will apply a little magic, hopefully get rid of the nuisance of page transitions where possible, and in the end treat the user to a better experience. Specifically, we will look at these **Process Flow** patterns:

- **Interactive Single-Page Process**
- **Inline Assistant Process**
- **Configurator Process**
- **Overlay Process**
- **Static Single-Page Process**

Interactive Single-Page Process

Consumer products come in a variety of shapes, sizes, textures, colors, etc. Online shoppers will not only have to decide that they want shoes, but do they want blue suede shoes? And what size and width do they want them in? In the end the selection is constrained by the available inventory. As the user makes decisions, the set of choices gets more and more limited.

This type of product selection is typically handled with a multi-page workflow. On one page, the user selects a shirt and its color and size. After submitting the choice, a new page is displayed. Only when the user arrives at this second page does he find out that the "true navy" shirt is not available in the medium size.

The Gap accomplishes this kind of product selection in a single page (Figure 8-3) using **Interactive Single-Page Process**. The purple shirt is available in all sizes from XS to XXXL. Hovering over the dark blue shirt immediately discloses that this color is only available in XS and S sizes.

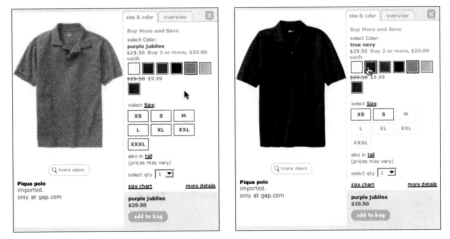

Figure 8-3. *The Gap uses Interactive Single-Page Process to reflect the sizes for each product color choice in real time*

Considerations

There are some issues to consider when using an **Interactive Single-Page Process**.

Responsiveness

The user's taste preference comes first. Either the color or the size can be chosen. If the item is out of stock for any color/size combination, it is displayed as unavailable (by showing the color or size as disabled). By placing this process in a few simple interactions, the user can quickly find something available to buy. With any online shopping experience, the potential for the user to bail out is a real concern. In-place interactions like this reduce these *bailout moments*.

In *Designing Interfaces* (O'Reilly), Jenifer Tidwell uses the term **Responsive Disclosure** to describe this same pattern. According to Tidwell, **Responsive Disclosure** is good when:

> *The user should be walked through a complex UI task step-by-step, perhaps because he is computer-naive, or because the task is novel or rarely done (as in a Wizard). But you don't want to force the user to go page-by-page at each step—you'd rather keep the whole interface on one single page.**

---

* See *http://www.oreilly.com/catalog/9780596008031* or page 123 in printed book.

Amazon's interface for selecting a shirt also uses **Interactive Single-Page Process** with a slightly different interface (Figure 8-4).

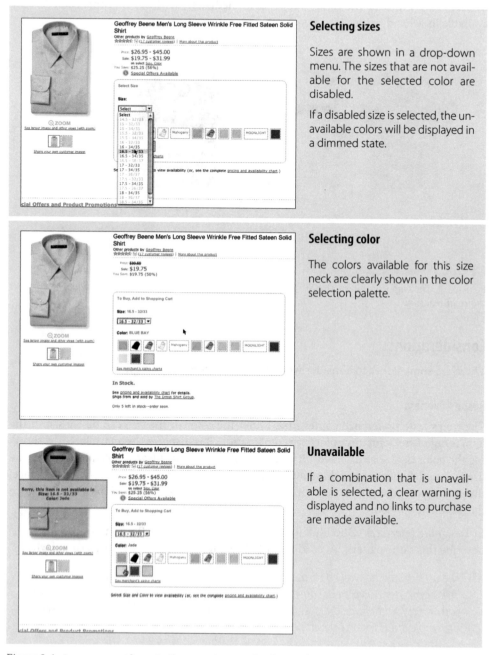

Selecting sizes

Sizes are shown in a drop-down menu. The sizes that are not available for the selected color are disabled.

If a disabled size is selected, the unavailable colors will be displayed in a dimmed state.

Selecting color

The colors available for this size neck are clearly shown in the color selection palette.

Unavailable

If a combination that is unavailable is selected, a clear warning is displayed and no links to purchase are made available.

Figure 8-4. *Amazon provides a similar experience to the Gap, utilizing Interactive Single-Page Process*

The idea is the same: make the experience for selecting a product painless by providing inventory disclosures as quickly as possible, and doing it all in a single-page interface.

─── Tip ───

Interactive, single-page process flows improve user engagement and increase conversion rates.

───

Keeping users engaged

Broadmoor Hotel uses **Interactive Single-Page Process** for room reservations (Figure 8-5).

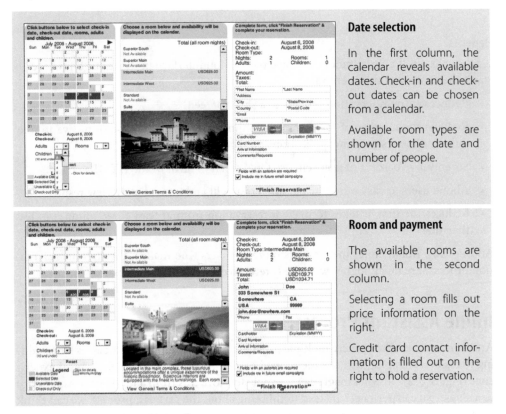

Date selection

In the first column, the calendar reveals available dates. Check-in and check-out dates can be chosen from a calendar.

Available room types are shown for the date and number of people.

Room and payment

The available rooms are shown in the second column.

Selecting a room fills out price information on the right.

Credit card contact information is filled out on the right to hold a reservation.

Figure 8-5. *Broadmoor Hotels provides a one-page interactive reservation system*

Each column represents what would normally be presented on a separate page. In the first column, a calendar discloses availability up front. This prevents scheduling errors. Selecting the room from the second column updates both the room picture and the pricing. The pricing is reflected back on the calendar days (Figure 8-6) as well as in the third column where credit card and contact information is entered.

Figure 8-6. *The Broadmoor calendar shows availability and pricing information*

Benefits

Adobe calls out the Broadmoor one-page reservation interface in its Adobe Showcase.* It states the benefits of this method:

- Reduces entire reservation process to a single screen.
- Reduces the number of screens in the online reservation process from five to one. Other online reservation applications average 5 to 10 screens.
- Seventy-five percent of users choose OneScreen in favor of the HTML version.
- Allows users to vary purchase parameters at will and immediately view results.
- Reduces the time it takes to make a reservation from at least three minutes to less than one.

Additionally, Adobe notes that conversion rates (users who make it through the reservation process) are much higher with the **Interactive Single-Page Process.**

Inline Assistant Process

Another common place where multiple pages are used to complete a process is when adding items to a shopping cart. As mentioned earlier, Amazon provides the typical experience (Figure 8-2). So what magic can we apply to move this from a multi-page experience to a single-page experience? Instead of thinking about the cart as a process, we can think about it as a real-world object. Given this mindset, the cart can be realized in the interface as an object and be made available on the page. The Gap employed an **Inline Assistant Process** pattern for its shopping cart when it re-launched its site a few years back (Figure 8-7).

---

* Other benefits are highlighted in the case study. See *http://www.adobe.com/cfusion/showcase/index.cfm?event =casestudyprint&casestudyid=2486.*

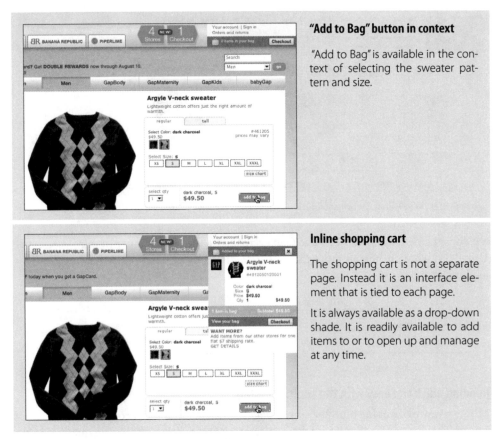

"Add to Bag" button in context

"Add to Bag" is available in the context of selecting the sweater pattern and size.

Inline shopping cart

The shopping cart is not a separate page. Instead it is an interface element that is tied to each page.

It is always available as a drop-down shade. It is readily available to add items to or to open up and manage at any time.

Figure 8-7. *The Gap's single-page "Add to Bag" process*

Considerations

There are some things to consider when using the **Inline Assistant Process**.

Quick and easy

The Gap integrates the shopping cart into its entire site as a drop-down shade. In fact, the Gap, Old Navy, Banana Republic, and PiperLime all share the same **Inline Assistant Process**-style shopping cart. The Gap is betting that making it quick and easy to add items to the cart across four stores will equal more sales.

Additional step

Amazon, on the other hand, is betting on its recommendation engine. By going to a second page, Amazon can display other shirts like the one added—as well as advertise the Amazon.com Visa card (Figure 8-8).

Figure 8-8. *Amazon shows recommendations when confirming an add to its shopping cart*

Which is the better experience? The Gap seems to be the clear winner in pure user experience. But which brings in more money? It's a question we cannot answer, but the right one for any site to ask.

Tip

Use a quick and easy approach to get users to finish a task. Use additional steps when there are opportunities to engage the user further (as with recommendations).

Blending quick and easy with the additional step

Is there a way to combine both the single-page experience and the recommendation experience? This is what Netflix does when a user adds movies to his shipping queue (Figure 8-9).

Figure 8-9. *Netflix displays its recommendations in an overlay*

Each movie on the site has an "Add" button. Clicking "Add" immediately adds the movie to the user's queue. As a confirmation and an opportunity for recommendations, a **Dialog Overlay** is displayed on top of the movie page.

Just like Amazon, Netflix has a sophisticated recommendation engine. The bet is that since the user has expressed interest in an item (shirt or movie), the site can find other items similar to it to suggest. Amazon does this in a separate page. Netflix does it in an overlay that is easily dismissed by clicking anywhere outside the overlay (or by clicking the close button at the top or bottom).

In a previous version of Netflix (or if JavaScript is disabled), this becomes a multiple-page experience (Figure 8-10).

Figure 8-10. *Without JavaScript enabled, you can see the original multi-page flow for the "Add to Queue" process on the Netflix site*

Each movie add leads to a separate recommendation page. Clicking on "Add" for a movie on a recommendation page takes the user to a secondary recommendation page. This process can continue, on and on. Eventually, the user has to hit the back button a number of times to get back to the original context. In the **Overlay** example (Figure 8-9), the multi-page flow is encapsulated in the overlay and can be easily dismissed at any point, quickly returning the user to the originating page.

Best Practices for
Interactive Single-Page Process and Inline Assistant Process

Here are some best practices to keep in mind:

- Use these patterns to simplify user flow.
- Use these patterns to improve conversion rates.
- Show previews in context.
- Show invalid choices in real time. This informs users of the impact of their decisions.
- Show shopping carts inline where possible.
- Treat shopping carts as first-class interface elements and not just as an extra process.
- Show an additional step if recommendations are relevant and important.

Dialog Overlay Process

As mentioned before, any page switch is an interruption to the user's mental flow. In addition, any context switch is a chance for a user to leave the site. We seek an experience that has as little mental friction as possible. But sometimes the step-by-step flow is necessary.

The Netflix approach just described (Figure 8-9) uses a **Dialog Overlay Process** to encapsulate a multi-step flow inside a **Dialog Overlay**. We looked at **Overlays** in detail in Chapter 5. **Overlays** allow us to keep the context of the page yet present a virtual space to conduct a conversation with the user.

Discover.com recently expanded its account section with a more detailed profile. The profile captures things like your payment date, mobile fraud alerts, paperless statements, and general contact information (Figure 8-11). The overlay pops up when you first enter your account.

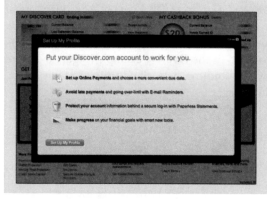

Invitation to set up profile

When entering an account, a **Dialog Overlay** is presented with an invitation to set up a profile.

A **Lightbox Effect** is used to focus the user on the task of profile setup. The pleasing visuals add a level to the engagement factor.

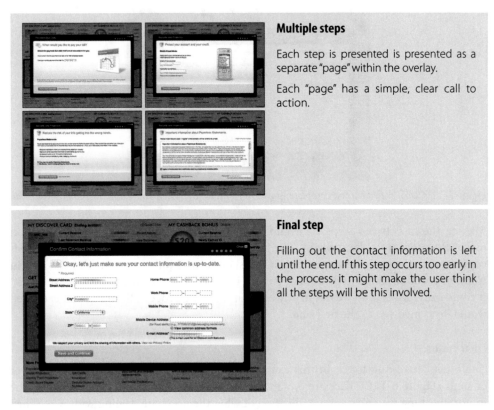

Multiple steps

Each step is presented is presented as a separate "page" within the overlay.

Each "page" has a simple, clear call to action.

Final step

Filling out the contact information is left until the end. If this step occurs too early in the process, it might make the user think all the steps will be this involved.

Figure 8-11. *Discover encapsulates its "Create Your Profile" flow in a Dialog Overlay*

Considerations

There are some issues to consider when using the **Dialog Overlay Process**.

Making it feel lightweight

The **Lightbox Effect** is nice because it focuses the user on the task. But what is smart about the flow is the first page is colorful and rendered in a simple, pleasing manner. The process looks like it might be simple and feels engaging.

The in-between steps are usually a single action. There is a whole page dedicated just to selecting the due date for payments (Figure 8-12).

Figure 8-12. *Discover dedicates a complete "page" to just selecting when you would like to pay your bill*

Making the in-between steps clear and visually appealing with a single call to action makes the process feel lightweight. The last step is the biggest. By this time the user has committed to the process to some degree. Most of the user information is already filled in from the account, so the step does not feel too involved. But imagine if this step were first. It could cause users to more frequently bail out from the process, thinking that each step would be as involved as the first one.

Clear status

The other interesting touch in this example is providing an indication of the number of steps (Figure 8-13). There are any number of ways to indicate this information; the important thing is to give some indication of what the users are dealing with when they start. Usually three steps are ideal. In this case, there are five steps. But as we mentioned, the early steps are single actions.

Figure 8-13. *Discover uses the orange dot to indicate how far the users are in the process and gray dots to indicate what they have left*

Netflix probably has one of the simplest overlay flows. When a user purchases a previously viewed DVD, a one-page overlay appears. Since the only way for a user to get to this purchase dialog is by being a member, Netflix has all the information it needs (shipping and billing information, for example) to complete the purchase in a single step (Figure 8-14).

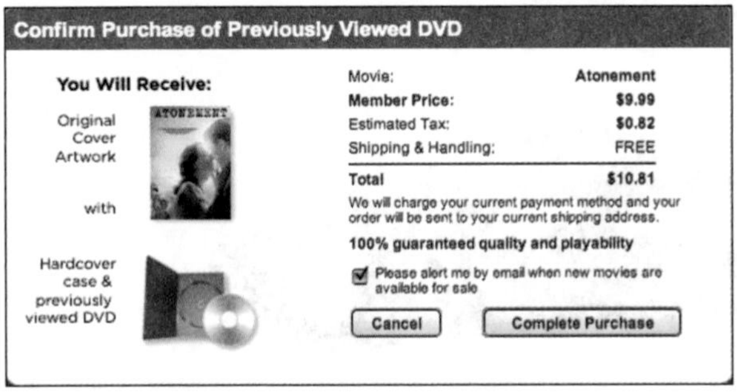

Figure 8-14. *Netflix has a single-step purchase flow for previously viewed DVDs*

Best Practices for Dialog Overlay Process

Here are some best practices to keep in mind:

- Use **Dialog Overlay Process** to make multiple steps appear in context of the page.
- Use **Dialog Overlay Process** to make the process feel lighter than moving to different pages.
- Use a **Lightbox Effect** to focus users on the workflow.
- Keep the users informed throughout of their location in the process.

Configurator Process

Sometimes a **Process Flow** is meant to invoke delight. In these cases, it is the engagement factor that becomes most important. This is true with various **Configurator Process** interfaces on the Web. We can see this especially at play with car configurators. Porsche provides a configurator that allows users to build their own Porsche (Figure 8-15).

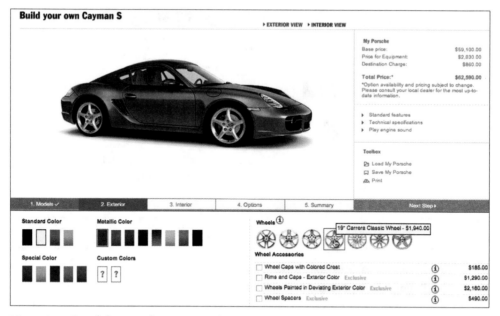

Figure 8-15. *Porsche's car configurator provides an engaging way to customize a car*

Being able to tweak the colors, wheels, interior, and options for a car and see the results in real time is an engaging experience. In Chapter 14, we discuss **Live Previews**. **Live Previews** allow the user to see the effect of his changes on a simulated version of the real thing.

Considerations

There are some issues to consider when using a **Configurator Process**.

Immediate feedback

In the case of the Porsche site, when the user clicks on various body colors, the car is re-configured in the selected color and rendered in photorealistic shading. Most configurators allow a 360-degree view of the car as it is configured.

— Tip —

Use immediate feedback (**Live Previews**) to simulate real-world choices.

Imagine if this was turned into a multi-page experience. Each panel would ask for the color, the wheel style, the interior material, dashboard configuration, and various other options. At the end, you would see your car. Not compelling? By making the experience engaging, users are more apt to experiment and fall in love with the car they have "designed."

It should be noted that the Porsche color configuration experience is actually part of a multi-page process flow. This highlights the fact that the decision between a single-page experience and a multi-page experience are not mutually exclusive. Single-page workflows can live within a multi-page workflow.

Out of view status

Apple has a **Configurator Process** for purchasing a Macintosh computer (Figure 8-16).

Figure 8-16. *Apple provides a one-page configurator for computer purchase*

There is a dynamic nature to this **Configurator Process**. As the user selects items to add to the computer, the price is dynamically updated using a **Spotlight** technique (discussed later in Chapter 11). In the upper-right corner of the page, the system configuration and price are highlighted to indicate updated information. The downside is that if this user is scrolled too far down, she can't see the update **Spotlight** since the summary panel is not visible.

Static Single-Page Process

The Apple example illustrates another way to get rid of multiple pages in a **Process Flow**. Just put the complete flow on one page in a **Static Single-Page Process**. The user sees all the tasks needed to complete the full process. This can be both good and bad. Seeing just one step to complete the process can encourage users to finish the task. But if the single step seems too long or too confusing, the user will most likely bail out of the process early. In other words, if placing all the tasks on a single page is enough to cause the user to bail out, it is not a good idea. In the case of the Apple store, each item is optionally set, and it's just a single click to include or exclude an item from the purchase.

eBay provides two ways to sell an item. An introductory panel (Figure 8-17) gathers the description of the item for sale. The "Customize your listings…" option takes the user through a traditional multi-page process (Figure 8-18).

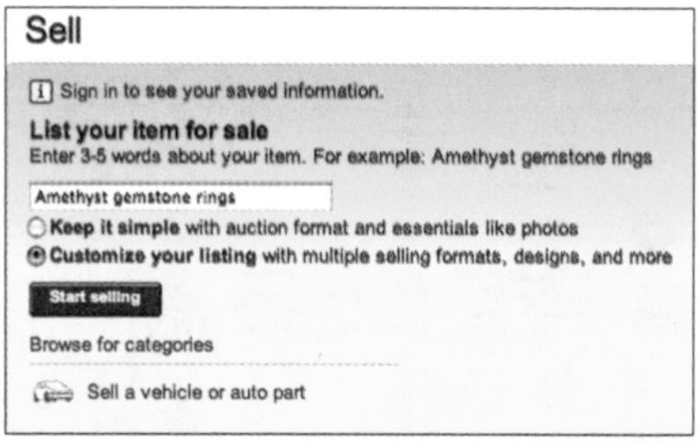

Figure 8-17. *eBay's simplified one-page flow*

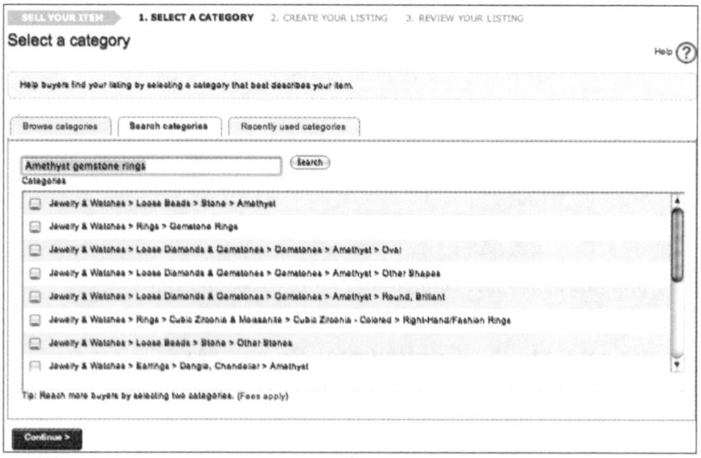

Figure 8-18. *The customized flow is a traditional multi-page process*

Since the customized flow contains many options for listing an item, it requires a good deal of handholding. A multi-page process fits well with guiding the user through a complex set of tasks.

The other flow provided by eBay is a simplified **Static Single-Page Process** (Figure 8-19).

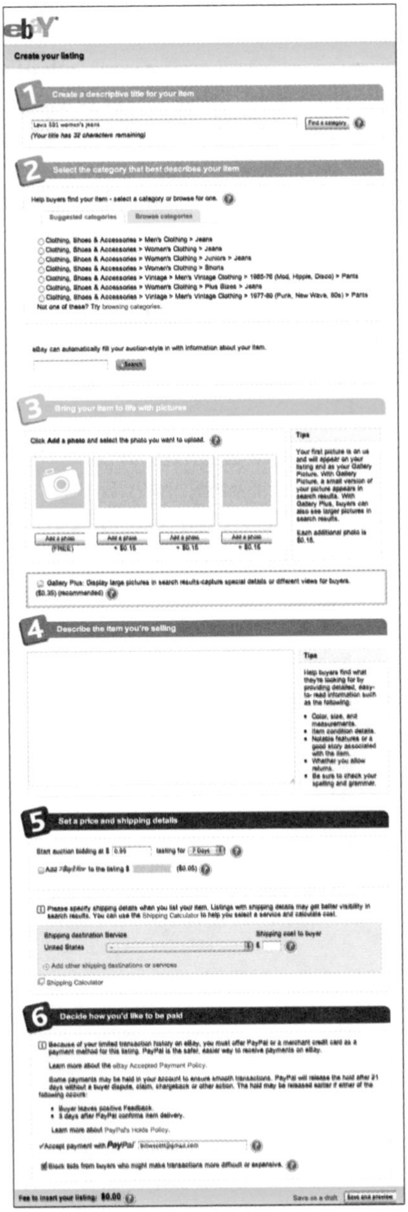

Figure 8-19. *eBay displays a simplified "Sell Your Item" as a Static Single-Page Process*

Considerations

There are some issues to keep in mind when using a **Static Single-Page Process**.

Making it feel lightweight

In this **Static Single-Page Process**, many options are defaulted and a simplified form is presented to the user. Multiple pages are compressed into a single page. Of course a long page like this can also be daunting. But eBay did a good job of getting the essentials into a single page. Each step is clearly called out with a clear border and a large step number. In addition, color is used to further simplify the steps. The two steps in green are about the item the user is selling. The last two steps in blue are about money. The color coding gives the impression there are only four steps total: item, photo, description, and pricing.

Multiple pages are not necessarily evil

The eBay example (Figures 8-16 through 8-18) illustrates that there is more than one way to deal with a step-by-step **Process Flow**. For a very complex flow, a **Static Single-Page Process** may work well.

Sometimes it is good to break what could be a **Static Single-Page Process** into a multi-page process. Multiple pages can provide the natural chunking needed. They say "You are done with that step, now move onto the next." Netflix has a problem-reporting interface that does just that. When reporting a scratched disc, clicking on the "DVD is damaged…" link takes the user to a secondary page (Figure 8-20).

First page

The first page focuses the users on just deciding what the issue is.

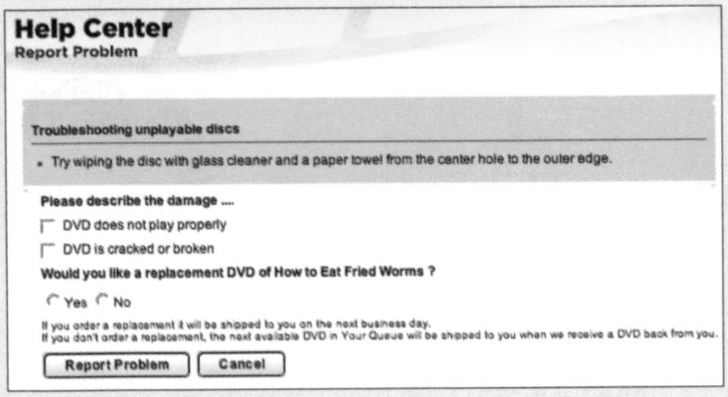

Final page

The second page allows them to describe the details of that problem.

Figure 8-20. *Netflix provides a multi-page approach to reporting disc problems*

Why is it good to have a multi-page process in this case? Confirmation is a critical step in the process. The user needs a place to focus just on reporting a problem. Suggestions can be provided here without the context of all the other possible problems.

Best Practices for Static Single-Page Process

Here are some best practices to keep in mind:

- Use a multi-page process when the process is complex.
- Use a multi-page process when you want to hide the previous context (and the next) and bring the focus to a single task in the steps.
- Use a **Static Single-Page Process** when you only have a few steps and want to avoid taking the chance that a user will quit while moving from page to page.
- Use visual treatments to make the number of steps seem fewer.
- Provide clues as to where the user is and how much is left in a multi-step operation.
- Gather as many defaults as possible to simplify a flow.
- Use engagement, color visuals, interactivity, and simple visual styles to make the steps seem fewer.
- Put lightweight tasks up front in a multi-step operation.

Principle Four

Provide an Invitation

Recently I had the chance to travel to Germany. It had been over 15 years since my last trip, so one of the things on my agenda was to take some time and tour by car. Not wanting to figure out local maps or ask for directions, I requested a car with a GPS navigational system.

The system turned out to be dead simple. However, at first I was disappointed: it did not contain a street map view. Instead it displayed a simplified set of arrows indicating the correct turn and audible instructions just when I needed it. But the system worked perfectly. I found the experience delightful. Instead of trying to look at an in-dash map, I simply let it tell me what to do next. It provided just the right amount of directions without taking away my travel experience.

One reason I needed these just-in-time cues was due to lack of familiarity with the streets of Germany. Being in an environment with different cultural conventions (not the least of which was the language barrier) added to its total necessity. If I moved to Germany, learned the language, and used the roads on a daily basis, then my dependence on the GPS would diminish.

We need a similar experience for our web applications.

An Invitation

In earlier chapters we discussed **Drag and Drop**, **Inline Editing**, and **Contextual Tools**, as well as other patterns of interaction. A common problem with many of these rich interactions is their lack of discoverability.

Let's look again at the way Flickr introduces the ability to edit a photo description (Figure P4-1). Just below each photo is a description area. This area can be edited directly. But how does the user know the area is editable? In the first panel of Figure P4-1 there is no cue or invitation telling users that they can edit the photo description. But notice in the second panel—when users hover their mouse over the description area, a cue to edit appears.

Figure P4-1. *Flickr provides an invitation to edit the photo description*

The background of the editable areas becomes highlighted in light yellow. A tool tip appears, cueing the user to "Click to edit". If users follow these cues to the next level of interaction (from mouse hover to mouse click), they will be able to edit the photo description directly.

Invitations are the prompts and cues that lead users through an interaction. They often include just-in-time tips or visual affordances that hint at what will happen next in the interface.

Providing an invitation to the user is one of the keys to successful interactive interfaces.

In the Flickr example, the designers chose to reveal the feature during mouse hover. This **Invitation** is revealed just in time, when the mouse is paused over the editable area. The downside is that the feature is not visible when the mouse is not over the area. The other choice is to make the **Invitation** visible at all times. There is an obvious tension between the two styles of invitations, *static* and *dynamic*, which we explore in the next two chapters:

Chapter 9, *Static Invitations*
> These are invitations that are offered on the page using visual techniques to invite interaction.

Chapter 10, *Dynamic Invitations*
> These invitations come into play in response to what and where the user is interacting.

Static Invitations

By providing cues for interaction directly on the page we can statically indicate to the user the expected interface behavior. **Static Invitations** provide cues directly on the page. There are two broad patterns of **Static Invitations**:

Call to Action Invitation
    Invite users to primary task or tasks.

Tour Invitation
    Invite users to explore new features.

Call to Action Invitation

Both Yahoo! Answers and Discover card provide a simple 1-2-3 step explanation of their site (Figure 9-1). These clear steps provide a **Call to Action Invitation**. For Yahoo! the individual calls to action are *ask*, *answer*, or *discover*.

Figure 9-1. *Yahoo! Answers and Discover Card use a clear 1-2-3 set of call to action invitations*

Call to Action Invitations are generally provided as static instructions on the page. But visually they can be provided in many different ways (Figure 9-2).

Flickr Organizr

In the Organizr, the user can drag items from a photo set to a work area. When the work area is empty, the area serves as a **Call to Action** for dragging items to edit.

Yahoo! Movies "Rating" widget

In a similar manner, Yahoo! Movies provides a static area that invites the user to rate movies. Once the user engages, this area dynamically shows the potential rating.

Netflix "Rate Your Recent Return"

A top banner invites the Netflix user to rate recent returns. A clear **Call to Action** to rate is important because ratings information is central to the underlying recommendation engine.

Yahoo! Hot Jobs Call to Action button

The "Search Jobs" button is indicated with a larger-than-normal button, a bright color, and clear typography.

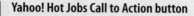

Idea Bob Vote Now

Idea Bob has an extremely clear **Call to Action**: "Vote for it now."

Figure 9-2. *Textual invitation, interactive ratings, and Call to Action buttons are different ways to create Call to Action Invitations*

Considerations

There are some issues to keep in mind when using a **Call to Action Invitation**.

Visual noise

The problem of course with a **Call to Action Invitation** is that it competes with everything else on the page. Thinking through what actions you want to call out on a page (before any interaction) is a healthy design exercise that brings clarity to both visual and information hierarchy on the page.

> —— **Tip** ————————————————————————
> Use a **Call to Action Invitation** for a primary action or to call out main 1-2-3 steps.

Like.com is a site for finding items that are similar to other items. Users can shop for similar colors, shapes, and patterns. Given a particular kind of watch, the users can draw a box around some physical feature they really like about it. Like.com will then find similar watches that match the characteristics that were highlighted. For example, highlighting the chronograph face will find more chronograph-style watches (Figure 9-3).

Since this feature is unique, a **Call to Action Invitation** is placed just above the watch. Titled "Refine by Visual Detail", it contains a **Static Invitation** that says "Draw a box on the item to focus your search on that area."

Figure 9-3. *Like.com allows users to highlight what they like visually about a product; it will then return items visually similar: the black watch matched the face style highlighted*

As with any **Static Invitation**, the question is: does it get lost on the page? The additional graphic that represents a mouse dragging a box adds some visual contrast to grab the user's attention. In situations like this, only user-testing can verify whether users get it or not.

Blank Slate Invitation

Another type of **Call to Action Invitation** is a **Blank Slate Invitation**. 37 Signals utilizes this in its Backpackit application (Figure 9-4).

Figure 9-4. *Backpackit uses a blank page to invite the user to start adding content*

It's a simple idea: starting with a blank slate invites the user to fill it in. Recycling what would normally be a blank area to provide clues on how to personalize it is a great way to entice users to create content. The use of the arrow is a nice touch as it allows the user to read the page as normal, but visually ties the invitation back to the toolbar above.

— **Tip** —

Recycle blank areas with invitations to interact.

Unfinished invitation

Yahoo! has a security feature that helps users confirm that they are indeed logging in to the official site (and not a spoof site). The setup is simple. Provide an image associated with the login page, an image known by only the user and Yahoo!. When users are on the official site, they will see the image uploaded for the login page.

— **Tip** —

Leave an area unfinished to invite the user to complete a task.

The Login team has gone through a couple of iterations on how to cue the user to add a sign-in seal. You can see these two approaches in Figure 9-5. The first renders the corner of the login area as a page turned down. The idea is that something appears out of place, which draws the user to interact with the security feature. We can only speculate, but given the latest revision to the invitation it appears that the first design did not work as well as expected (Figure 9-5, left). In the second iteration, messaging, visual style, color, and proximity have all been combined to create a clear invitation (Figure 9-5, right).

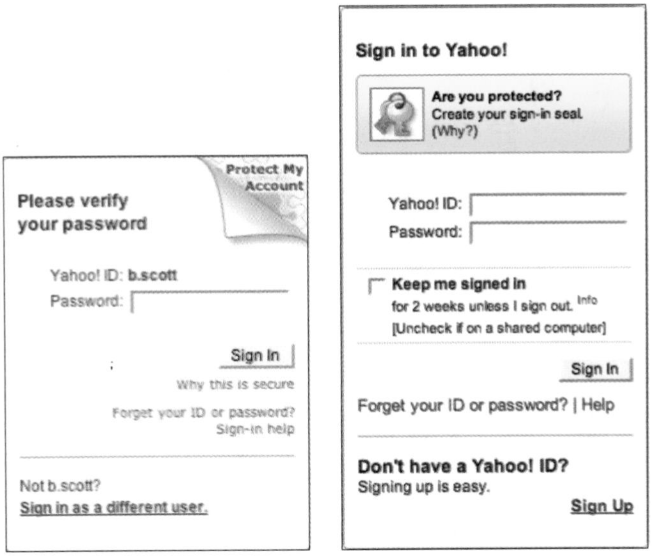

Figure 9-5. *Yahoo! Login provides a Call to Action Invitation to add a sign-in seal: the first version (left) used a dog-ear graphic to get the user's attention; later versions (right) used a rectangular area with a different color background*

Best Practices for Call to Action Invitation

Here are some best practices to keep in mind:

- Use **Call to Action Invitations** for a single primary action.
- Use **Call to Action Invitations** for a simple 1-2-3 call to action.
- Make **Call to Action** areas visually stimulating to get the user's attention. Avoid competing visual clutter.
- Use empty areas as opportunities to call the user to action.
- Use partially completed areas as a way to call users to action. Human nature will lead them to want to "fix" it.

Tour Invitation

Closely related to **Call to Action Invitations** are **Tour Invitations**. The situation: you have a newly redesigned site or a whole range of new features. How do you invite the user to interact with the new site correctly and discover these new features?

When Yahoo! Maps went through a major interface change they included an **Tour Invitation** (Figure 9-6). Tours are a great way to introduce new features.

Invitation to take tour

A drop-down shade partially obscures the map. It has a slight transparency to reveal the map underneath. It provides a **Call to Action** button ("Take Tour") and the four parts to the tour.

Animated transitions

Each step is animated into place and slides slightly up and to the right.

This extra animation is intended to get the user's attention.

Tour steps

Once the tour starts, the shade slides out of the way and an overlay describes a specific feature.

Taking the next step

The overlay provides familiar play, rewind, and forward video-style controls to navigate the tour. Clicking the "Next" button leads the user to the next tour step.

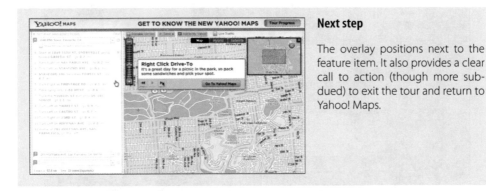

Next step

The overlay positions next to the feature item. It also provides a clear call to action (though more subdued) to exit the tour and return to Yahoo! Maps.

Figure 9-6. *Yahoo! Maps provides a Tour Invitation for its features; the tour provides a way to invite users to interact with new features*

Considerations

While tours can be a nice way to explain design changes to a web application, they are too heavy-handed for showing features at the moment the user interacts with them. And they run the risk of not being used since they are optional to the user's flow.

Not a Band-Aid

Be careful. It is tempting to use tours as a Band-Aid for a poor interface. If users don't get it, then creating more instructional text and providing tours will not solve the real problems an interface may have during interaction. But coupled with a well-designed interface, a tour can be just what is needed for users to get started.

Tip ────────────────────────────
Tours don't make a difficult site easy to use.

The key to tours is keeping them simple, easy to start, and easy to stop. A tour should just illustrate the live site. Going into a "tutorial" mode separate from the site rarely works.

Keep it simple

When Yahoo! changed its home page in 2006, it launched a way to tour the live interface with a **Dialog Overlay** (Figure 9-7). The overlay provides a three-step interface: "Search Smarter", "Find it Faster", and "Get Personal". Each step highlights a different part of the interface with a bubble callout explaining the feature (Yahoo! calls this a "Feature Cue").

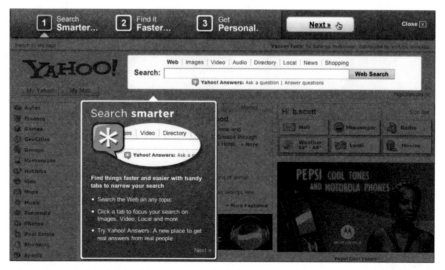

Figure 9-7. *The redesigned Yahoo! home page included a tour interface at launch; the tour provided a nice way to invite users to use the main features of the site*

Simple visual techniques like dimming the page and highlighting the key areas works well. Using a **Lightbox Effect** (discussed more thoroughly in Chapter 11) to highlight features and clearly explaining them are great techniques for keeping tours simple.

Introducing new idioms

Like.com introduces its key features in a large area at the top of the home page: "Detail Search", "Color Match", "Shape Match", and "Pattern Match" (Figure 9-8). Each has a postcard that explains the concept graphically. Each concept is automatically rotated through.

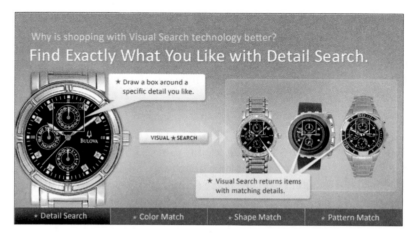

Figure 9-8. *Like.com displays its four key features ("Detail Search", "Color Match", "Shape Match", and "Pattern Match") in a large section at the top of the page; each feature is displayed in rotation*

While visually stunning, there are a few issues with this approach:

- Users tend to view visually treated areas at the top of a page as an advertisement. In tests of several products that employed this type of site introduction, users failed to even notice the area.

- Since the tour is completely disconnected from the site, it is harder for users to map these feature descriptions to the actual site.

However, Like.com is trying to introduce completely new idioms. Creating a nice visual, bold explanation does a very good job of making these features easy to discover and interact with. The real key is that the features are easy to use in the site. The tour becomes secondary and as such may overcome the limitations noted.

Best Practices for Tour Invitation

Here are some best practices to keep in mind:

- Use **Tour Invitations** when you have a newly redesigned site or are launching a new site and need to take the user through a series of features.
- Integrate **Tour Invitations** with the live site as much as possible.
- Make **Tour Invitations** short and sweet, easy to exit, and clear to restart.
- Don't depend on tours to fix interface issues.
- Keep tours simple.

Chapter 10

Dynamic Invitations

Static Invitations are useful for cueing the user about what the interface has to offer. However, it is a fact established by many independent tests that users often don't read instructional text. A good way to get the users' attention is to provide invitations to interact at the moment when they need it. **Dynamic Invitations** engage users at the point of the interaction and guide them through the next step of interaction.

There are several ways to engage the user with a **Dynamic Invitation:**

Hover Invitation
> During mouse hover.

Affordance Invitation
> Using the familiar as a bridge to the new.

Drag and Drop Invitation
> For drag and drop.

Inference Invitation
> During interaction.

More Content Invitation
> For revealing more content.

Hover Invitation

One way to engage the user is by using the mouse hover to show a **Hover Invitation**.

The Gap uses the mouse hover event to invite its shoppers to take a more detailed look at an item (Figure 10-1).

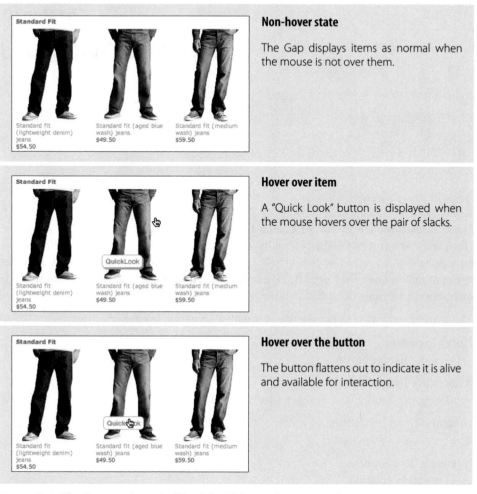

Non-hover state

The Gap displays items as normal when the mouse is not over them.

Hover over item

A "Quick Look" button is displayed when the mouse hovers over the pair of slacks.

Hover over the button

The button flattens out to indicate it is alive and available for interaction.

Figure 10-1. *The Gap provides a nice "Quick Look" feature that is exposed as a Hover Invitation*

Considerations

There are some issues to keep in mind when using a **Hover Invitation**.

Visual cues

The button revealed uses inviting language. The term "Quick Look" makes it seem quick and easy. The button also looks like a button. The affordance of a button is clear; buttons have a clear connection with providing an action. It says to the user "click me" without saying it directly. The button also visually contrasts with the item hovered over. Finally, the proximity of the invitation clarifies which item can be inspected.

Another nice touch is that the button changes visual depth when the mouse hovers over it. This detail hints that the button can be clicked. It gives a signal to what the next level of interaction should be—clicking the button. It provides a **Hover Invitation**.

Notice also that this employs the best practice we discussed in the last chapter: using familiar idioms to bridge the gap to new interactions.

Interactive versus static

Like.com takes a different approach. For every product, it displays a "Visual Search" button. Instead of revealing the invitation on hover, it uses a **Static Invitation (Call to Action)**. Is this the right approach?

Like.com has a very different model for search. Most likely in the interest of exposing this feature, it chose to show the button at all times on all products (Figure 10-2). This strategy does have a downside, though. It makes the page elements compete with the product. Each button becomes a "visual speed bump." And by having buttons everywhere, they run the risk of the actions not being seen at all. If Like.com chose to reveal the button on hover, it might actually be more effective at grabbing the user's attention.

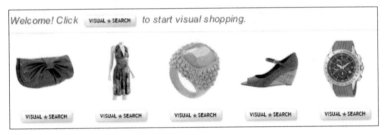

Figure 10-2. *Like.com chose to display the "Visual Search" button at all times, most likely because it is a key feature on the site*

The tension between revealing a feature statically on the page versus more subtly during interaction is based on how primary the action is, and is best resolved through user testing.

Netflix uses **Static Invitations** to reveal star ratings and the "Add" button for every movie shown on the page (Figure 10-3). As with Like.com, this setup has the negative effect of making the page visually heavier. But as with Like.com, priority is clearly placed on the exposed features.

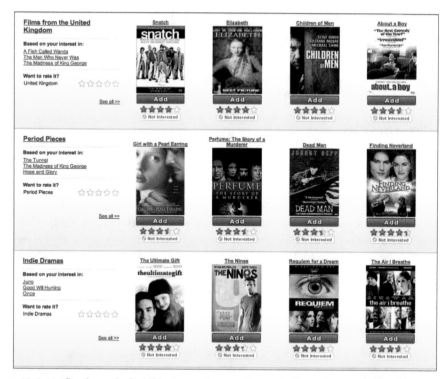

Figure 10-3. *Netflix shows the "Add" button and star rating statically on the page; both adding movies to the queue and rating them are important to the user's experience with the service*

Both Like.com and Netflix have specific reasons that drove them to not use a **Hover Invitation** to reveal these actions but instead to use the **Call to Action Invitation**. An egregious example can be contrived by changing the design of Backpackit to show all of its in-context tools at the same time (Figure 10-4).

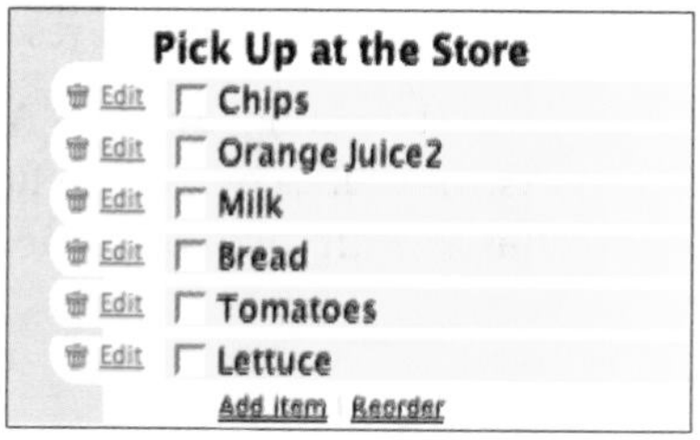

Figure 10-4. *A portrayal of what Backpackit would look like if it displayed all actions at once (this is not the approach Backpackit took)*

This setup would not work at all as it is so visually dense it distracts from the to-do list itself. Looking at this extreme example helps us to evaluate the tension between being visually explicit and interactively subtle:

- Choose being visually explicit if your actions are key actions and you can do it in such a way as to not be too visually dense.

- Choose being interactively subtle whenever possible if the actions are secondary to the content and the primary goal is readability and visual simplicity.

Enhancing Hover Invitation

There are several ways you can enhance a **Hover Invitation** (see Figures 10-5 and 10-6):

- Highlight the background of the hovered area (Flickr's yellow background).

- Use a tool tip to describe the action that will happen on click (Flickr's "Click to edit" tool tip).

- Change the cursor to reflect the operation (Flickr's insertion cursor).

- Provide an in-context preview for the action (Yahoo! Movie's rating widget).

Figure 10-5. *Flickr highlights the background, displays a tool tip, and changes the cursor to invite the user to edit*

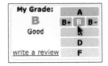

Figure 10-6. *Yahoo! Movies previews what the rating will look like after it gets chosen*

Previewing what effect the action will have is a really nice way to invite the user to engage with a feature. Yahoo! Movies does this by showing the grade in the left pane as it will appear after the grade is chosen (Figure 10-6). LandsEnd.com does just the opposite. When the user hovers over a color swatch, the slacks do not change color; only after a click does this happen. The downside is that the user can't just quickly roll over the swatches and see what each looks like. Additionally, the user only knows if a color is unavailable after clicking on the color swatch (Figure 10-7).

Figure 10-7. LandsEnd.com does not show colors on hover; only on click will the color be shown

---

Best Practices for Hover Invitation

Here are some best practices to keep in mind:

- Use **Hover Invitations** when the actions are secondary to content and you want to keep the visual style uncluttered.
- For **Hover Invitations**, use cursor change, background change, and tool tips to clearly indicate the invited action.
- During **Hover Invitations**, try to preview what the change will be if the user clicks.
- Sprinkle familiar idioms throughout the various stages of an interaction. Bridging the new with the old will make the new become familiar more quickly. The most common idioms to use are buttons, links, drop-down arrows, and familiar icons.
- Use proximity to clarify what an invitation is referring to. Changing the cursor while over an object indicates that the invitation applies to the object being hovered over.

Affordance Invitation

In his book *The Design of Everyday Things* (Basic Books), Donald Norman applied the term *affordance* to design. The original use of the term goes back to J. J. Gibson, a perceptual psychologist. Gibson used the term to describe the actionable properties of an object. The classic example is that of a doorknob. To humans the affordance provided is the ability to grasp, turn, or pull the handle. In Gibson's view the property did not have to be visible, it just needed to be something the actor (human or animal) perceived as a way to interact with the object. Norman used this term to describe the idea of a *perceived affordance* for a user interface element. He hastened to add that the perceived affordance on screen elements does not have physical properties, but on some level users will perceive that they can interact with them largely due to convention, terminology, metaphor, and consistency.*

Considerations

There are some issues to consider when using an **Affordance Invitation**.

Bridging the new with the familiar

An **Affordance Invitation** plays off of the familiar to provide an invitation to interact. It works since following understood conventions helps introduce new interaction techniques. By bridging new interaction styles with familiar idioms, the user can be led through a sequence of interactions.

Flickr allows users to perform a number of actions with other Flickr users. Anywhere a user's picture is displayed, a set of actions is revealed on mouse hover. The familiar idea of a drop-down arrow (normally leading to a set of choices or a menu) invites the user to click to see the available actions (Figure 10-8).

Non-hover state

A user's photo is displayed in a visually non-cluttered style. Just the picture, not interface tools, is visible.

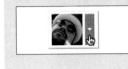

Hover state

When the mouse enters the photo, an additional interface element (a drop-down arrow) is revealed. The photo gets treated with visual depth: this creates an affordance that this is an interface control and not just content.

Arrow hover state

When the mouse enters the drop-down arrow, additional highlighting (arrow background inverts to blue) is revealed. Again, this reinforces visually that this is indeed a button. Buttons are familiar idioms.

---

* For a fuller discussion of the nuance between an affordance and a perceived affordance, see *http://www. interaction-design.org/encyclopedia/affordances.html.*

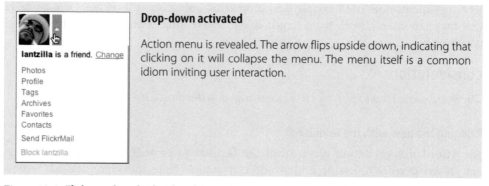

Drop-down activated

Action menu is revealed. The arrow flips upside down, indicating that clicking on it will collapse the menu. The menu itself is a common idiom inviting user interaction.

Figure 10-8. Flickr employs the familiar drop-down affordance when the user hovers over another Flickr user's profile picture; clicking the drop-down reveals a menu of actions

---

Tip

Bridge new interactions with familiar idioms.

Multiple idioms

During this interaction sequence, several idioms are revealed. Each revealed idiom is familiar and naturally leads the user to the next level of interaction. In the Flickr example the **Contextual Tool** for contacts has these affordance attributes:

Looks like a button
> When the user hovers over a photo, it gets a visual depth treatment that looks like a button.

Has a drop-down arrow
> A drop-down arrow is part of the visual button treatment. It is slightly separated (by whitespace) to emphasize that it has a specific function.

Provides a drop-down menu
> When the menu is revealed, it is an obvious idiom that the user knows how to interact with.

Inverts the arrow
> The drop-down arrow is flipped upside down to indicate that the menu can be closed.

At each step in the interaction, a familiar idiom is revealed. Each tugs the user forward into the interaction.

Another common idiom used throughout the Web is the hyperlink. It clearly indicates a possible "click" (Figure 10-9).

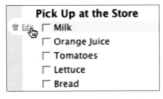

Figure 10-9. *Backpackit uses the familiar idioms hyperlink and trashcan to indicate each tool's purpose (edit and delete)*

Recall from our earlier examples of Backpackit that hovering over a to-do item reveals contextual tools. The "Edit" tool is represented as a hyperlink. The interaction is fairly obvious. Clicking the link will do something. The link is labeled "Edit" so it should edit something. Because it is revealed when the mouse is over the "Milk" item and the "Edit" link is placed in proximity to it, we can assume it will edit the "Milk" item.

Perceived affordance

The other tool revealed is a trashcan icon. Again, most users are familiar with the trash-can icon idiom. It has been in use since the early 1980s, and was popularized by the Apple Macintosh. It is fairly obvious that clicking the trashcan will delete "Milk" from our to-do list.

While dynamically revealing contextual tools might initially be unexpected, the use of these **Affordance Invitations** serves as a bridge to invite the user to understand how to complete a task.

Best Practices for Affordance Invitation

Here are some best practices to keep in mind:

- Bridge new, unfamiliar interactions with classic, familiar idioms (e.g., revealing a hyperlink for an action on **Contextual Tools**).
- Use perceived affordances to cue an invitation (e.g., an arrow that points down before drop-down, then up to cue that the arrow will close the menu).
- Place **Invitations** in context, in proximity to the interaction.

Drag and Drop Invitation

When we discussed drag and drop in Chapter 2 we stressed the challenge of getting the interaction right. There are more than a dozen interesting moments of interaction in any drag and drop interaction (see Figure 2-2). Many of these moments are opportunities to provide **Drag and Drop Invitations**.

The Events

In Chapter 2, we listed 15 different events that are available to the designer to cue the user during a drag and drop interaction. Here are the 15 drag and drop events we listed in that chapter:

- **Page Load**
- **Mouse Hover**
- **Mouse Down**
- **Drag Initiated**
- **Drag Leaves Original Location**
- **Drag Re-Enters Original Location**
- **Drag Enters Valid Target**
- **Drag Exits Valid Target**
- **Drag Enters Specific Invalid Target**
- **Drag Is Over No Specific Target**
- **Drag Hovers Over Valid Target**
- **Drag Hovers Over Invalid Target**
- **Drop Accepted**
- **Drop Rejected**
- **Drop on Parent Container**

As with any complex interaction, it is key to guide the user through each step. Given this many interactions, it's important to show invitations at key moments.

While at Yahoo!, I (Bill) worked on the Yahoo! for Teachers product. A key feature is the Yahoo! Gobbler™, which allows teachers to grab text clippings, images, and links from pages around the Web and "gobble" them back to their classroom projects (Figure 10-10).

Non-drag state

The Yahoo! Gobbler allows teachers to grab elements from the page (images, text clippings, links) and drag them into the Gobbler tool. Items dropped into projects in the Gobbler are saved automatically to the Yahoo! for Teachers portfolio of projects.

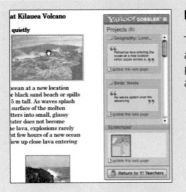

Hover over draggable object

To indicate that an image can be dragged from the page, an orange border highlight and a selection color tint is applied to the image. This indicates to the users that the image is draggable and invites them to initiate a drag.

Drag initiated

Once the drag is initiated, a small thumbnail representation can be dragged around.

There is an additional opportunity missed for an invitation, however. When drag is initiated, all of the valid drop objects could be lightly highlighted. This would indicate to the user where it is valid to drag items.

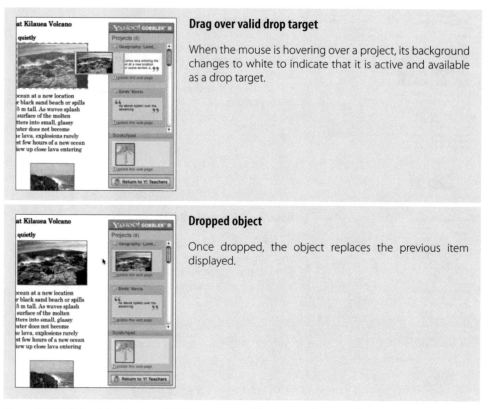

Drag over valid drop target

When the mouse is hovering over a project, its background changes to white to indicate that it is active and available as a drop target.

Dropped object

Once dropped, the object replaces the previous item displayed.

Figure 10-10. Yahoo! for Teachers Gobbler uses several invitations during a drag and drop interaction

Considerations

The challenge is how to indicate that items on the page are draggable and what to do with them once they are dragged. The interaction is made clear by highlighting draggable items on hover, indicating where something has been ripped from, showing a miniature version of the clipping (as it would be represented once saved), and highlighting the project that is ready to receive the clipping.

Thinking through each of these microstates in an interaction is really a navigation problem. How do we subtly prompt the user about what to do next? This is the power of invitational design when intertwined with the interaction. A common mistake is to provide drag and drop with little or no cues during operation. This leads to confusion.

Invitation to drag

For any drag to work, there needs to be a way to indicate draggability. In the prior ex-amples the only indication that something was draggable was the cursor change on mouse hover. In observing user-testing, the step of providing the cursor change is a key way users can find out whether something is draggable. The cursor change is subtle and seems to only cue users who know the page allows drag and drop. The continued challenge is to make drag and drop discoverable for users not expecting it.

In the same round of testing we experimented with various styles for module headings to indicate a "grip" area. Surprisingly this seemed to have a negligible effect.

The key element to indicating draggability is answering the question, *where do you grab to drag a module?* In iGoogle (Figure 10-11), the title contains a link to the module's origin as well as three controls (menu drop-down, collapse, and remove). That leaves a small space (or in some cases almost no space) for grabbing the module for drag and drop. It also means a smaller space to see the cursor change and allow the feature to be discovered.

HowStuffWorks: Daily Stuff Feed

Figure 10-11. *In iGoogle the area users can grab a module for dragging is sometimes very small if the title is long; the drag area is between the word "Feed" and the menu drop-down arrow*

One solution would be to reserve an always-visible grab texture on the lefthand side of the header (Figure 10-12).

⊹ HowStuffWorks: Daily Stuff Feed

Figure 10-12. *Adding a drag control to the left of the header for modules would provide a discoverable and standard way to drag each module*

The grab area plays on users' spatial memory: it indicates that they should always go here to start dragging. Coupled with the cursor change indicating draggability, the grab area creates a complete invitation for drag.

It's OK to be extremely explicit. Concept Share does this for associating a concept with an image the user has added to a concept workspace. Saying "Drag me" is a clear invitation to drag (Figure 10-13)!

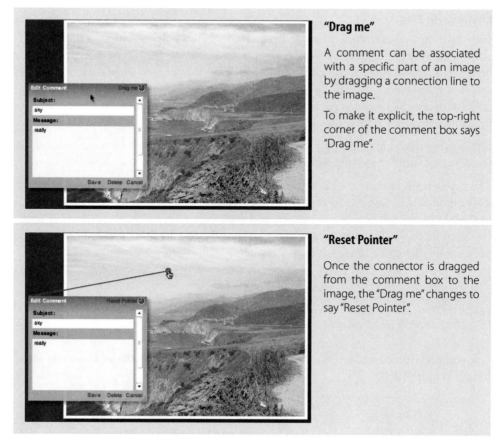

"Drag me"

A comment can be associated with a specific part of an image by dragging a connection line to the image.

To make it explicit, the top-right corner of the comment box says "Drag me".

"Reset Pointer"

Once the connector is dragged from the comment box to the image, the "Drag me" changes to say "Reset Pointer".

Figure 10-13. *Concept Share explicitly invites the user to "Drag me" in order to tie comments to a part of the image*

Google Maps recently added a feature that allows users to change driving directions by dragging the displayed route to connect through different roads (Figure 10-14). A connector object (represented as a circle) provides a tangible object to drag. Changing the cursor indicates draggability. The tool tip states plainly "Drag to change route". Since the route actually changes dynamically as the user drags it, the effect of dragging is immediately reinforced: changing the route on-the-fly.

Figure 10-14. *Google Maps displays a draggable circle, changes the cursor, and displays a tool tip*

Advertising drag and drop

When drag and drop is used to start an action (delete, upload, copy, and so on), the drop target can often advertise its ability to accept a dropped item.

In Flickr's Organizr the workspace area is initially blank. The workspace area is recycled to invite drag and drop (Figure 10-15).

Figure 10-15. *Flickr's Organizr provides a place to move photos that users wish to perform actions on; a typical action involves adding them to a set*

Yahoo! Photos had a nice upload feature that allowed direct drag and drop from the user's desktop into the upload page. Since this is new functionality that is not typically supported by browsers, the designers chose to prominently advertise drag and drop. The invitation to drop photos the easy way was placed in the spot where photos could be dropped. Using a stylized arrow and image to illustrate the procedure helped to make the feature clear (Figure 10-16). Both examples use the **Blank Slate Invitation** (discussed in Chapter 9).

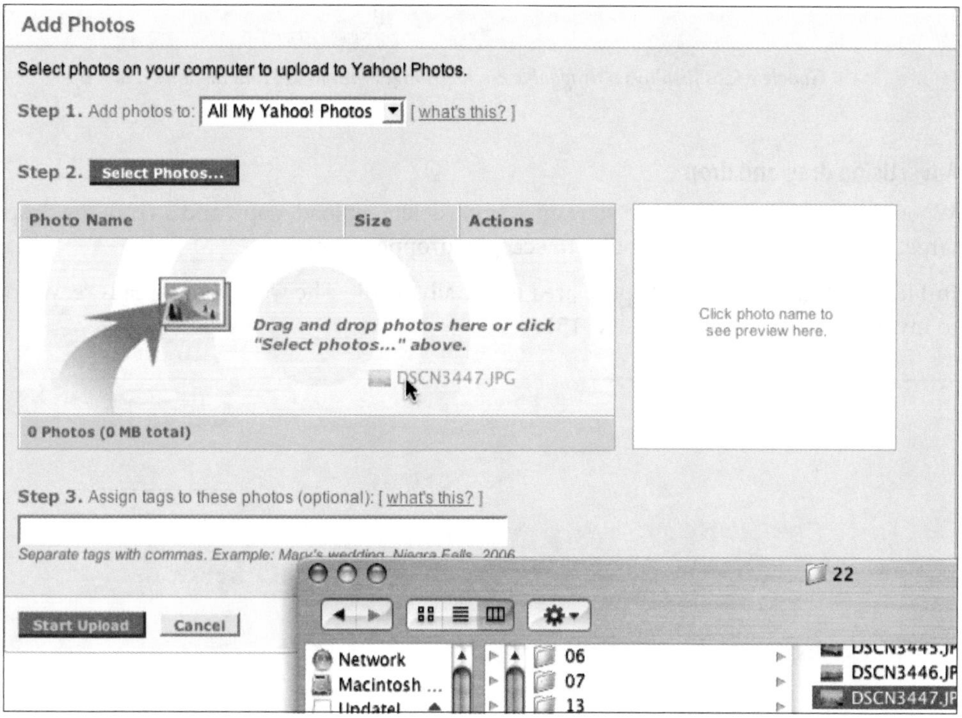

Figure 10-16. *Yahoo! Photos provided an easy upload feature through drag and drop, and advertised it prominently*

This only works if the message is clear and simple. The Flickr invitation has other instructions that may detract from the main message. In Yahoo! Photos there are two ways to upload: the select and upload model and the drag and drop model. To avoid confusion between the two models, the drop text reads "Drag and drop photos here or click 'Select photos...' above." One slight improvement would have been to place each choice on a line by itself and make the "or" all-caps (Figure 10-17).

Figure 10-17. *Slightly altered messaging to make the two upload interactions more explicit*

Invitation to drop

Another place that invitations can happen is during the drag. If there is a single drop target, you can repurpose the area by changing the messaging there to indicate this is where to drop.

In the Flickr Organizr tool (Figure 10-18), once dragging starts, the bottom pane (containing all the photos) gets overlaid with a message "Drop a photo here to remove it from the batch." This is a straightforward way to invite the user to take the next step. At a more general design level, there are other possible ways to remove a photo from the work batch area. One would be to provide a small [X] next to the photo on hover, allowing the user to click to remove it from the temporary area. Dragging is consistent here since it was used to place it in the area to begin with.

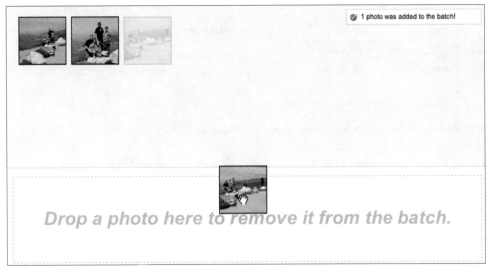

Figure 10-18. *Flickr contains a slightly confusing drop invitation: users have to drag the photos from the temporary work area (batch) to their set of photos in order to "remove" them*

The problem with temporary areas like this is that users can often be confused about what it means to remove the items after they are done working with them. What is odd about this is having to use drag and drop to "remove" the item from the batch by dragging it back into the photo area (when in reality it was not actually removed). Flickr completes this action by showing an animated nuclear explosion. This seems to indicate the photo has been "nuked," when in reality it is just no longer in the temporary area.

An alternate approach is to have a set of actions that only work on objects that are directly selected (see Chapter 3). This removes the need for drag and drop to simulate selection.

The more common use for drop invitations is like the one used by Yahoo! Mail (Figure 10-19). When dragging a mail message to folders, the dragged message representation contains a drop status icon indicating what will happen on drop.

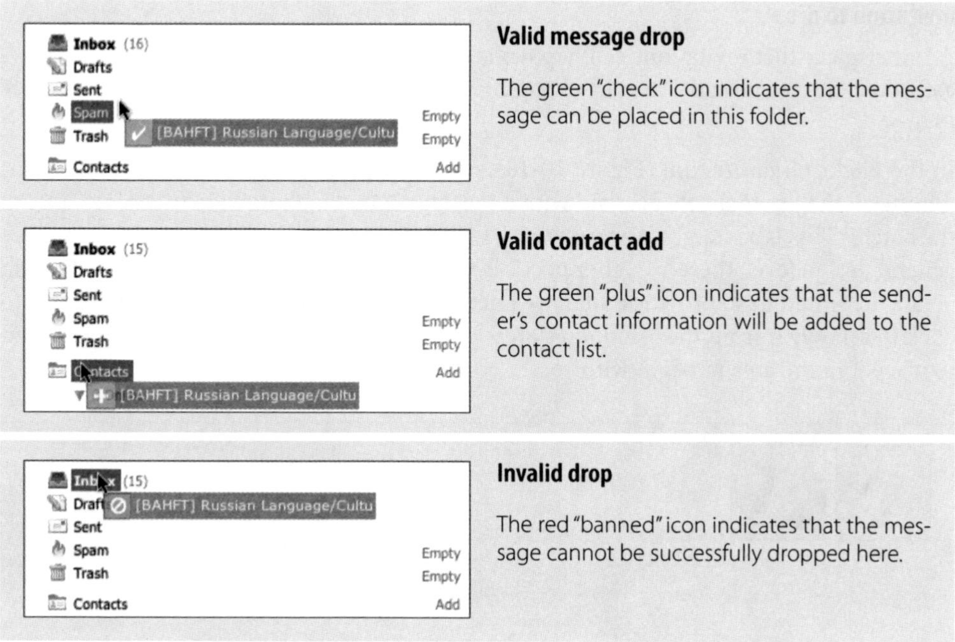

Valid message drop

The green "check" icon indicates that the message can be placed in this folder.

Valid contact add

The green "plus" icon indicates that the sender's contact information will be added to the contact list.

Invalid drop

The red "banned" icon indicates that the message cannot be successfully dropped here.

Figure 10-19. *Yahoo! Mail provides drop invitations embedded with the drag object*

Green is used to indicate a valid drop target; red indicates invalid. The "check" indicates that the message can be moved here. The "banned" icon indicates that the item will not be dropped here. The "plus" icon is a special case. Dragging a message to the Contacts folder will add the sender to the contact list.

Best Practices for Drag and Drop Invitation

Here are some best practices to keep in mind:

- During drag and drop, use as many moments as possible to keep the user engaged through subtle invitations.
- Provide a cursor change over draggable areas.
- Provide an unambiguous space to grab items for dragging.

Inference Invitation

Another challenge to providing invitations is not over-anticipating the user's intent. When you couple the different actions a user may perform with the fact that you cannot always know what the user is going to do next, you find the problem much more difficult than you first imagined.

What you don't want to end up with is the infamous *Clippy*, Microsoft Office's attempt to determine what the user wanted to do next. Clippy was overaggressive with its suggestions as well as visually distracting (and annoying). It was eventually removed from the product suite.*

> ── **Tip** ──
>
> Use visual inferences during interaction to cue users as to what the system has inferred about their intent.

For a counterexample, Google Sketchup does a really nice job of inferring user intent. When the user is drawing 3D objects, the interface provides cues (called **Inference Invitations**) as he moves his mouse around (Figure 10-20).

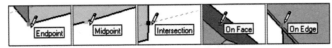

Figure 10-20. *Google Sketchup does an amazing job of inferring what the user might want to do next while drawing*

Considerations

There are some issues to keep in mind while using **Inference Invitations**.

Intelligent interaction

The inference engine uses *help cues* that appear automatically while the user is working on the sketch, to identify significant points or geometric conditions. These cues make complex inference combinations clear as the user draws. Besides point-based inferences, the interface also provides inferences for the linear space or for planar space.

The result is a very intelligent way to draw. When sketching real-world objects, the user will want to play off of existing spaces. The inference engine plays off of this real-world metaphor. Even smarter, users can cue the inference engine as to their interest in real

---

* Clippy's official name was Clippit. For the full scoop on Clippy, see *http://en.wikipedia.org/wiki/Office_Assistant*.

time, allowing it to respond to what they are doing. When they start drawing a line, they can hover over another line edge telling Sketchup that this is their reference. Then it is trivial to draw a line parallel or perpendicular to the reference line (Figure 10-21).

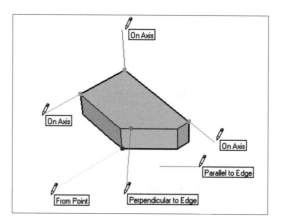

Figure 10-21. *Google Sketchup uses just-in-time inferences while the user is drawing*

More Content Invitation

In Chapter 6 we discussed **Virtual Pages**, a technique for making more content available to a page than is currently visible. The Yahoo! home page employed this in its redesign in 2006 (Figure 10-22).

Figure 10-22. *Yahoo! home page contains more content than is statically visible*

The Yahoo! home page contains more than 20 pages of hidden content and previews from 6 other Yahoo! sites in a small space.

In the Personal Assistant (top right, Figure 10-22), whenever the mouse hovers over a Yahoo! site tab, it automatically animates open. This provides a **More Content Invitation** revealed through a simple **Hover Invitation**.

Yahoo! Games provides an interesting approach to exposing more games. Featured games are shown two at a time. A carousel component is used to slide more games into view. But to give the idea that there are more games, a small thumbnail viewer shows six games at a time. The two main games in view are highlighted in the thumbnail viewer (Figure 10-23).

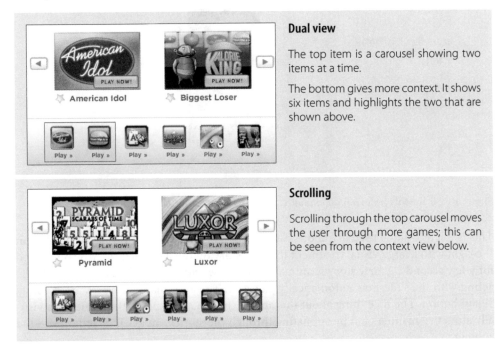

Dual view

The top item is a carousel showing two items at a time.

The bottom gives more context. It shows six items and highlights the two that are shown above.

Scrolling

Scrolling through the top carousel moves the user through more games; this can be seen from the context view below.

Figure 10-23. *Yahoo! Games uses a two-level viewer: the top shows two games; the bottom gives context indicating that more games can be viewed*

Considerations

There are some issues to keep in mind when using **More Content Invitation**.

Hinting with animation

In both techniques, the challenge is how to indicate to the user that there is more content available. The one exposes content on hover. The other gives a visual sneak peek indicating that more content is available.

Tip ——————————————————————————————————————

Where appropriate, use animation to indicate that there is more content.

Animation is a powerful way to indicate that more content is available. When Yahoo! Games starts up, this two-level game viewer gets kicked off by sliding in content. Every few seconds (if the viewer is not interacted with), an animation rolls in new content. Since animation grabs visual attention, it works as an invitation to indicate to the user that there is more content (Figure 10-24).

Figure 10-24. *Yahoo! Health has an animated slideshow that reveals the top health stories*

This is the technique used at Yahoo! Health. The top 10 stories are displayed in a list on the right with a large visual treatment for each story on the left. Each story is spotlighted for a few seconds. A new story is animated into view with a cross-fade animation. Interacting with the slideshow automatically pauses it. The auto-play can be restarted with a "Play" button. The nice thing about this approach is that it exposes the stories in a visually attractive manner, and by animating through the stories, invites interaction with the content.

Tip ——————————————————————————————————————

When there is more content, use hover to reveal its existence or allow a little of the other content to be slightly revealed.

Hinting by providing a sneak peek

A final way of creating a **More Content Invitation** is to reveal partial content on the edges of the page (Figure 10-25).

Figure 10-25. *Starz reveals a little bit of the next movie in its carousel to invite users to go to more content*

Showing just a little of the off-page content (providing a peek) at the edge adds a visual cue that there is more content before and after the visible area. This strategy can also be used with content outside of carousels. Slightly revealing an additional row of content at the natural fold for a web page invites the user to interact with what would normally not be seen.

The Advantage of Invitations

Invitations are an integral part of the nuance that well-designed applications exhibit. Using a natural affordance, providing good static invitations, revealing more invitations during interaction, using tour invitations for newly designed sites, taking advantage of all the interesting moments in a drag and drop interaction, and using invitations to reveal more content are all effective ways to naturally lead the user to the next level of interaction.

Use Transitions

Kathy Sierra writes a blog called "Creating Passionate Users."* She does an amazing job identifying what is happening in the typical user's head. I had the good fortune to attend a workshop by Kathy Sierra of the same name. She puts the spotlight on the "brain." Not just the mind, but the physical, chemically driven brain.

In her talk she recommends the book *Mind Hacks* by Tom Stafford and Matt Webb (O'Reilly), which pulls back the curtain to see how the mind works. I quickly added it to my shortlist of must-have books. Fortunately, at the same conference, O'Reilly was giving away books at its booth. I could only choose one—and guess what they had? That's right, *Mind Hacks*.

Mind Hacks contains 100 short experiments (or hacks) you can do on your own brain. Each hack provides a glimpse at the inner workings of our gray matter. But the hack that really got my attention was Hack #37, "Grab Attention":

> *Sudden movement or light can grab your attention, thanks to a second region for visual processing.*

It turns out that besides the normal visual-processing region of the brain (you are using the occipital lobe right now while reading this book), there is a second region that deals with attention capture.

We experience it every day. While talking with a friend at a park, someone throws a Frisbee to another person in the background. You cannot help but notice this change of motion even though you are not looking directly at it. You can thank the superior colliculus for this little attention interruption.

As the authors describe it, this region of the brain is not very sophisticated. But it does a good job of telling you to pay attention because something may be coming at you. You aren't sure what it is but you know you better watch out. This response is automatically generated deep within the chemistry of the brain. It is something that happens naturally without any conscious thought.

---

* Kathy no longer blogs actively; however, her excellent work is archived at *http://headrush.typepad.com/*.

Hack #37 explains why there are so many unfortunate advertisements with dancing silhouettes (such as the one in Figure P5-1): motion catches your attention, whether you want it to or not! As stated in a *New York Times* article, "Don't Like the Dancing Cowboys? Results Say You Do":[*]

> *Rogers Cadenhead, an author and blogger, resorted to tinkering with his computer to block all ads from the company. "I was trying to read a news article and realized the dancing mortgage people were eliminating all rational thought from my brain," he said.*

Figure P5-1. *Dancing cowboy silhouettes from mortgage advertisers grab attention*

If animation is this powerful for advertisers, it can certainly be harnessed and, used in moderation, become an effective part of a rich web interface. The question for us is how do we use these **Transitions** (cinematic effects, animations, and so on) to *improve* the user experience? It's not enough to bring animation into an application: there must be a reason.

In the next two chapters, we will explore a set of common **Transition** patterns and the rationale for when and how to apply the principle *Use Transitions* in your application:

Chapter 11, *Transitional Patterns*
> Introduces the **Transition** patterns, such as **Brighten and Dim, Expand and Collapse, Self-Healing Fade, Animation**, and **Spotlight**.

Chapter 12, *Purpose of Transitions*
> Further explores the reasons for using these powerful effects and where they are most appropriate.

* *http://www.nytimes.com/2007/01/18/business/media/18adco.html*

Transitional Patterns

We have chosen to use the term **Transitions** to describe special effects that happen over a specified period of time. The term *transition* seems to catch the right spirit of how these cinematic effects get applied. They provide the grease that smoothes out what happens in the interface. Without transitional effects the user can be left to wonder what just occurred.

There are a number of **Transitions** available for our use. Let's take a quick survey of the most popular.

Brighten and Dim

Two patterns that go hand-in-hand are **Brighten** and **Dim**.

Brightening an area of the screen focuses attention there. Since there is no way to raise the brightness of a part of the screen, this is typically accomplished by dimming the entire application window and exposing a part of the interface at normal, full-brightness level.

Color changes do not generate the same level of attention in the brain as movement changes. How much attention the dimming and brightening of an area on the screen will get depends on the speed of the color change (faster is more eye-catching) and the contrast between the dimmed and brightened state (greater contrast equals more attention).

Tip

Use **Brighten** and **Dim** to control the user's point of reference.

Considerations

Dimming and brightening an area is an effective way to communicate subtle or second-ary changes in an interface. Using **Brighten** focuses attention on an area. Using **Dim** in an area causes the elements to be treated as secondary or not in use. Dimming reduces attention to an area. **Dim** and **Brighten** can communicate importance, whether an object is in use, and if an interface is ready for interaction.

Importance

A common technique is to **Dim** a page and show an overlay in the normal, non-dimmed state. The effect seems to brighten an area and dim the rest. This interaction pattern is called a **Lightbox Effect**.

Wayfaring uses the **Lightbox Effect** when a user attempts to log in (Figure 11-1).

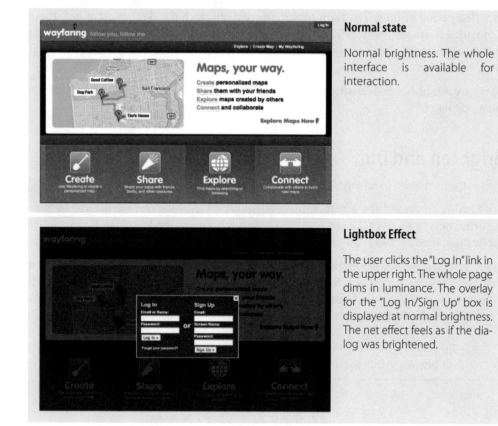

Normal state

Normal brightness. The whole interface is available for interaction.

Lightbox Effect

The user clicks the "Log In" link in the upper right. The whole page dims in luminance. The overlay for the "Log In/Sign Up" box is displayed at normal brightness. The net effect feels as if the dia-log was brightened.

Figure 11-1. *Wayfaring uses a Lightbox Effect to focus the user on login or signup*

The login box appears brightened (again, in reality the background is the only thing changed—it is dimmed). Brightening an area with this technique makes it the primary focus. Dimming the background indicates that the rest of the interface is not currently part of the interaction at hand.

Recall the Yahoo! home page tour we discussed in a Chapter 9. Each part of the interface introduced is highlighted with the **Lightbox Effect** (Figure 11-2).

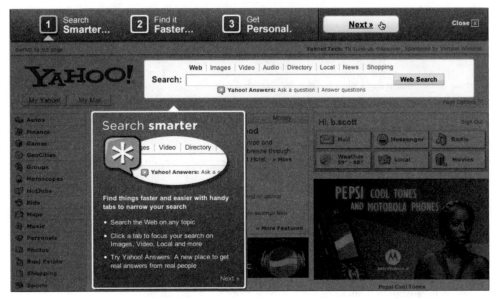

Figure 11-2. *The Yahoo! home page tour uses the Lightbox Effect to highlight each of the three areas it introduces*

One issue to consider when using the **Lightbox Effect** is how jarring the change in luminance will be to the user. Dimming the interface and brightening an overlay calls a lot of attention to the dialog. In some ways it can make the overlay feel like a big context switch. If the goal is to quickly show a dialog, get input, and get out of the way, then do not use the **Lightbox Effect**. Instead use a normal **Dialog Overlay**.

Active

Another use of **Dim** and **Brighten** is to show when an object is being interacted with. An object can be dimmed when it's not in use and brightened when it is in use. The original version of Measure Map (now a part of Google Analytics) provided a graph detailing the number of visitors to a blog over time. In order to decrease visual noise, the graph was dimmed when not in use (Figure 11-3).

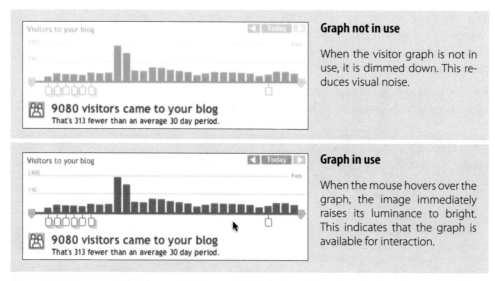

	Graph not in use
	When the visitor graph is not in use, it is dimmed down. This reduces visual noise.
	Graph in use
	When the mouse hovers over the graph, the image immediately raises its luminance to bright. This indicates that the graph is available for interaction.

Figure 11-3. *Measure Map dims and brightens the Visitor Graph based on whether the user is interacting with it or not*

When the mouse moves outside the graph, the image begins to fade in luminance. When the mouse re-enters the graph area, the graph quickly brightens. The dim and brighten effects take about a fourth of a second to transition.

Tip

Use **Brighten** and **Dim** to indicate whether or not an interface is active.

Not ready

You can also use **Dim** to indicate that a part of the interface is not ready for interaction. When searching for hotels in Yahoo! Travel's Farechase tool, the map displaying the found hotels is dimmed until the search is finished (Figure 11-4).

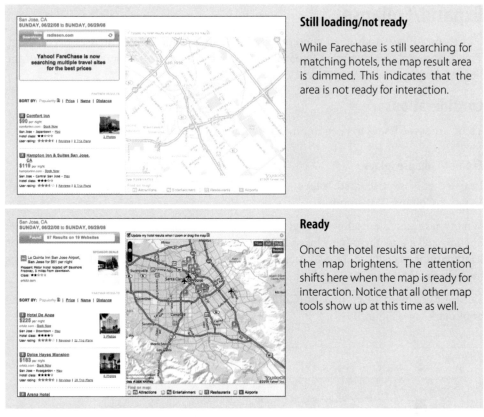

Still loading/not ready

While Farechase is still searching for matching hotels, the map result area is dimmed. This indicates that the area is not ready for interaction.

Ready

Once the hotel results are returned, the map brightens. The attention shifts here when the map is ready for interaction. Notice that all other map tools show up at this time as well.

Figure 11-4. *Yahoo! Travel's Farechase uses Dim to communicate that search results are not ready and Brighten to communicate when they are ready*

Once the search is finished, the map result area is brightened and all interaction tools for the map are displayed (zoom, map styles, etc.) Dimming the map is coupled with other indications that the search is not completed.

Brighten/Dim transitions are very useful. You can use them when you:

- Need to focus attention on a particular part of an interface (or detract attention from another part of the interface).

- Need to provide feedback indicating that an object is being interacted with. A common interaction is to brighten an object when the mouse is hovered over it.

- Decrease visual noise in an interface. Elements that are secondary can be dimmed when not in use.

- Indicate that a part of the interface is not ready to be interacted with, perhaps when an application is being loaded.

Expand/Collapse

It's helpful to have additional content or other panels hidden until the user needs them. This is accomplished by using **Expand** and **Collapse** to control a panel's visibility in the flow of the page.

Considerations

There are some issues to keep in mind when using **Expand** and **Collapse**.

Expand/Collapse Inlays

In Chapter 5 we discussed **Inlays**. A typical way to bring an **Inlay** into a page is with **Expand/Collapse** transitions.

When these panels are shown, providing an animated transition for expanding the panel open or collapsing the panel closed helps connect the panel to the control that activates it. **Expand** is visually more eye-catching than **Brighten/Dim** (because the movement is more dramatic than reducing color slightly).*

Yahoo! Bookmarks uses **Expand/Collapse** to hide and show its edit panel for editing bookmark tags (Figure 11-5).

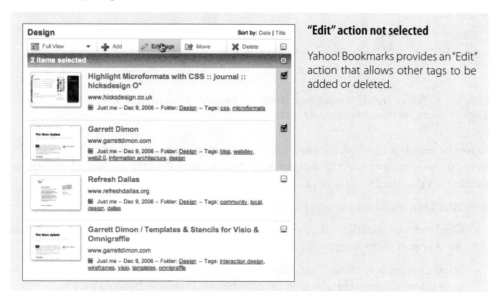

"Edit" action not selected

Yahoo! Bookmarks provides an "Edit" action that allows other tags to be added or deleted.

---

* You can try this for yourself. Put your left hand straight in front of you. While keeping your eyes straight ahead, move your hand to the side until you can just no longer see it from your peripheral view. Now wiggle your fingers. Did you see it? Movement makes something normally invisible, visible.

Edit action activated; Panel slides open

Instead of using an overlay, the "Edit" panel expands in place, pushing down other content on the page.

Panel fully open

After the opening transition is finished, the "Edit" panel allows tag editing.

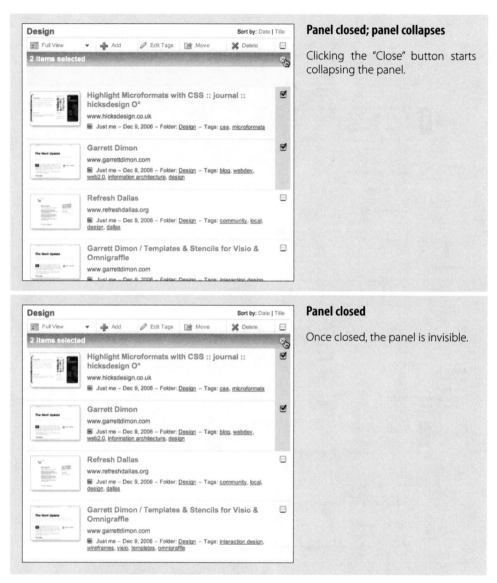

Panel closed; panel collapses

Clicking the "Close" button starts collapsing the panel.

Panel closed

Once closed, the panel is invisible.

Figure 11-5. *Yahoo! Bookmarks expands and collapses the "Edit" panel in place with the page*

While the same result could have been accomplished with a normal **Overlay**, the **Expand** in context makes it apparent that it is connected to the "Edit" button as well as applied to the content. By making it inline, the context is preserved and not hidden.

Tip

Use **Expand** and **Collapse** to extend the available screen real estate in the application.

Expand and **Collapse** within the flow of the page is often used to open details about items within the page. It provides a nice way to toggle open additional content without losing the context of the summary information.

Expand/Collapse as Overlay

A slight variation is to have content **Expand/Collapse** appear as an **Overlay** on the page. Instead of pushing content down or out of the way, the panels simply slide out from some part of the page into a layer above the rest of the items on the page. The panel slides out, anchored to the activating control.

Five Runs is a Ruby on Rails application-monitoring tool. It provides a window into the inner workings of Rail's apps, helping IT groups track down system issues. The Five Runs web application uses slide-out panels for additional controls (Figure 11-6).

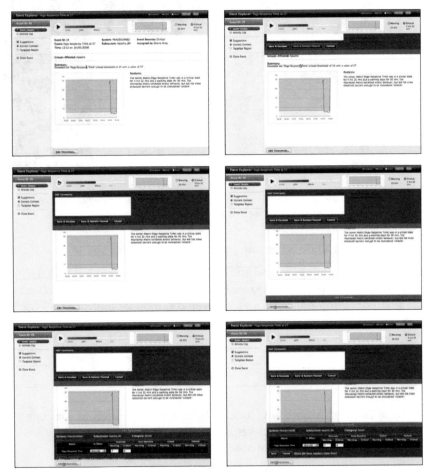

Figure 11-6. *Five Runs animates expanding and collapsing panels with additional controls as overlays to the interface*

Be careful to not overuse **Expand**. For example, in a photo application, if you provide a rollover to expand photos from thumbnail to a larger size, the transitions will become annoying because the user will see them back-to-back. Either remove the transition altogether or make it extremely fast.

An especially egregious example of overuse of **Expand/Collapse** is when it is applied to normal drop-down menus. The primary purpose of transitions is to communicate, and no amount of graphic trickery will make a noisy interface compelling. In a recent incarnation of the Nasa.gov website, we can see **Expand** and **Collapse** abused with their overuse of animated menus (Figure 11-7).

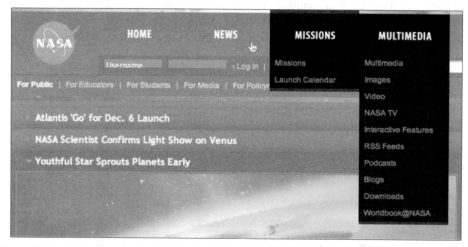

Figure 11-7. Nasa.gov animates its menus: each menu animates its expand and collapse, resulting in situations where multiple menus can be open at a time

This type of animation abuse is the anti-pattern **Animation Gone Wild.**[*]

One problem with animating **Expand** and **Collapse** like this is that it makes the interface feel sluggish. It is also superfluous. Do we really need the menus animated? Does it communicate anything? Drop-down menus have been common for more than 25 years. Adding animation is simply gratuitous and unnecessary.

—— Tip ——
Avoid gratuitous **Animation** when expanding and collapsing content.

Buzzword also employs **Animation Gone Wild** by animating each toolbar button open and closed on hover. While it is a clever way to conserve space when the items are not interacted with, it feels like a series of **Mouse Traps** (Figure 11-8).

---

[*] No, there is no companion DVD available on late-night TV for this anti-pattern ;-).

Figure 11-8. *Several tool items get animated open at the same time by moving the mouse through Buzzword's toolbar*

Expand and **Collapse** can be used to:

- Manage lots of content or modules.

- Manage real estate on the screen.

- Emphasize the currently hovered-over object (e.g., photos in a photo album) as part of a rollover system.

- Provide details about an item in a list.

- Make content available for edit. Use instead of a pop up if the content being expanded is one of many items and there is a benefit to showing the detail in context with the other items.

Self-Healing Fade

When deleting or moving items, it is often helpful to temporarily expose a "hole" where the object being removed once lived. Animating the remove of the item and the closing of the hole reinforces where the deleted item was removed.

Considerations

This **Self-Healing Fade** pattern is used when deleting to-do items in Backpackit. Once an item is removed from an area, a hole is left. Next, the hole seals up, effectively healing itself (Figure 11-9).

Delete selected

The list item is selected for delete by clicking the trashcan.

Item starts to fade

The list item starts to fade out to indicate that it is being deleted.

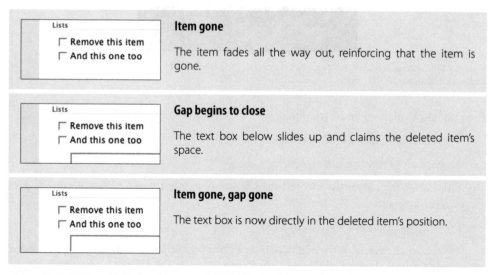

Item gone	The item fades all the way out, reinforcing that the item is gone.
Gap begins to close	The text box below slides up and claims the deleted item's space.
Item gone, gap gone	The text box is now directly in the deleted item's position.

Figure 11-9. *37 Signals' Backpackit uses a Self-Healing Fade to reinforce that an item has been deleted*

Self-Healing transitions can be used to:

- Remove an object from a list or grid.
- Convey that the removal happened and where the object was removed from.
- Indicate the completion of a drop operation in which the dropped object was moved from one place to another.

Animation

In our everyday world, objects occupy real space and don't normally instantly appear and disappear. We throw a piece of trash into the trashcan and see it leave our hand and go through the air into the trashcan.

Considerations

In our interfaces, we do not need to mimic every movement from the real world. Interfaces would be dreadfully slow. But by using **Animation** to show where an object came from or is going, we can make it easier for the user to find the object again or feel confident putting the object away in the future. Using animation to position an object in a grid confirms that it went into the slot. This type of feedback clarifies the user interaction.

Zoom back

My Yahoo! uses a zoom-back **Animation** if a drop fails. It communicates simply that the module returned from where the user attempted to drag it (Figure 11-10).

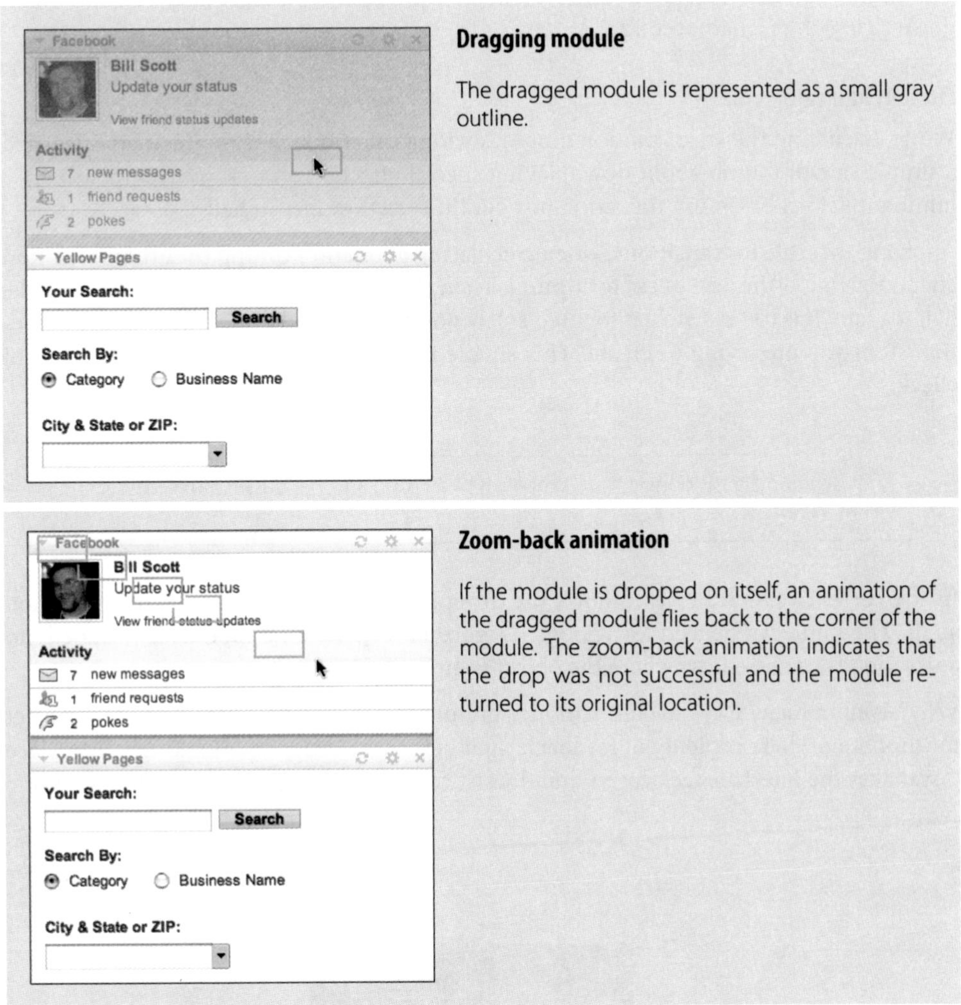

Dragging module

The dragged module is represented as a small gray outline.

Zoom-back animation

If the module is dropped on itself, an animation of the dragged module flies back to the corner of the module. The zoom-back animation indicates that the drop was not successful and the module returned to its original location.

Figure 11-10. *My Yahoo! uses a zoom-back animation to show that a module did not get moved, but instead returned to its original location*

While the use of a small gray rectangle for the drag object is less than helpful (a thumbnail of the object being dragged would be better), the image of a gray rectangle flying back to the module's original spot is simple and clear enough to communicate what happened.

—— **Tip** ——————————————————————————————
Build association between elements on the page with **Animation**.

Drop animation

Another place to use **Animation** is when dropping modules on a web page into new locations. In earlier versions of My Yahoo!, the dropped module would animate into place. The earliest version took about one second to animate into place. A later version took it down to less than a half-second.

Cut it in half rule

While discussing the art of motion graphics with a practitioner from the field, I learned a simple rule of thumb about downplaying special effects. To avoid over-emphasizing a luminance effect or timing transition just cut the effect's values in half.

Applying this rule to transitions, when calculating animation timing (or other transition effects), arrive at the best guess for timing. Then simply cut the effect in half. And maybe half it again. It is too easy to get focused solely on the effect and forget the overall interaction story you are trying to create. This simple rule is a nice way to keep transitions in check.

Tip

After defining a transitional effect, simplify it by making another pass to cut the effect's values in half.

In the current version of My Yahoo!, the dropping modules process uses no animation at all. The same can be said for iGoogle (Figure 11-11). When a module is dropped, no animation is used to show where the object went.

Why? Well in many ways the animation is gratuitous. The user has positioned the object for dropping. There is plenty of feedback right before the drop, so animating it into place just makes the interface feel slower and doesn't communicate anything new to the user.

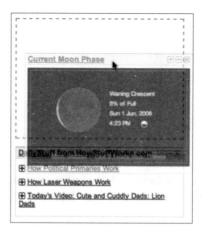

Figure 11-11. *It's obvious where the dropped object will land in iGoogle, so it is not necessary to animate the drop*

Animation is a great technique when used correctly. It can be used to:

- Smooth out a transition when a direct remove-and-appear in another place on the page would be a jarring or confusing way to show what just happened.

- Show how an object has changed places or containment on a page.

Spotlight

Spotlights are useful when a change has occurred in an interface. By momentarily highlighting an object, you can subtly notify the user of a change in the interface. The **Spotlight** is often accomplished by first highlighting the background of an object, then fading out the highlight. An example of this technique is in Backpackit (Figure 11-12).

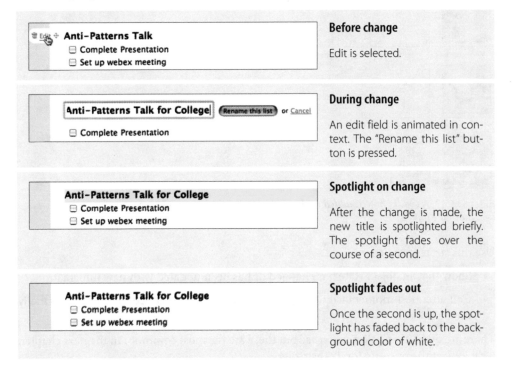

Figure 11-12. *Backpackit uses spotlighting to highlight modifications*

Considerations

When the title of the list is changed, it is momentarily spotlighted by highlighting its background in yellow. The color fades to the background color in about one second. This does a nice job of communicating that a change has occurred without keeping the notification around a long time. It avoids the **Idiot Boxes** anti-pattern we discussed in Chapter 5 by using a very subtle indication of change.

—— Tip ——————————————————————————————

Use **Spotlight** to temporarily call attention to a change in the interface.

Signaling change

Flickr uses **Spotlight** when adding photos to the Organizer. A status message is placed in the upper right. If another action is taken, a second status message appears. The first message moves down (visually swaps location with the first) and then fades out. The current message will fade out as well after time passes. This is a simple way to provide confirmation that requires no action and removes itself automatically (Figure 11-13).

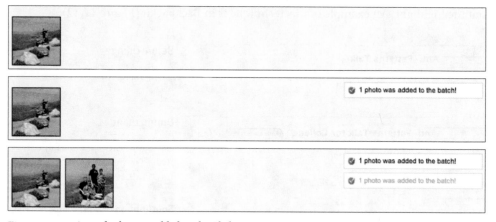

Figure 11-13. *As each photo is added to the Flickr Organizer, a status message is added; as messages age, they fade out*

Use this strategy in order to:

- Show that an object state has changed or has been updated with new information.

- Call attention momentarily to a different part of the interface that might normally not be noticed.

There are other **Transition** patterns,* but these are the most common. In the next chapter, we'll look at the purpose for **Transitions**.

---

* See *http://developer.yahoo.com/ypatterns/parent.php?pattern=transition* for the **Transition** patterns in the Yahoo! Design Pattern Library.

Chapter 12

Purpose of Transitions

We pointed out in the previous chapter that objects don't just pop in and pop out in the real world, appearing and disappearing suddenly. We usually see them go away or go somewhere in particular. An interface that does not mimic some aspect of this real-world behavior will be harder to understand.

Our eyes are wired to react to movement. The world doesn't flicker. It doesn't disappear or suddenly change and force us to look for the change. Things move smoothly in the real world. They do not "pop up." **Transitions** smooth out the jarring world of the Web, making changes appear more natural.

The main purpose for **Transitions** is to provide an engaging interface and reinforce communication.

Engagement

Transitions can be used to increase engagement.

Interacting with an area on the screen that responds by growing slightly, or seeing an accordion pane "snap" into place creates a richer and more compelling experience. The interface seems more alive and reactive. Of course, going overboard with these techniques can distract from what is being communicated and become just a Web 2.0 version of the horrendous blink tag.

Certain contexts tip the scale more toward the engagement side and less toward the communication side. In areas like game or car sites, engagement can take on a more important role. However, in most websites, communication is the most important purpose for transitions, with engagement being a secondary consideration.

Communication

Transitions are first and foremost about communication. Harry Marks, award-winning broadcast designer, stated:[*]

> *If you don't have a story, no amount of graphic trickery will make it interesting.*

The *story* is the key. **Transitions** are for making the story more compelling, filling in the hard jumps, and making an action more concrete and believable. Transitions communicate in the following ways:

- If an object fades away, users know it changed state from visible to invisible even if they are not staring directly at the object.

- If an object fades into view, users know the object has arrived. It was not there but now is.

- If an object fades rapidly, it is seen as an important event. If it fades slowly, its importance is lower.

- If an object is "coming at" users (getting larger and appearing to go past them), then users think of it as something that is important (and perhaps dangerous).

- If an object zooms down in size rapidly and disappears, it will capture the users' attention immediately.

Given the way transitions *can* communicate, what exactly *do* they communicate? They give us a way to:

- Maintain context while changing views

- Explain what just happened

- Show relationships between objects

- Focus attention

- Improve perceived performance

- Create an illusion of virtual space

---

[*] See Sarah Allen's presentation on Cinematic Interaction Design at *http://www.slideshare.net/sarah.allen/cinematic-interaction-design/*. The quote is from slide 8.

Maintain Context While Changing Views

We discussed several techniques in Chapter 3 for creating a virtual space larger than the static page. An essential ingredient to pulling off this effect is the proper use of **Transitions**, which allow views to change while maintaining overall context.

Slide In and Slide Out

Most monitoring applications have pages and pages of charts and tables. Five Runs takes a virtual page approach and pulls it off by using **Slide In** and **Slide Out** effects (Figure 12-1).

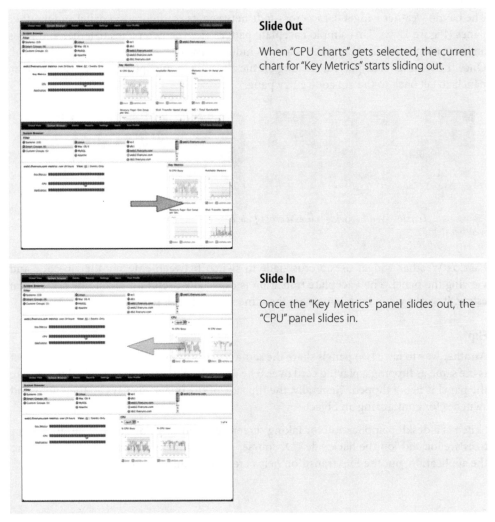

Slide Out

When "CPU charts" gets selected, the current chart for "Key Metrics" starts sliding out.

Slide In

Once the "Key Metrics" panel slides out, the "CPU" panel slides in.

Figure 12-1. *Five Runs switches between metric views by a simple Slide Out/Slide In transition*

Different charts can be selected by clicking on the bar graph summary. In reality, this process is the same as flipping through a series of tabs. But instead of a tab controlling the visibility of each panel, clicking on the associated metrics bar causes the content to switch in. The transition of sliding out the old and sliding in the new causes a clear mental connection. The surrounding context does not change so the switch in views stays in context.

Another just as effective (and possibly more effective) approach would be to simply cross-fade between the two panels. This method creates a faster transition while clearly communicating that the panels are associated with the different bars clicked.

Faceplate

The Laszlo weather widget uses a cross-fade between its configuration panel and weather panes (Figure 12-2). This simple **Faceplate** pattern ties the two panes together and gives an indication that the other pane is always hidden just below the currently visible panel. Once the weather is displayed, clicking on the zip code in the upper right cross-fades the panels to get back to the zip code entry pane.

Figure 12-2. *Laszlo's Weather widget uses a cross-fade between the configuration faceplate and the weather details*

Laszlo's Weather widget uses a cross-fade to switch between entering the zip code and viewing the panel. The **Faceplate** transition is especially useful for extending screen real estate. It works when both panels are the same size and each panel is independent.

Flip

Another way to have two panels share the same space is to use a **Flip** transition. The effect is the same as flipping a playing card over. The animation is effective if it actually feels like the panel is being flipped. Generally, the flip side of the image displays all the knobs and switches for configuring an object.

Skitch is a desktop application for taking screen snapshots. All of the configuration controls are located "on the back side." Of course, in reality there is no physical back side to the application, but the Flip transition helps create this illusion (Figure 12-3).

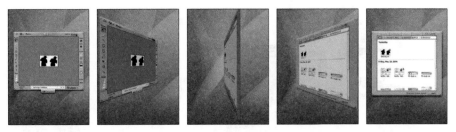

Figure 12-3. *Skitch uses a Flip transition between the application and configuration details*

The **Flip** transition is rarely seen in Ajax/DHTML applications, as it is a CPU-intensive effect. However, with Flash or Silverlight technologies, the effect is more easily achievable.

Carousel

We have discussed **Carousels** in previous chapters. **Carousels** are great for extending virtual space. But what effects reinforce this virtual extension? Let's look at four carousel implementations to discuss different approaches to animating carousels.

One of Amazon's many carousels actually does not use any animated transitions at all. Each arrow click just shows the next batch of books (Figure 12-4).

Figure 12-4. *This particular carousel on Amazon does not use any animation; it provides no clue to the direction users are moving through the content*

This one is rather disconcerting. Without the visual effect of content sliding in, it is easy to get confused about whether content is moving in from the left or the right. Adding the effect creates the illusion that content is being pulled into the page through the carousel.

Another Amazon carousel takes just the opposite approach (Figure 12-5). Visually it represents the items in a circular fashion to attempt to create a "true" carousel effect. And it uses lots of animation. In fact it uses animation in a way that appears to be gratuitous. Each click of the arrow moves the carousel around a few pixels at a time. Clicking and holding a little longer spins the carousel faster. In fact, it generally spins it too fast to stop on a desired book.

Figure 12-5. *Amazon uses a circular carousel as a widget for its associates to use; the carousel has the opposite problem as the last one: it animates too much*

A simpler implementation is to just animate the movement through the content space. In Flickr, clicking the arrow animates content into view. Since all content to the left is earlier in time and all content to the right is later in time, animating the movement through time is helpful in finding photos (Figure 12-6).

Figure 12-6. *Flickr employs the more common approach to use animation to flip through carousel content, in this case, back and forth chronologically*

How fast should **Carousels** be when they animate*? It's not easy to quantify. But the carousel should be fast enough that it will be finished animating by the time a normal user is ready to click the arrow again. Usually this is much less than half a second and never more than a second.

---

* For a reference on animation timing, see *Timing for Animation* by Harold Whitaker and John Halas (Focal Press).

The Starz on Demand carousel animates one image at a time (while displaying four images at time) and takes about a second to complete the animation. This is painfully slow, especially since it only brings in one item at a time. You find yourself clicking a lot of the arrows to see available movies (Figure 12-7).

Figure 12-7. *Starz on Demand animates one image at a time and takes about a second to complete the animation*

Accordion

Another component that helps maintain context while switching views is the **Accordion**. We discussed this pattern briefly in Chapter 6 on the topic of **List Inlays**. The **Accordion** is a variation on a **Tab** panel. Each panel title is the activation to slide open its associated panel. The currently visible panel and the panel being opened transition to closed and open states at the same time. This allows the carousel to take up a fixed amount of space (Figure 12-8).

Figure 12-8. *Opening Rico's Accordion widget shows one panel at a time; it animates opening and closing each panel simultaneously*

Accordions are good for collapsed modules of content. However, they should be used sparingly, as they have a strong visual style. If you scatter them around or make them too beveled, they will quickly clutter the interface.

Normally, accordions activate on click. However, a trend of late is to activate accordions on hover. This is normally a bad idea. Elsewhere we have written about the anti-pattern **Mouse Trap** and this can easily become one. However, you can see a nice implementation of a hover-based **Accordion** on Apple.com's Mac store (Figure 12-9).

Figure 12-9. *Apple.com uses an accordion to provide content for "Where to Buy", "Hot News" and "Mac@work"; each panel is activated on mouse hover*

A less-than-helpful implementation of a mouse hover-activated **Accordion** is on the Nasa.gov site (Figure 12-10).

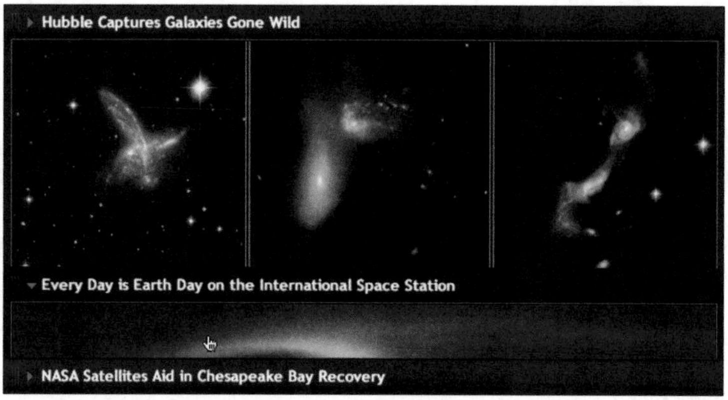

Figure 12-10. *Nasa.gov activates its accordion panels on hover*

The Nasa.gov accordion contains panels that are three times wider than the Apple accordion and are the centerpiece of the home page. This means that when users move their mouse over the accordion panel titles, panels fly open and closed. Since the targeting is three times as wide, twice as high, and the main part of the page, this process becomes very disorienting. The interaction is not helped by how visually heavy the accordion is compared to Apple's more-subtle styling. Apple's accordions are in the right sidebar, and the point is to get users to discover the hidden content.

—— Tip ——
Don't automatically open accordion panels on hover if the panels are large or central to the site content.

Explain What Just Happened

What do you do when one part of the interface affects another part of the interface? This is what happens in the Apple.com store when users configure a computer for purchase (Figure 12-11). Whenever users make a change to their configuration (main part of the page), the values in the summary and specifications update (left side of the page). To indicate that a change occurred, the changed values get spotlighted.

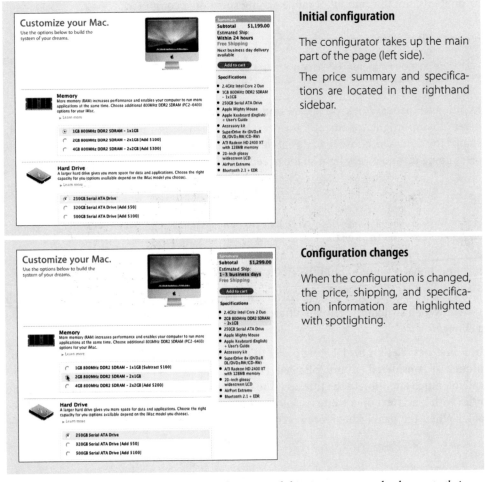

Initial configuration

The configurator takes up the main part of the page (left side).

The price summary and specifications are located in the righthand sidebar.

Configuration changes

When the configuration is changed, the price, shipping, and specification information are highlighted with spotlighting.

Figure 12-11. *Apple.com spotlights changes to the price and shipping as users make changes to their configuration*

Recall the yellow **Spotlight** used by Backpackit: it fades out after about one second. Contrast that to Apple's approach of highlighting in blue and keeping the spotlight in effect (Figure 12-12).*

Anti-Patterns Talk for College
☐ Complete Presentation
☐ Set up webex meeting

Figure 12-12. *Backpackit spotlights change*

Why the difference? Some of the differences are just stylistic choice. But in Apple's case, users want to know that they changed the default configuration and price. The change itself is important enough to keep spotlighted. In Backpackit's case, users are just changing to-do items, not the amount of money being spent on a computer.

> **Tip**
>
> Keep the last change highlighted (don't fade out with **Spotlight**) if there is a chance the change happened off-screen and the user might not see it.

In Yahoo! Finance, stock values are updated in real time. When a stock value changes, it gets the **Spotlight** treatment. However, to avoid making the interface feel extremely chatty, the designers chose to use a subtle color change, a very light shade of green for the price going up and a very light shade of red for the price going down (Figure 12-13).

At 10:56AM ET: **30.45** ↓ 0.67 (2.15%)

Figure 12-13. *Yahoo! Finance uses a very subtle color change and a quick change back to the original background color (half a second)*

Just how bold or subtle should the change be?

Jason Fried (founder of 37 Signals) dealt with this issue when designing Basecamp's Help system. When switching between different Help panels, there was little to visually indicate a change.

In a first-pass design for labeling panel titles (Figure 12-14), the yellow **Spotlight** technique was considered but not followed. For one thing, it was *too* subtle. And it seemed to call too much attention to the title, as if the title was the object being changed. Leaving the titles with black text on a white background made switching panels completely unnoticeable. When the panel titles were inverted (white text on a black background), the titles

---

* In the latest version of the Apple store, the highlight fades out just as with Backpackit. This adjustment is actually unfortunate, as changes made below the fold are not highlighted by the time the user scrolls back to the top.

became highly visible during a switch (Figure 12-15), not only because of the contrast of inverted text, but since the black background calls out the length of the title (by its bounding box), any variance in title length is readily apparent.

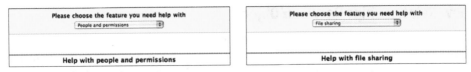

Figure 12-14. *Switching between the panels "Help with people and permissions" and "Help with file sharing" is not apparent with this design of Backpackit's Help section*

Figure 12-15. *Changing the background of the panel titles to be inverted causes them to get noticed when a switch occurs*

Opposite effect

Not every attempt to highlight change works. Flickr Daily Zeitgeist is a blog sidebar plug-in (Figure 12-16). As new photos show up, they fade slowly in place, overlaying four photos within the tile of photos. Not bad. Users may or may not notice the photo showing up, but that's OK. That detail is secondary. However, when the photo goes away, it rapidly scales down, revealing the images underneath while replacing one of the four images. The sudden rapid movement once again gets the superior colliculus to say "What the…?" Users look at the photos, and by the time they glance they are not really sure what happened. In reality they're seeing the new photo fading into place, but the effect makes it feel as if they missed something important.[*]

Figure 12-16. *Flickr Zeitgeist rapidly scales down the image going away and slowly fades in the new image*

---

[*] This is discussed in detail by Tom Stafford and Matt Webb (the authors of *Mind Hacks*) at *http://www.oreillynet. com/pub/a/network/2004/12/06/mndhcks_1.html*.

Tip ———————————————————————————————————————

Movement gets more attention than a simple color change.

Show Relationships Between Objects

Transitions can also tie objects together and indicate that they are related. On the Macintosh opening, an icon creates a genie-like effect when it swooshes up and out (like the genie coming out of the bottle) into the full-size application window. Once users have seen it, it is obvious that the icon and the application are related.

Zoom is a simple way to create this effect. Transmit uses this on its site when a user wants to take a look at the screenshot for the product. Instead of going to a different page or just providing a pop up, the screenshot zooms and fades up from the thumbnail. It is clear that the screenshot is the detailed view for the thumbnail (Figure 12-17).

Thumbnail view

"Transmit shopping page" shows a small set of thumbnail views of the application.

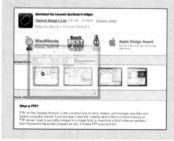

Zoom and fade up

Clicking on a thumbnail causes the screenshot to fade in and zoom out.

Screenshot displayed

Even after the screenshot zooms to full size, it is obvious that it is tied to the thumbnail below because of the transitions that were employed.

Figure 12-17. *Transmit uses Zoom and Fade to tie the thumbnail and the screenshot together in the shopper's mind*

The Gap ties a thumbnail to a detailed product view by using a series of **Zoom** rectangles when a shopper selects an item. The **Zoom** rectangles tie the object to the detail box displayed (Figure 12-18).

Figure 12-18. *The Gap shows details about an item; it ties the details to the item by using Zoom boxes as a transition effect*

Focus Attention

Sometimes you would just like to make sure the user sees something. It's not necessarily a change in the interface, but just something to be aware of.

In the earlier example of Transmit, the "Close" box is placed on the upper left of the snapshot detail view. The overlay uses a **Fade** transition to fade in the close button after the it appears. By waiting until the other animation is finished, the "Close" box gets readily noticed (Figure 12-19).

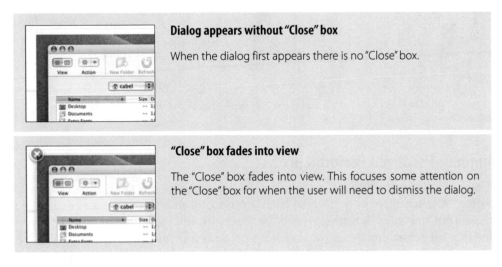

Dialog appears without "Close" box

When the dialog first appears there is no "Close" box.

"Close" box fades into view

The "Close" box fades into view. This focuses some attention on the "Close" box for when the user will need to dismiss the dialog.

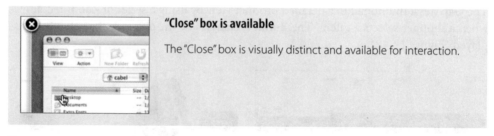

Figure 12-19. *Transmit fades in the "Close" box after the dialog is displayed to focus attention on how to dismiss the dialog*

Focusing attention can also be associated with what the user is currently interacting with. In Chapter 11 we discussed the MeasureMap graph that used **Brighten** when the mouse hovered over it and **Dim** when the mouse moved away from it (Figure 11-3). Similarly, the Gap uses **Spotlight** when focusing the user's attention on the selected pair of jeans (Figure 12-20).

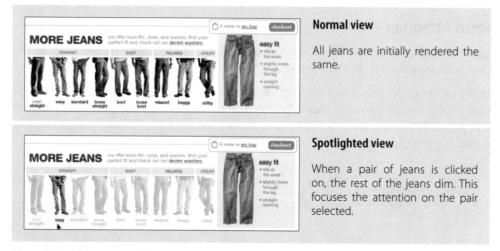

Figure 12-20. *The Gap spotlights the selected pair of jeans to focus the shopper's attention on the selected merchandise*

Improve Perceived Performance

There is a difference between actual performance and *perceived* performance. The old saying, "A watched pot never boils" is true. Diverting the user's attention is a good way to make a pot boil faster. Something that takes 10 seconds will appear to go by much faster if the user has something to read or is shown a progress animation during the delay. Without such a diversion, the time seems to pass much more slowly because the user is not sure the system is still responding. User testing has confirmed that **Transitions** improve the perceived time an operation takes.

—— Tip ——
Keeping the user engaged during a long process improves the perceived performance time.

A good example of this technique at work is with Yahoo! Travel's Farechase tool. Searching for a hotel can take a long time. In this example, it took 30 seconds to complete (Figure 12-21).

Progress bar displayed

The progress bar is the first interface element shown. It initially displays 0% progress.

Searching status animated in

As the progress bar animates, a status message expands down like a window shade.

Additional status area appears

An additional status area that reveals which service is currently being searched is animated in as well.

Searching services

A spinning set of arrows adds additional feedback that something is happening.

Rolling through services

The "Now Searching" progress bar begins to roll through various services being searched. (Services are animated into place similar to the way an odometer works.)

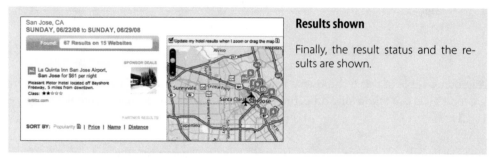

Results shown

Finally, the result status and the results are shown.

Figure 12-21. *Yahoo! Travel's Farechase tool steps through five stages of animation before producing the search results*

Since Farechase is actually retrieving results from a number of different hotel search services, the search can take quite a while. Farechase cleverly goes through five stages of **Transitions** to make the time appear to go faster. The result is that the users are kept informed and engaged throughout the process and report a much better experience, since they're less frustrated with the time it takes to get results.

Create Illusion of Virtual Space

We devoted all of Chapter 9 to the **Virtual Space**. Transitions can assist in creating the illusion of **Virtual Space**.

A significant improvement to the Yahoo! home page in the last few years has been the additional content packed in. One of the ways this is done is with the **Personal Assistant**. The **Personal Assistant** appears at the top right of the Yahoo! home page and contains a mini-view of six Yahoo! sites. Hovering over any of the site buttons causes the panels to animate open (Figure 12-22).

Not activated state

The Yahoo! Personal Assistant shows six collapsed mini-views of Yahoo! sites.

Activated by hover, expand starts

On mouse hover the hidden panel starts to animate open, creating a new virtual space.

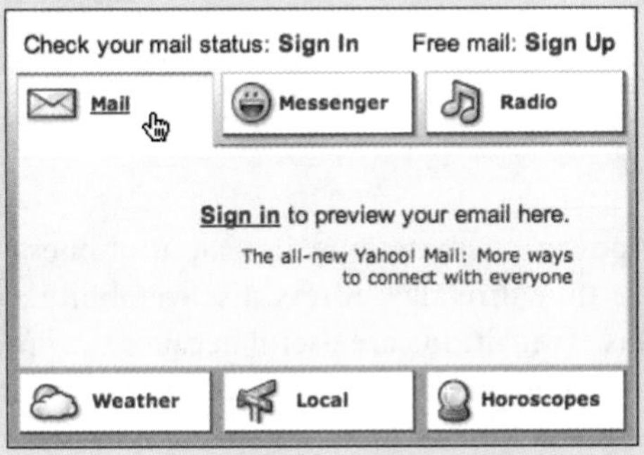

Expand finishes

The site panel animates to full open position. It allows the user to interact with the mini-view.

Figure 12-22. *Yahoo!'s Personal Assistant uses Expand and Collapse to create a virtual mini-space for other Yahoo! sites*

Expanding content with an animation emphasizes that the content is associated with the button that activated it. In this case, hovering over the "Messenger" button animates a preview of the Yahoo! Messenger site. **Transitions** are key to underpinning the concept of **Virtual Pages** we discussed in Chapter 7.

Best Practices for Transitions

Transitions are a powerful way to communicate and engage the user. While they can be abused, they can also be beneficial. Here is a set of best practices for employing transitions in your applications:

- The more rapid the change, the more important the event.
- Rapid movement is seen as more important than rapid color change.
- Movement toward the user is seen as more important than movement away from the user.
- Very slow change can be processed without disrupting the user's attention.
- Movement can be used to communicate an object's new home. By seeing the object moving from one place to another, users understand where it went and therefore will be able to locate the object in the future.
- Transitions should normally be reflexive. If an object moved and collapsed to a new spot, users should be able to open it and see it open up with the reverse transition. If users delete an object and it fades, then if they create an object it should fade into place. This illustrates the concept of Symmetry of Interaction.
- The misuse of effects by ads should teach us to be cautious about overusing transitions.
- Try not to rely solely on transitions for communicating change in the interface.
- Keep the transitions near the users' area of focus . This will make the transitions more discoverable and feel less like advertising.
- Gimmicky effects annoy and distract rather than communicate.

Principle Six
React Immediately

The previous two principles introduced the power of invitations and the usefulness of **Transitions**. **Invitations** are powerful because they directly address discoverability and provide feedback *before* an interaction happens. **Transitions** are useful because they provide visual feedback *during* an interaction. But another class of feedback exists. It is the feedback that happens immediately *after* each interaction with the system—an immediate reaction paired with the user's action.

Newton's Third Law of Motion states:

For every action, there is an equal and opposite reaction.

This law explains how a bird flies. Its wings push air downward. At the same time the air pushes the bird upward. The amount of force downward on the air equals the amount of upward force from the air. For every action there is an equal and opposite reaction. These are often called *action-reaction force pairs.*

While we can't literally extend Newton's law to the world of user interfaces, we certainly can apply this principle to the way we should interact with users. When users click on a button, they expect the button to depress. When they type in a field, they expect to see characters show up in the text box. When they make a mistake, they want the application to tell them where they goofed. When they start to search, they would like the results to show up as they type. When they start an unknown process, they hope they will be guided step by step with clear, timely, and contextual feedback.

In short, users want the application to react to their every action. The interface should *React Immediately*.

While there is a possibility of too much feedback (or, more accurately, too much of the wrong feedback—a concept we will discuss in the upcoming chapters), a system with little or no feedback feels sluggish and thickheaded. Immediate reactions are an expected part of intelligence. You can't have an intelligent interface without them.

Wundrbar.com is an example of an interface that reacts immediately (Figure P6-1). Wundrbar provides a search layer to a number of third-party services such as purchasing flight tickets, renting cars, or checking gas prices. As the user types a flight search in an input field, the interface formats a flight search form in real time. The tight loop between input and immediate feedback makes it easy to create a correct search (Figure P6-1).

> wundrbar beta

fly boston to dfw on american a

Expedia flight search   redirect ✕

Don't want Expedia? You can also use CheapTickets, Kayak, Orbitz, Sidestep or Travelocity. Just say so!

From Boston, Logan, MA (BOS)
To Dallas/Ft. Worth, TX (DFW)

Dates: **Passengers:**
leaving ....   1 adult
returning n/a (one-way)

Other trip details:
Economy class on American Airlines

Figure P6-1. *As the user types in a flight search, Wundrbar immediately displays what it understands; the user is able to express all the needed input*

It should be noted that while interfaces built in this style have only recently shown up on the Web, this principle is not new to the world of user interfaces. The Mac OSX Human Interface Guidelines calls this principle "Feedback and Communication," and describes its goal as:

> …*keeping users informed about what's happening by providing appropriate feedback. When a user initiates an action, always provide an indication that your application has received the user's input and is operating on it.*[*]

Jakob Nielsen, in his widely recognized heuristics research, described a principle of "visibility of system status" in which:

> …*the system should always keep users informed about what is going on, through appropriate feedback within reasonable time.*[†]

Bruce Tognazzini, founder of the Human Interface Group at Apple, captured the essence of this in his design principle called **Latency Reduction,**[‡] in which the user is kept engaged throughout a lengthy process. The emphasis is on communication, feedback, and engagement.

The next two chapters will look at two areas where we can directly apply this principle:

Chapter 13, *Lookup Patterns*
  Discusses **Auto Complete, Live Suggest, Live Search,** and **Refining Search.**

Chapter 14, *Feedback Patterns*
  Covers **Live Preview, Progressive Disclosure, Progress Indication,** and **Periodic Refresh**.

---

[*] *http://developer.apple.com/documentation/UserExperience/Conceptual/AppleHIGuidelines/XHIGHIDesign/chapter_5_section_2.html*

[†] *http://www.useit.com/papers/heuristic/heuristic_list.html*

[‡] *http://www.asktog.com/basics/firstPrinciples.html#latencyReduction*

Chapter 13

Lookup Patterns

A good portion of application interfaces is involved in looking up information. Whether an application is performing direct searches, filtering search results, or aiding in input, there are a lot of opportunities to provide lookup assistance.

Since lookup is really a shot in the dark for the user, any real-time feedback will be valued as users work to complete their tasks. There are four lookup patterns we will apply the principle of *React Immediately* to:

- **Auto Complete**
- **Live Suggest**
- **Live Search**
- **Refining Search**

Auto Complete

Auto Complete is a powerful pattern that benefits from a reactive interface. As the user types input into a field, a drop-down menu of matching values is displayed. When done right, the choice that best matches will be auto-selected. The user can stop typing and accept the choice that has been matched or choose a different value from the list. The selected value is then entered into the field. Yahoo! Mail uses **Auto Complete** for email addresses (Figure 13-1).

Prompt shows suggestions

Typing the letter "z" immediately matches all contacts that start with that letter (in either first, last, or email fields).

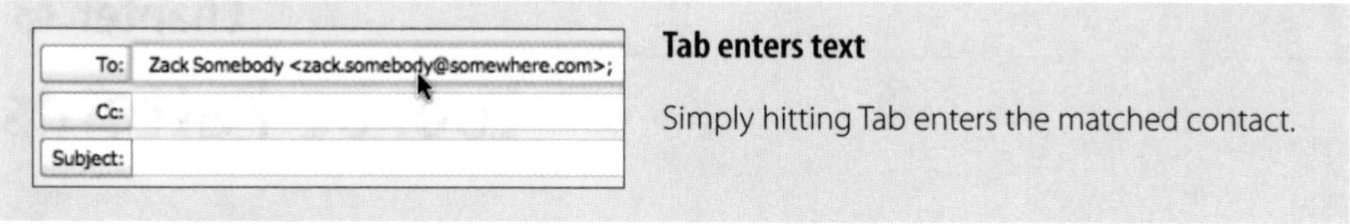

Tab enters text

Simply hitting Tab enters the matched contact.

Figure 13-1. *Yahoo! Mail automatically completes email addresses*

The Yahoo! Mail **Auto Complete** has a singular purpose: help users find an email address from their contact list. However, the user can choose to ignore the displayed value and instead enter a new email address. This distinguishes **Auto Complete** from a normal drop-down selection box. Selection boxes provide a limited set of valid values. Users are not free to add their own values. For example, entering a U.S. state is best done with a select box and not **Auto Complete** since you don't need to create new states.

Considerations

At first glance **Auto Complete** can seem like a simple interaction. However, there are a few key interesting moments to consider.

Typing

How long should you wait to display feedback as the user types? In the case of **Auto Complete**, feedback should be sent after each character is typed. Since the focus is on entering a value in a field, the set of choices should be shown instantaneously. However, it is acceptable to delay retrieving values between keystrokes if the user is a fast typist.

Matching

In the case of Yahoo! Mail, the typed character(s) are matched against any part of the contact's name and email address. This is important since sometimes the user recalls part of an email address and other times is typing the contact's first or last name.

Yahoo! Mail also highlights the matched contact as well as displaying the matched characters in bold text. This clearly indicates which contact was matched as well as how the match was made.

The Up and Down arrow keys can modify the matched value. They simply move up and down through the list of partially matched contacts.

Selecting

Once an item is matched, it should be straightforward for the user to accept the match. In the case of Yahoo! Mail, hitting the Tab key enters the matched contact into the input field.

This might seem obvious. However, it is not uncommon for **Auto Complete** interactions to miss this crucial step. A counterexample to Yahoo! Mail ironically comes from Yahoo! as well. The Yahoo! Travel Farechase product provides an **Auto Complete** feature for entering origin and destination airports (Figure 13-2).

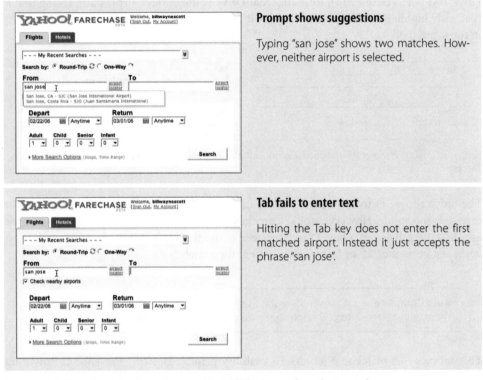

Prompt shows suggestions

Typing "san jose" shows two matches. However, neither airport is selected.

Tab fails to enter text

Hitting the Tab key does not enter the first matched airport. Instead it just accepts the phrase "san jose".

Figure 13-2. *Farechase's implementation of Auto Complete makes selection tedious*

Farechase handles the delay during typing well but fails in the way it handles matching and selecting. Neither of the two airports that match the phrase "san jose" gets highlighted. The only indication of which airport Farechase thinks is the best match is based on position. Since "San Jose, CA—SJC (San Jose International Airport)" is the first airport in the list, it seems that this might be the best match. But hitting Tab reveals that neither was considered worthy of choosing. Instead the user gets to keep a partially typed phrase, "san jose".

The only way to get it to work correctly is to use the Up and Down arrow keys (or the mouse) to explicitly choose an airport from the drop-down set of choices. This is a cumbersome, unnecessary step that is easily avoided by automatically selecting the first matched item in the list.

Kayak Auto Complete

Kayak.com is a good example of getting typing, matching, and selecting correct for **Auto Complete**. In Figure 13-3, the user wants to fly to Dallas, TX. He isn't sure what the airport code is, but he wants the one in Dallas/Fort Worth. Typing "dall" gets two matches: DFW and DAL (Love Field). Realizing that DFW is the correct airport and seeing that it is already highlighted, he hits the Tab key. It enters the correct value for the DFW airport in the input field.

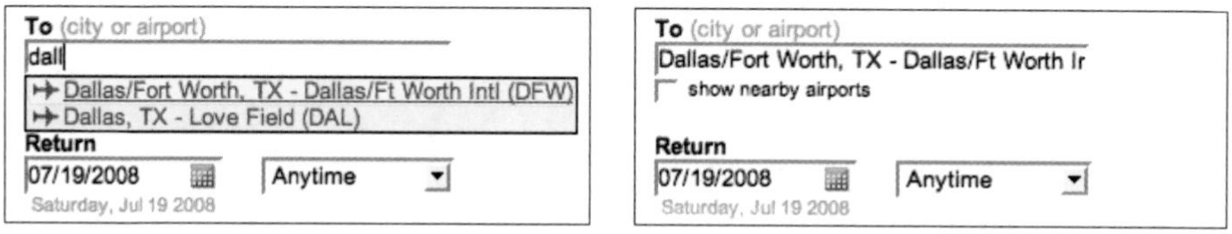

Figure 13-3. *Kayak shows the matched airport and allows the user to accept the selection by hitting the Tab key*

The only critique of this system is the use of light yellow for the selection color. In most cases it is too subtle. However, unlike Farechase, Kayak just does the right thing when the user hits the Tab or Enter key. There's no need to use the down arrow key to select the first item: just press the Tab or Enter key to accept the match.

Tip

Auto Complete should never make the user scroll through the drop-down to choose the already selected item! The Tab key should enter the matched item.

This follows one of Jakob Nielsen's 10 usability principles: *Error Prevention*. Providing immediate reactions and the proper cues prevents the user from entering the wrong value (e.g., "dall") and having to go back to correct a mistake that should have been avoided in the first place.

Best Practices for Auto Complete

Here are some best practices to keep in mind:

- Use **Auto Complete** for input assistance.
- Match on multiple fields.
- Show results when the user pauses typing.
- Allow selecting matched value on Tab key.

Live Suggest

A very close cousin to **Auto Complete** is the **Live Suggest** pattern (also known as *winnowing*). While **Auto Complete** provides suggested real-time values for an input field, **Live Suggest** provides real-time search term suggestions for creating a search. The context switch from input field to search box and from input value to term suggestion puts a different twist on the interaction.

Google Suggest was one of the first examples of **Live Suggest** on the Web. As the user types in the Google Suggest search box, the top search terms that match the user's input are shown in a drop-down. Figure 13-4 shows two versions of Google Suggest with different approaches to matching and choosing.

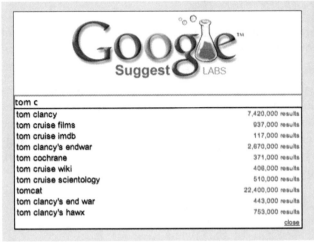

Early version of Google Suggest

In the earliest versions of Google Suggest, the best match was highlighted and the search field was populated with the matched value.

Later version of Google Suggest

In the more recent versions of Google Suggest, the closest match is not highlighted and the search box does not get auto-populated.

Figure 13-4. *Two versions of Google Suggest take different approaches for selecting a matched item*

Considerations

Just as in **Auto Complete**, **Live Suggest** has three interesting moments to focus on: typing, matching, and selection. Let's look at how both versions of Google Suggest handle these.

Typing

The two versions handle reactions to user input the same way. As the user types, suggestions are presented in real time with no noticeable delay. If the user pastes a phrase into the search box, it will just display results for phrase and not attempt to display results for individual characters.

Matching

The most powerful aspect of Google Suggest is its ability to narrow in on good search terms based on partial input. Here is how Google describes the service:

> As you type into the search box, Google Suggest guesses what you're typing and offers suggestions in real time. This is similar to Google's "Did you mean?" feature that offers alternative spellings for your query after you search, except that it works in real time. For example, if you type "bass," Google Suggest might offer a list of refinements that include "bass fishing" or "bass guitar." Similarly, if you type in only part of a word, like "prog," Google Suggest might offer you refinements like "programming," "programming languages," "progesterone," or "progressive."
>
> Our algorithms use a wide range of information to predict the queries users are most likely to want to see. For example, Google Suggest uses data about the overall popularity of various searches to help rank the refinements it offers.... Google Suggest does not base its suggestions on your personal search history.*

What this means is that by progressively applying the suggestion algorithm to the current input, the search terms are narrowed to yield a good search result. It also has the potential of producing novel or intriguing suggestions.

Providing real-time feedback can have a negative side effect. If what is shown diverges from what the user is actually looking for, instead of narrowing in, the process becomes distracting. This is the tension in all suggestion-based systems. Are you distracting the user or helping her narrow in on better results? You should continue to make live suggestions only if you are certain you can narrow and not distract. Otherwise, take a more conservative approach and change the suggestions less frequently.

--- **Tip** ---
Suggestions should always narrow toward the user's goal and avoid distracting her with needless information.

---

* See *http://labs.google.com/suggestfaq.html.*

Narrowing suggestions are powerful. For example, typing "tom cr" shows a number of common Tom Cruise searches. Continuing to type "tom cruise crazy" yields specific common searches (see Figure 13-5).

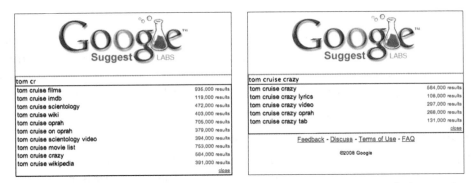

Figure 13-5. *Google Suggest progressively applies suggestions that help narrow in on the best search terms*

Yahoo! Search also provides a **Live Suggest** for its searches (see Figure 13-6). One difference between Google Suggest and Yahoo! is that Yahoo! provides feedback on matched terms.

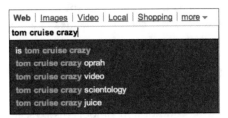

Figure 13-6. *Yahoo! Search highlights what is different between its suggestions and what the user inputs*

At first glance it seems that Yahoo! is highlighting the wrong thing. Recall the Yahoo! Mail **Auto Complete** example earlier in this chapter (see Figure 13-1). The characters that matched the user's input for each matched contact are displayed in bold. But in Yahoo! Search, just the opposite happens. Instead of highlighting the *matched* text, it highlights the *difference*. This twist shifts the focus to how each suggestion will narrow the search.

This illustrates how dependent interaction styles are on context. With **Auto Complete**, we are trying enter a direct value. The suggestions are possible matches. With **Live Suggest,** we are trying to formulate the right query for a search. Each suggestion has a unique context to offer. When the words "is", "oprah", "video", "scientology", and "juice" are highlighted, users can quickly scan and get the suggestion's context. Each suggestion provides a way to head off in a different direction.

Both **Live Suggest** implementations have another nice side effect. Spelling mistakes are caught earlier in the cycle since the guesses are based on implicitly correcting the spelling of the search query.

Selecting

In the earlier versions of Google Suggest, the best match (first item) was automatically chosen. Not only was the suggested term highlighted but also the full matching string was placed in the search box. Typing "tom c" produced "tom cruise" with "ruise" selected (see Figure 13-4). The idea of selecting the portion of the text not explicitly typed was to:

- Allow the user to hit Enter to accept the implicit match.

- Allow the user to hit Delete to remove the implicitly added string (e.g., "ruise").

More recent revisions have taken a different approach. Instead the best match is *not* selected and the search box is *never* modified by matches found. The idea is to:

- Avoid making assumptions that the guesses are what the user wants. Guesses have to be explicitly chosen with the arrow keys or the mouse.

- Allow the user a more normal search-box experience.

There are advantages to each approach. The first is more heavy-handed and assumes the guess has a high probability of being the user's intent. As we saw earlier with **Auto Complete**, selecting the suggestion as the value to accept makes for a more pleasant experience. But the current approach better captures the idea of a "suggestion"; it's just that—a suggestion, not an explicit choice.

More Considerations

Live Suggest doesn't have to look exactly like the preceding examples. It can come in other flavors. When users enter a new question in Yahoo! Answers, an alternate set of questions is suggested (see Figure 13-7).

Question entered

Suggestions are not made while the user is busy typing.

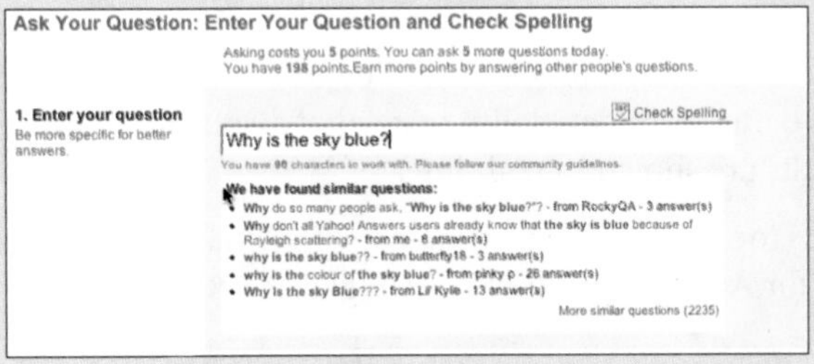

Suggested alternatives

Suggestions are triggered when the user stops typing.

Figure 13-7. Yahoo! Answers suggests already answered questions as an alternative to creating a new question

Typing

This method departs from the previous **Live Suggest** examples. Instead of triggering suggestions after each character is typed, suggestions are displayed whenever the user pauses typing. If a complete question is entered without a pause, no suggestions will be displayed until the very end. Showing suggestions too early would be distracting and would not help users narrow down to the question they are trying to formulate.

Matching and selecting

Instead of a drop-down, a list of similar questions is provided in context just below the question asked. The reason? If users pick an alternate question, they don't need to create a new question. Selecting an alternate question takes users directly to the question and its answers, and out of the task of creating a new question.

Best Practices for Live Suggest

Here are some best practices to keep in mind:

- Use **Live Suggest** for suggestion assistance, not for direct search results.
- Provide suggestions highlighting the context of each suggestion.
- Start showing suggestions after a reasonable delay (pause in typing, etc.).
- The interface should help users narrow down on a good choice without overly restricting them.

Live Search

Yet another close relative to both **Auto Complete** and **Live Suggest** is **Live Search**. As with **Live Suggest,** a search query is being formulated. But instead of displaying suggested search terms, actual live search results are shown in real time.

A clear example of this is ZUGGEST* for Amazon. Not affiliated with Amazon.com, Francis Shanahan created a Live Search for Amazon products (see Figure 13-8).

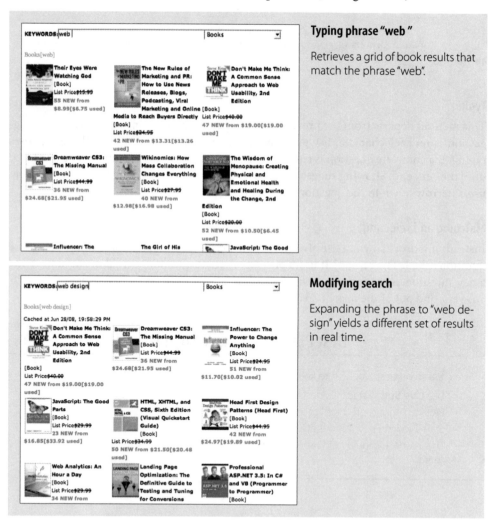

Typing phrase "web "

Retrieves a grid of book results that match the phrase "web".

Modifying search

Expanding the phrase to "web design" yields a different set of results in real time.

Figure 13-8. *ZUGGEST for Amazon is a third-party way to search Amazon using the Live Search pattern*

---

* See *http://www.francisshanahan.com/zuggest.aspx.*

Considerations

Providing in-context, real-time results to queries as they are typed is a powerful way for users to find what they are looking for. **Live Suggest** sets up a tight feedback loop for finding the right query. However, the actual search results are shown outside this iterative feedback loop. **Live Search,** on the other hand, creates a tight feedback loop directly with the search results themselves.

How does the handling of interesting moments differ between **Auto Complete** and **Live Suggest?**

Typing

Since returning search results generally takes longer than the time between typing characters, searching should wait for the user to stop typing. This allows feedback to happen at times when it will not be distracting, as well as providing better user experience performance. While ZUGGEST does not provide a Busy Indicator or Progress Indicator, it is a good idea to provide this feedback as soon as a search is initiated. Otherwise the interface will feel sluggish. Instant feedback improves the perceived performance.

Matching and selection

There is nothing inherently unique in the way search results are matched for **Live Search** or normal search. Nor is there anything unique about how items are selected. **Live Search** primarily affects the way searches are retrieved in response to typed queries.

Contextual results

While ZUGGEST presents a full search interface, sometimes the results can be shown in a more compact way. This is especially useful if you want to contain **Live Search** in a separate tool on the page or in a sidebar.

Firefox version 3 introduced search directly into the URL bar of the browser (Figure 13-9).

Figure 13-9. *Firefox's AwesomeBar uses Live Search to retrieve results based on previous interest in websites*

In the words of the Mozilla blog:*

> *Dubbed the "AwesomeBar", it lets you use the URL field of your browser to do a key-word search of your history and bookmarks. No longer do you have to know the do-main of the page you're looking for—the AwesomeBar will match what you're typing (even multiple words!) against the URLs, page titles, and tags in your bookmarks and history, returning results sorted by "frecency" (an algorithm combining frequency + recency).†*

While ZUGGEST bases its results strictly on a straight product lookup, the AwesomeBar bases its search on personalized information. Since the browser can keep track of the us-ers' interest in pages and knows how recently they accessed them, the **Live Search** can be a powerful aid to finding previous sites they have visited.

The variance in the way these two sites perform matches has to do with context. With a straightforward search, you don't know if users are looking for something they have seen before or not. And you would rather not limit their results. In the case of the browser URL, chances are that users are heading to a site they have been to before.

Previews in Live Search

When **Live Search** results are displayed in a drop-down or sidebar, users need enough context to choose the right result. Without the proper detail, users will have to click through to see whether they have really received the result they were looking for. If the result isn't correct, they have to return to the page and start the search all over again. While the initial live search is fast and easy, the ensuing click-through and failure can be slow and painful.

Any easy way to minimize this happening is to show some preview information for each search result.

In the AwesomeBar example (Figure 13-9), each URL is displayed with its favicon, docu-ment title, and the URL.

Another approach is to provide detailed previews on demand. As we discussed in Chapter 3, **Hover Details** are a way to reveal lots of additional information when the user hovers over an item.

Dunstan Orchard created one of the early **Live Search** examples on his blog, 1976design. com (Figure 13-10). Previews are displayed in a balloon pop up when the mouse hovers over one of the search results returned. This allows a more compact view of search results, yet helps the user find the right result before clicking through.

---

* See *http://blog.mozilla.com/blog/2008/04/21/a-little-something-awesome-about-firefox-3/*.
† See the Mozilla blog at *http://tinyurl.com/6mowhb*.

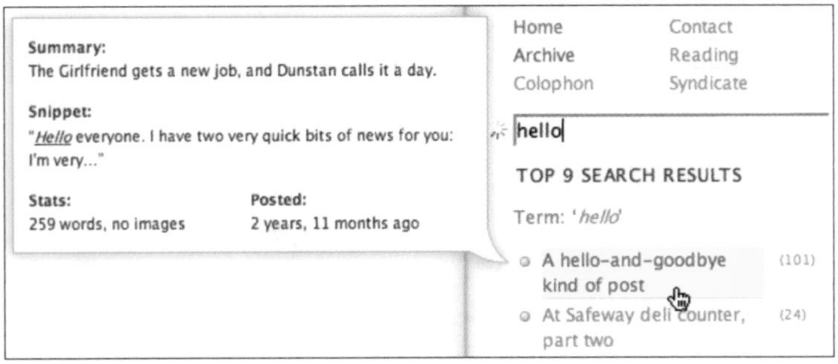

Summary:
The Girlfriend gets a new job, and Dunstan calls it a day.
Snippet:
"Hello everyone. I have two very quick bits of news for you: I'm very..."
Stats:
259 words, no images
Posted:
2 years, 11 months ago
Home
Contact
Archive
Reading
Colophon
Syndicate
hello
TOP 9 SEARCH RESULTS
Term: 'hello'
A hello-and-goodbye kind of post
(101)
At Safeway deli counter, part two
(24)

Figure 13-10. *Dunstan Orchard's blog provides details on blog posts with a balloon pop up on mouse hover*

Narrowing too quickly

Yahoo!'s Instant Search takes a narrower approach. A balloon pop up shows up with what it feels is the best single match. It's like an abbreviated Google Suggest and the Google "I'm feeling lucky" button merged into a single interface.

Typing "tom cruise" yields a single result from IMDb (Figure 13-11).

Instant Search BETA
tom cruise
Search the Web
1. IMDb: Tom Cruise
photos, filmography, and facts about the super star.
www.imdb.com/name/nm0000129

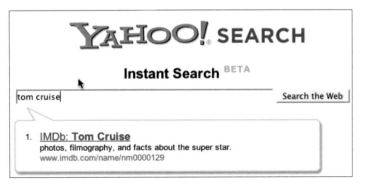

Figure 13-11. *Yahoo! Instant Search shows a single result based on what the user types*

Here are a few caveats:

- Users frequently have to type fairly specific, complete search terms. "tom c" does not cut it; "tom cruise" does.
- Having a single result is too narrow. In this example, users will always get the IMDb database result for Tom. Is that what they want?
- The balloon can be distracting since it calls so much attention to itself and draws users' eyes away from where they are typing. And when they don't get the suggestion, they may think they have made a mistake.

Combining Live Suggest and Live Search

It is possible to combine **Live Suggest** and **Live Search** in a single interface. In an experimental interface, Yahoo! released (for a short period of time in 2006) AllTheWeb LiveSearch (Figure 13-12).

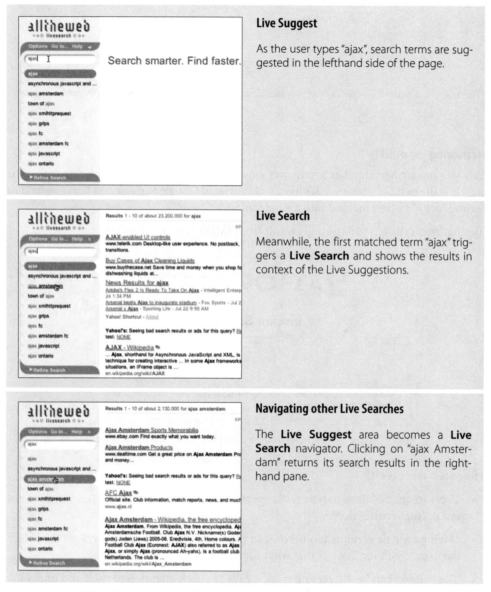

Live Suggest

As the user types "ajax", search terms are suggested in the lefthand side of the page.

Live Search

Meanwhile, the first matched term "ajax" triggers a **Live Search** and shows the results in context of the Live Suggestions.

Navigating other Live Searches

The **Live Suggest** area becomes a **Live Search** navigator. Clicking on "ajax Amsterdam" returns its search results in the righthand pane.

Figure 13-12. AllTheWeb.com LiveSearch was an experimental combination of Live Suggest and Live Search

AllTheWeb LiveSearch is no longer live on the Web,* however, Yahoo!'s search has evolved to incorporate a variation on combining **Live Suggest** and **Live Search** into a single interface.

> **Tip**
>
> Combining **Live Suggest** and **Live Search** is a good way to provide a dynamic search experience.

As we saw in Figure 13-6, the main page for Yahoo! Search incorporates **Live Suggest** in its interface. The search results page incorporates a pull-down shade that contains the **Live Suggest** results. Changing the search query brings new suggestions in the pull-down shade area. Clicking on any of the suggestions displays new search results for the page (Figure 13-13).

Figure 13-13. *Yahoo! Search combines Live Suggest and Live Search into a single interface*

Live Search can be expensive

It is a good idea to keep in mind that **Live Search** can be an expensive operation. Being able to search instantaneously with every user's keystroke (or some set of keystrokes) can greatly increase server load.

In an early version of Yahoo! Mail (Beta version), typing a mail search triggered search on each keystroke. This was removed due to heavy server load (Figure 13-14).

---

* You can find a screencast of it at *http://www.flickr.com/photos/designingwebinterfaces/2758155472/in/set-72157606696104907/*.

Figure 13-14. *Yahoo! Mail switched from a Live Search model to a traditional submit model for Search; performance considerations were the primary drivers*

Best Practices for Live Search

Here are some best practices to keep in mind:

- Use **Live Search** for free-form searches.
- Provide generous context for each result returned. Results need to be returned quickly.
- Show enough results to help narrow in on a solution but not too much to be distracting.
- Where possible, combine **Live Suggest** and **Live Search** into a single interface.

Refining Search

Another variation on **Live Search** is **Refining Search**. Also known as **Faceted Browse**, **Refining Search** provides a set of live filters that allow the search results to be tuned in real time.

One of the earlier applications that effectively used **Refining Search** on the Web was Kayak, an online travel search site. The filter bar on the left dynamically updates the flight results on the right (Figure 13-5).

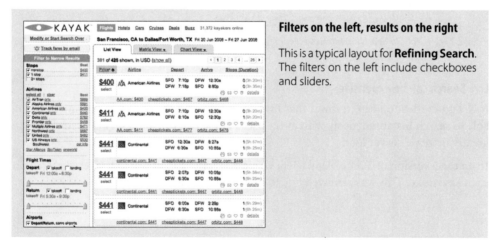

Filters on the left, results on the right

This is a typical layout for **Refining Search**. The filters on the left include checkboxes and sliders.

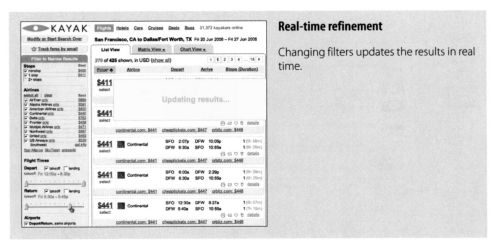

Real-time refinement

Changing filters updates the results in real time.

Figure 13-15. *Kayak uses a Refining Search model to allow users to tweak travel results in real time*

Considerations

As we have shown with **Auto Complete**, the **Live Suggest** and **Live Search** *React Immediately* principle is a powerful way to narrow in on a desired result. Kayak uses this technique effectively to allow the user to iteratively get a new set of results by tweaking a set of filters. While the filters can be placed anywhere on the page that makes sense, most sites (like Kayak) place the filters in a lefthand sidebar.

Avoid page refreshes

It is important that each iteration of the result is displayed without a page refresh.

eBay uses a **Refining Search** (Figure 13-16). However, refinements are triggered only after hitting a "Submit" button. Each search generates an in-between page refresh. While this step may sound minor, it is very disruptive to the action-reaction feedback loop. The page result throws a blank page in the mix and usually scrolls the page back to the top. After each iteration, users have to relocate some element on the page to get their bearings, reposition the page, and analyze what changed. Generally any updates to the results after one of these page refreshes is not immediately noticed by the user. It's as if the page refresh also refreshed the user's mind!

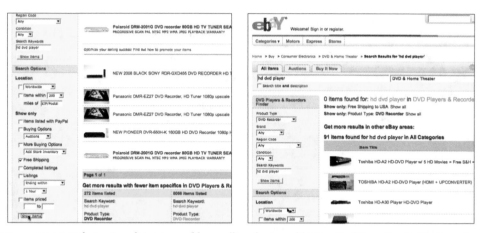

Figure 13-16. *Refining Search is triggered by scrolling down and hitting the "Show Results" button; the results are shown after a page refresh that scrolls the page back to the top*

Tip

Avoid page refreshes in **Refining Search**. The point is to quickly iterate to a result. Refreshing the page causes the user to lose her context.

Even smoother transitions

On the opposite end of the spectrum from the eBay page refresh model, Viewzi, a search interface, uses **Transitions** to smooth out **Refining Search** iterations. In the "4 Sources View," results from Yahoo!, Google, Ask, and MSN are shown on the same page. In the first panel of Figure 13-17, only results from Ask are initially shown.

Figure 13-17. *Viewzi uses animated transitions to "smooth out" the changes between each Refining Search iteration*

Clicking the pink bar (denoting "display Google results") brings the Google results into the mix. Notice that the second panel shows the Google results flying into the page. The final panel shows both Ask and Google results displayed on the same page. The in-between fly in **Transition** makes it clear what got added during the **Refining Search**.

Custom filters

Roost, a real estate search site, provides an interface similar to Kayak's. One nice addition is the ability to add custom search terms. Typing custom attributes in the "Custom Search Terms" panel adds them to the set of filters. The terms can then be checked on and off in real time. Like Kayak, Roost makes use of sliders for the **Refining Search** (Figure 13-18).

Figure 13-18. *Roost uses sliders and a custom search area to refine searches*

It should be noted that, while visually attractive, sliders can be hard for users to control. If you employ them, you should:

- Display a tool tip or other real-time feedback while dragging a slider knob.
- Allow clicking anywhere on the background or along the range to set the slider.
- Make sure any background graphic gives additional feedback for the values along the range.
- Consider an input field for accessibility considerations.
- Allow double sliders (a knob for minimum value and a knob for maximum value) to overlap. Otherwise certain ranges can't be entered. Endless.com is one of the few sites that gets this technique right (Figure 13-19).

Figure 13-19. *Endless.com allows its dual sliders to overlap; as a result, any range of values can be set*

Think outside the box

Filters in a **Refining Search** don't have to be just text fields, sliders, and checkboxes. They can be visual controls that provide clear feedback as to what the result will be before it is actually selected.

Like.com is a good example of this approach (Figure 13-20). Colors, shapes, sizes, and textures all are various ways to refine the search. You can even highlight a part of a product to find more like it.

Figure 13-20. *Like.com uses colors, textures, shape, and sizes to refine product searches*

Endless.com provides filters for finding shoes (Figure 13-21). The filters include things like shoe sizes, widths, and color families. The filters more closely represent the values than just simple checkboxes, sliders, or drop-downs.

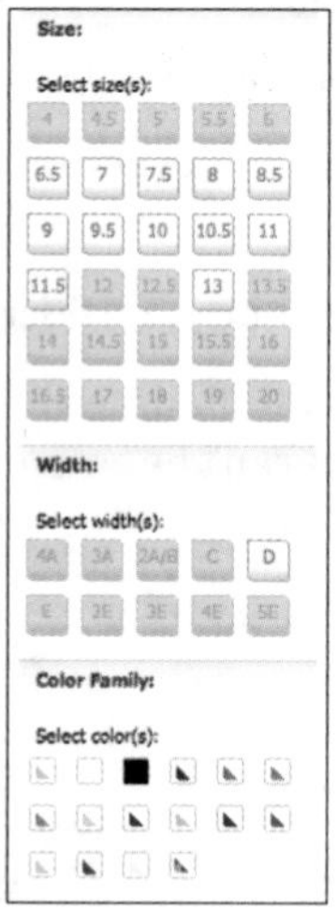

Figure 13-21. *Endless.com provides visual representations for filtering shoe sizes, widths, and color families*

When to trigger a search

While eBay requires the "Show Items" button to trigger a search and Kayak and Roost perform the search immediately after each refinement, there is a middle ground. Just as in **Live Search**, sometimes it makes sense to wait before triggering a **Refining Search**.

In Yahoo! for Teachers, a **Refining Search** is used for finding other teacher's projects and lesson plans (Figure 13-22). Clicking various grade levels in succession only fires the search after the user has stopped interacting (for about half a second). The interface feels responsive, but not too chatty.

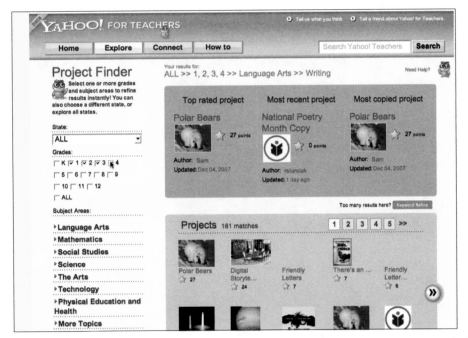

Figure 13-22. *Yahoo! for Teachers triggers Refining Search following a burst of user interaction with the refinement filters*

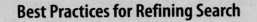

Best Practices for Refining Search

Here are some best practices to keep in mind:

- Use **Refining Search** for product searches when there are multiple facets to filter.
- Use visually compelling filter controls.
- Be careful with sliders, as they tend to be harder for users to control.
- Use animations to smooth out refining iterations.
- Use proper delays to limit unnecessary refinements (wait until the user stops tweaking).

Chapter 14

Feedback Patterns

Reacting immediately to the user is not only needed for lookup patterns, but in order to provide interactive feedback in other situations. There are several patterns that help keep the user informed about what is happening in the application:

- **Live Preview**
- **Progressive Disclosure**
- **Progress Indicator**
- **Periodic Refresh**

Live Preview

A **Live Preview** gives the users a glimpse beforehand of how the application will interpret their input once submitted.

We mentioned Jakob Nielson's Error Prevention principle earlier. This principle says:

> *Even better than good error messages is a careful design which prevents a problem from occurring in the first place.*[*]

Benjamin Franklin seemed to be speaking about the same principle when he uttered the famous quote, "An ounce of prevention is worth a pound of cure."

—— **Tip** ————————————————————————————————

Use **Live Previews** to prevent errors.

———

---

* Nielsen, Jakob. "Ten Usability Heuristics." See *http://tinyurl.com/aruty*.

Being reactive to user input is an excellent way to provide that ounce of prevention. **Live Previews** dispense just the right amount of information, in context and just in time to keep users informed, preventing unnecessary mistakes.

Wundrbar.com is an example of an interface that reacts immediately (Figure 14-1). Wundrbar provides a search layer to a number of third-party services such as purchasing flight tickets, renting cars, or checking gas prices in Des Moines.

Search invitation

The "examples" help area serves as an invitation to discover how to interact with Wundrbar.

Reaction: Flight form

Typing the word "fly" triggers Wundrbar to display an Expedia flight search form. Notice three inputs are displayed: "Origin", "Destination", and "Departure date".

Reaction: Origin

Typing "fly boston" automatically fills in the Origin with "Boston, Logan, MA (BOS)".

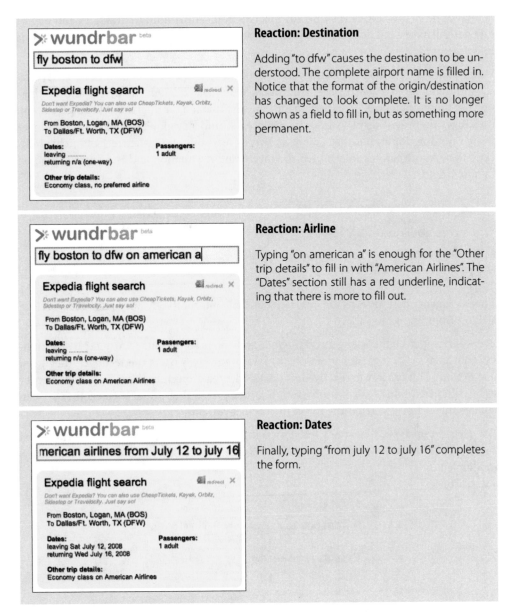

Reaction: Destination

Adding "to dfw" causes the destination to be understood. The complete airport name is filled in. Notice that the format of the origin/destination has changed to look complete. It is no longer shown as a field to fill in, but as something more permanent.

Reaction: Airline

Typing "on american a" is enough for the "Other trip details" to fill in with "American Airlines". The "Dates" section still has a red underline, indicating that there is more to fill out.

Reaction: Dates

Finally, typing "from july 12 to july 16" completes the form.

Figure 14-1. *Wundrbar provides an immediate reaction to each user input*

Note that before we start seeing action-reactions, we get a nice **Static Invitation** in the "Examples" section. Once we start typing, this interface perfectly illustrates the principle of action-reaction pairs. Our action of typing the word "fly" leads to the reaction of an Expedia flight search panel being displayed. The panel is shown immediately in context.

A total of three invitations is shown in this reaction. The origin, destination, and departure date all have a red dotted underline. This cues the user that the application needs this information.

Emboldened by the intelligence displayed, let's experiment with some more text. Typing "boston" and "to dfw" each get a reaction as Wundrbar fills out the origin and destination. At this point it does an interesting thing. Sure that it has understood the user's intent, it changes the way it displays these two pieces of information. The fields are no longer shown needing input, but instead are shown as read-only text (Figure 14-2). This indicates that Wundrbar has interpreted the origin and destination and is ready to move on to other input.

```
Origin: Boston, Logan, MA (BOS)
Destination: ..........
Departure date: ..........
```

```
From Boston, Logan, MA (BOS)
To Dallas/Ft. Worth, TX (DFW)
```

Figure 14-2. *The origin and destination are displayed as an input form before the user types them; afterward they are changed to display not as input, but as static text*

The intelligence continues as the interface correctly interprets "fly bos to dfw on american airlines from July 12 to July 16".

But what happens if the user gets off the rails and enters something incorrect? By continuing to display what it thinks users mean, Wundrbar gives users the feedback they need just in time. This is a key to reactive interfaces. The reactions must be in real time in order to be effective. In this case, if users see it has interpreted their input incorrectly, they can change their phrase in real time to get the correct response.

If a user did mistype, she would see something like Figure 14-3. The red underline next to the "To" field is very visible. It serves as a nice way to cue the user that the input is incomplete.

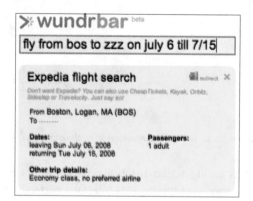

Figure 14-3. *Typing "zzz" for an airline just leaves the "To" field displaying a red-dotted underline*

Considerations

There are some issues to consider when using **Live Previews**.

Immediate feedback

Instead of users entering a password, hitting the "Submit" button, and then finding out that their password is "too short," the Google signup process (Figure 14-4) keeps users informed as they modify their entry. The nice thing about this interface is that it lets users make an informed decision about their password strength before making their final choice.

Google uses a **Live Preview** to help users choose an adequate password during the signup process.

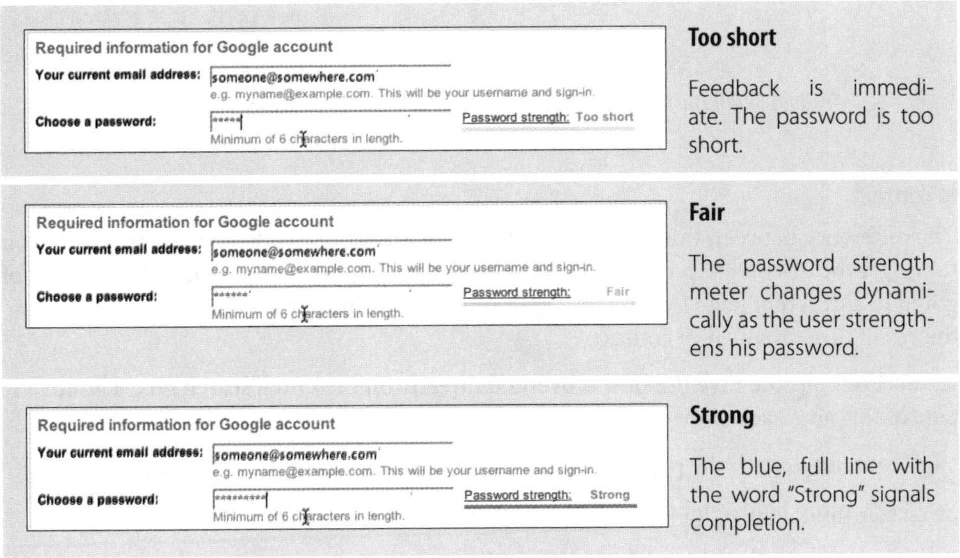

Too short

Feedback is immediate. The password is too short.

Fair

The password strength meter changes dynamically as the user strengthens his password.

Strong

The blue, full line with the word "Strong" signals completion.

Figure 14-4. *Google uses Live Preview to show password strength before creating an account*

Engagement

The use of a bar that fills up as users strengthen their passwords is reminiscent of the "ring-the-bell" carnival game, where you swing the hammer and try to hit the bell—only getting to a strong password is much easier.

> —— **Tip** ——
> Use **Live Previews** to improve user engagement.

Yahoo! Small Business uses **Live Preview** to help users find a domain name without leaving the current page (Figure 14-5).

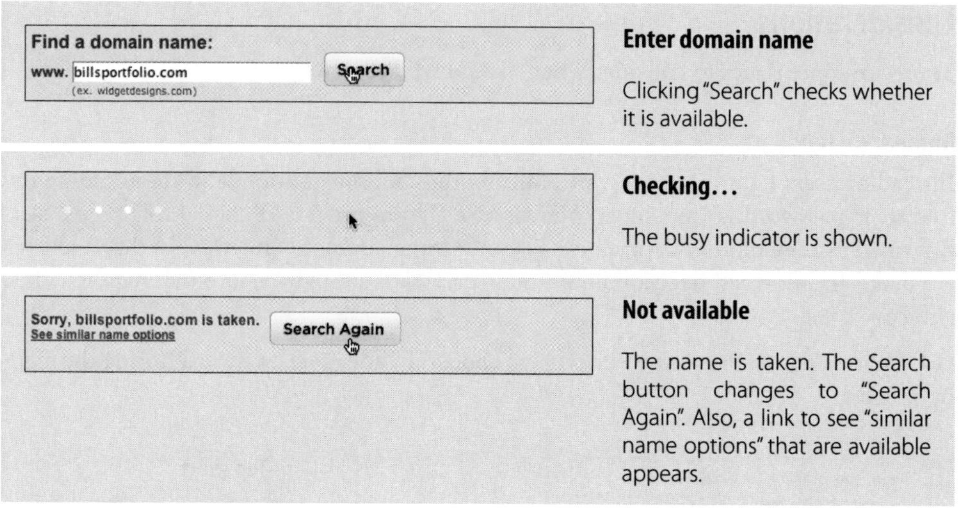

Find a domain name: www. billsportfolio.com **Search** (ex. widgetdesigns.com)	**Enter domain name** Clicking "Search" checks whether it is available.
• • • • ▶	**Checking…** The busy indicator is shown.
Sorry, billsportfolio.com is taken. **Search Again** See similar name options	**Not available** The name is taken. The Search button changes to "Search Again". Also, a link to see "similar name options" that are available appears.

Figure 14-5. *Yahoo! Small Business uses Live Preview for domain name search*

In context

The difference between this example and the Google example is the use of a search button to trigger the in-context preview. The search button removes the ambiguity. But instead of going to a different page for showing the results of the attempted domain name creation, the results are provided in context.

In this example, the **Live Preview** is overlaid directly on the initial search box. The advantage of this approach is that it:

- Does not disturb the page by adding more content into the flow of the page.
- Feels more lightweight than a page transition.
- Gives a clear place to put a progress indicator.
- Provides room for a status message and two courses of action: "Search Again" or "See similar name options".

Last.fm also uses a button to check the validity of a field during its "Sign up" flow (Figure 14-6). Typing into the username field immediately reveals a "Check Availability" button. Pressing the button triggers a **Live Preview** check of whether this username is available. If it is not, a red exclamation point is placed beside the field and the button changes to say "Try another name".

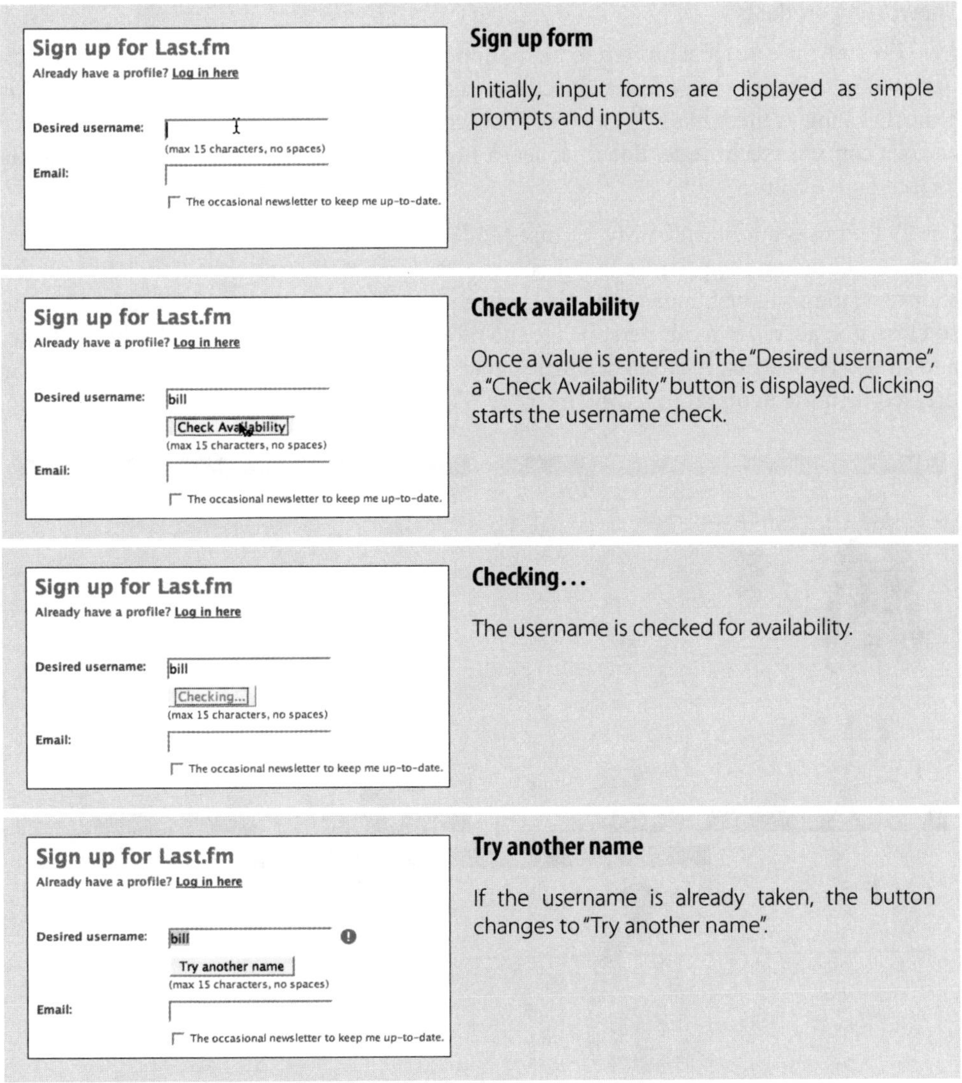

Sign up for Last.fm
Already have a profile? Log in here

Desired username:
(max 15 characters, no spaces)
Email:
☐ The occasional newsletter to keep me up-to-date.

Sign up form

Initially, input forms are displayed as simple prompts and inputs.

Sign up for Last.fm
Already have a profile? Log in here

Desired username: bill
Check Availability
(max 15 characters, no spaces)
Email:
☐ The occasional newsletter to keep me up-to-date.

Check availability

Once a value is entered in the "Desired username", a "Check Availability" button is displayed. Clicking starts the username check.

Sign up for Last.fm
Already have a profile? Log in here

Desired username: bill
Checking...
(max 15 characters, no spaces)
Email:
☐ The occasional newsletter to keep me up-to-date.

Checking...

The username is checked for availability.

Sign up for Last.fm
Already have a profile? Log in here

Desired username: bill ❗
Try another name
(max 15 characters, no spaces)
Email:
☐ The occasional newsletter to keep me up-to-date.

Try another name

If the username is already taken, the button changes to "Try another name".

Figure 14-6. *Last.fm uses a Live Preview to help the user pick a valid username*

Notice that a tight feedback loop was created in all three examples. For each significant action, there is an equal and opposite reaction. This is fundamental to the success of using **Live Previews** in your application.

Showcasing products

Live Previews are not just limited to form input. They also can be used in an online product catalog to preview a product. Strictly speaking, previews have been used on sites for almost as long as there has been a Web. Showing a close-up of a camera on an electronics site is a common technique. But what sets a **Live Preview** apart from a simple preview is its interactive nature.

Land's End uses a tool called My Virtual Model* to bring **Live Previews** to clothes shopping. It is based on the premise that if you can show what the clothes will look like on the shoppers, they will be happier with their purchases. While virtual models can only come so close to reality, users can personalize the model with their height, weight, body shape, and so on. Then when they select shirts, pants, and shoes, their virtual model will appear dressed with the items (Figure 14-7).

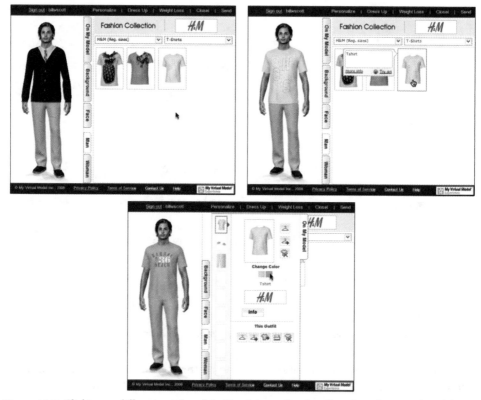

Figure 14-7. *Clicking on different articles of clothing is immediately reflected on the virtual model*

---

* My Virtual Model is a third-party tool for online clothing stores. See *http://www.mvm.com/*.

The MINIUSA site uses the **Live Preview** pattern in a similar way. Displaying how different models of Mini Coopers will look with different color combinations instantaneously is a powerful marketing tool (Figure 14-8).

Figure 14-8. *MINIUSA.com sports a Live Preview for selecting Mini Cooper models and altering color combinations on the fly*

The site also lets the user spin the car around 360 degrees to get a look at the car from every angle (Figure 14-9).

Figure 14-9. *Changing perspective is as easy as moving a slider; the feedback is in real time*

The ability to react instantaneously to the user's color or perspective changes fits well into the marketing message of cool and zippy. Imagine an old-style interface of "make the change," and "go to another page and see the result". **Live Previews** allow users the freedom to experiment.

Best Practices for Live Preview

Here are some best practices to keep in mind:

- Use **Live Previews** to prevent errors.
- Use **Live Previews** to engage users.
- Make feedback immediate.
- Place the preview in context of the action.
- If possible, have the real object change on the fly.
- Use **Live Previews** to avoid page transitions.
- If performance permits, provide real-time previews during character input for input fields. Alternatively, trigger on leaving the field or provide a clear **Call to Action** button to initiate preview.

Progressive Disclosure

The **Progressive Disclosure** pattern is related to **Live Previews**. When users are faced with a series of steps, it is often best to provide hints only when they are needed, instead of cluttering the interface by displaying all the hints at once.

Picnik is a photo manipulation tool that adds photo-editing features to a number of photo-sharing sites. During the "Create Account" flow, it provides **Progressive Disclosure** of hints and feedback all along the way to keep the user engaged and successfully filling out the signup form (Figure 14-10).

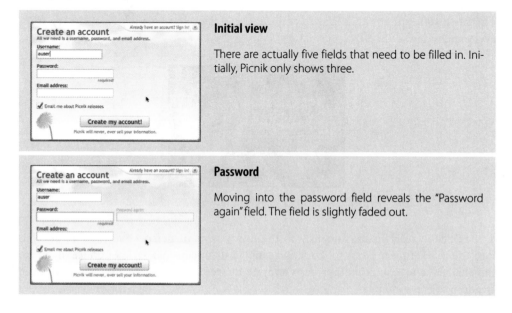

Initial view

There are actually five fields that need to be filled in. Initially, Picnik only shows three.

Password

Moving into the password field reveals the "Password again" field. The field is slightly faded out.

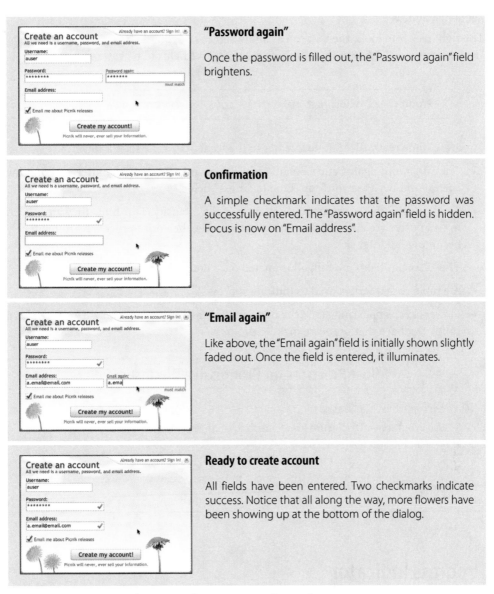

"Password again"

Once the password is filled out, the "Password again" field brightens.

Confirmation

A simple checkmark indicates that the password was successfully entered. The "Password again" field is hidden. Focus is now on "Email address".

"Email again"

Like above, the "Email again" field is initially shown slightly faded out. Once the field is entered, it illuminates.

Ready to create account

All fields have been entered. Two checkmarks indicate success. Notice that all along the way, more flowers have been showing up at the bottom of the dialog.

Figure 14-10. *Picnik provides a series of Progressive Disclosures during account creation*

Considerations

Typically, login interfaces get little dynamic treatment. All fields for input are shown with every possible hint revealed. Unfortunately, this kind of full disclosure creates a very cluttered interface.

Keeping it lightweight

The right idea is to make the task feel as lightweight as possible. The Picnik interface says, "It is as easy as 1-2-3," even though there are really five fields to be entered, not three.

> ── **Tip** ────────────────────────────────
> Use **Progressive Disclosure** to make a heavier process feel more lightweight.

There are some really nice subtle touches to the feedback in the Picnik form:

- The "Password again" and "Email again" fields are revealed only after entering the corresponding "Password" or "Email address" fields.
- The "…again" fields are shown at about half the intensity. This hints they are related to what users are entering but does not take over the entire process by immediately becoming full intensity.
- The "…again" fields are fully illuminated once entered.
- A simple checkmark is used to indicate success.
- Flowers keep appearing along the bottom after each successful entry. This provides a subtle feedback that users are making progress.

Best Practices for Progressive Disclosure

Here are some best practices to keep in mind:

- Use **Progressive Disclosure** to lead users through lengthy processes.
- Reveal help information just as it is needed.
- Remove help information as soon as the user leaves the input field.
- When appropriate, hint at what is about to be revealed (e.g., "Password again" field in Picnik).

Progress Indicator

Another opportunity for creating a reactive interface occurs when the application is busy with a lengthy process. **Progress Indicators** keep a conversation going with the user when the rest of the interface is currently unavailable. This is a common situation on travel sites, as well as many search-based applications.

In Chapter 12, we discussed the way Yahoo! Travel Farechase used transitions to improve perceived performance. Let's look at a similar example from another travel site, Microsoft's Farecast service. It provides a variety of **Progress Indicators** throughout the search process (Figure 14-11).

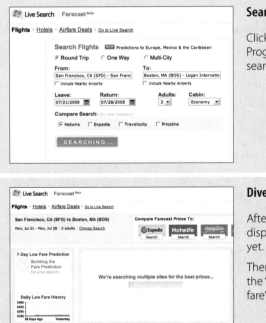

Search initiated

Clicking the "Search" button triggers the first Progress Indicator, which simply changes the search button to say "Searching…".

Diversion

After a few seconds, the search results page is displayed. But notice that there are no results yet.

There are actually three **Progress Indicators**: the "showing results" page, the "animating the fare" predications, and a progress bar.

Results trickle in

The first set of results now appears. The fare predictor panel finishes animating into place. The progress bar collapses to a small bar just above the results.

Finished

Results are displayed. The progress bar goes away.

Figure 14-11. *Farecast makes use of a number of different Progress Indicators to make the interface feel snappier and more reactive*

Considerations

There are some issues to consider when using **Progress Indicators**.

Perceived performance

There are actually nine **Progress Indicators** used by Farecast in this one flow:

1. Search button label changes to "Searching…".

2. Switch to search results page.

3. "We're Searching…" animated progress bar.

4. Daily Low Fare History chart animates from flat line to trend line.

5. 7-Day Low Fare Prediction spinning wheel.

6. 7-Day Low Fare Prediction spinning wheel changes to the "Tip: Wait" graphic.

7. Progress bar collapses to single line, changes to read "Still searching…".

8. First set of results trickle in.

9. Progress bar disappears.

When I went through this process, it took 24 seconds from the time I clicked the Search button until I got all the results. But because there are so many reactions to my one action, the process seemed much faster.

> —— **Tip** ——
> Keeping the user informed improves the overall experience.

Compare this to the traditional approach by Orbitz (Figure 14-12).

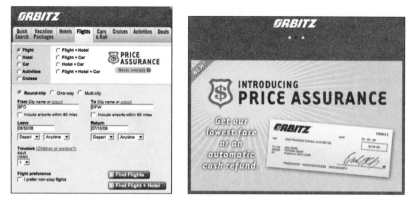

Figure 14-12. *Orbitz displays a single interstitial while it retrieves results*

Orbitz is generally twice as fast as Farecast at retrieving flight results. Orbitz pulls results from its own service, while Farecast pulls from multiple services. However, in Orbitz, there is sometimes a noticeable delay before the Progress Indicator is shown. And since there is only one indicator, it stays on the stage longer than any single one of Farecast's indicators. The net result is that Farecast can *feel* at least as fast, if not faster, than Orbitz.

Of course **Progress Indicators** can be really simple. When users search their mail folders in Yahoo! Mail, a simple busy indicator is displayed next to the search box (Figure 14-13).

Figure 14-13. *Yahoo! Mail uses a simple spinning wheel to indicate a search is in progress*

Placing progress indicators next to the place the action was initiated is common. Another variation is to place the **Progress Indicator** over the area that will be affected by the operation. In the Yahoo! Mail example, this would mean placing a Progress Indicator over the search results area. This technique is common in **Refining Search** and can be seen in Kayak (Figure 14-14).

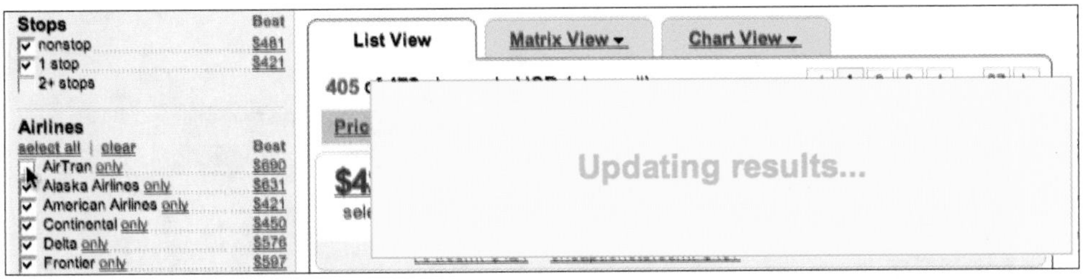

Figure 14-14. *Kayak places the progress indicator over the results area*

Immediate feedback

Progress indication can come in many forms. It is a way to keep the user informed of changing status. In Yahoo! Answers, user are restricted to 110 characters for the question. As users type in the question, the number of characters they have left is updated (Figure 14-15).

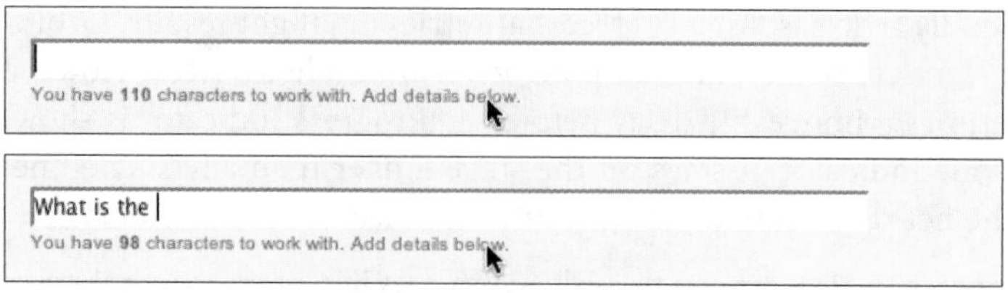

Figure 14-15. *Yahoo! Answers displays real-time feedback on how much longer a question can be*

This simple feedback loop encourages users to formulate short questions.

Showing upload status

Progress Indicators are really helpful for showing upload status. Due to constraints on the way files are usually uploaded to the Web, showing status is often hard to do. However, some products have overcome the challenge and provide constant updates on individual file upload status, as well as overall file upload status. The Yahoo! Photos uploader provides this kind of dynamic status (Figure 14-16).

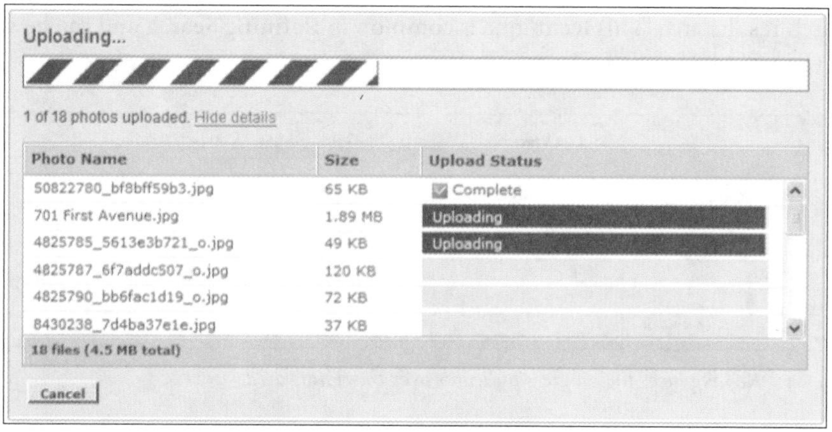

Figure 14-16. *Yahoo! Photos provided multiple file upload status*

Deferred loading

A final example of a **Progress Indicator** is one that is useful when there are external services you would like to defer loading until after the page is shown. An earlier design of Technorati used this technique to load its own content quickly, and then used loading indicators in place of the external content (Figure 14-17).

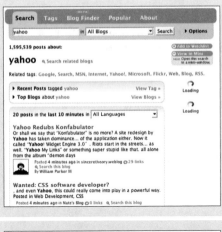

Loading

All local content is loaded immediately. Two busy indicators spin as the content that has been deferred gets loaded.

Deferred content loads

External services return content and load into the page-replacing busy indicator.

Figure 14-17. *An earlier version of Technorati used loading indicators for deferred content-loading of external services*

Best Practices for Progress Indicators

Here are some best practices to keep in mind:

- Use **Progress Indicators** to improve perceived performance.
- Keep indicators simple.
- Keep indicators in close proximity to where the action is.
- When the focus is on user input, show progress indicators next to the input field.
- When the focus is on the result of an input or activity, show progress indicators over the results area.
- If possible, have the indicators show actual progress. Alternatively, do something cyclical (spinning wheel, back and forth animation, and so on).

Periodic Refresh

Sometimes an interface needs to showcase new content or new community activity. In such a case, the interface is not really reacting to the users' input but to the larger community as a whole. **Periodic Refresh** brings in fresh content on a periodic basis without direct user interaction.

Digg Spy is a feature of the Digg site that allows users to observe real-time activity in the Digg community (Figure 14-18).

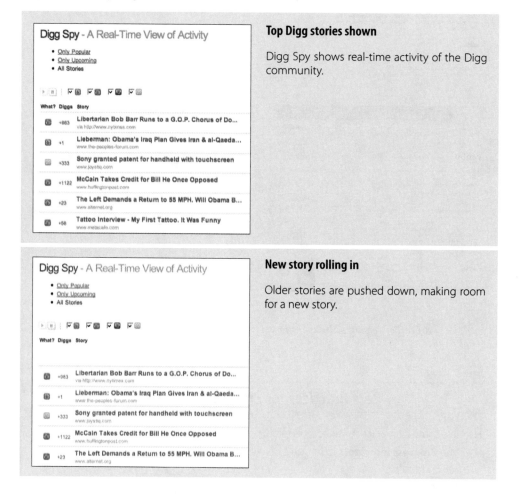

Top Digg stories shown

Digg Spy shows real-time activity of the Digg community.

New story rolling in

Older stories are pushed down, making room for a new story.

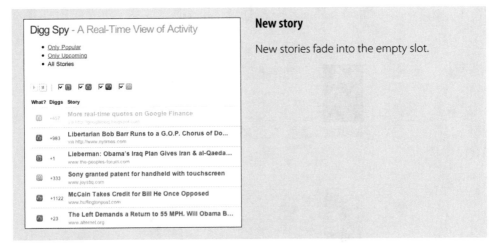

New story

New stories fade into the empty slot.

Figure 14-18. *Digg Spy uses Periodic Refresh to show top stories as they come in*

Digg Spy generally shows new stories every few seconds. Each story is a single row in a list of other stories. Keeping the rows compact makes it easier to roll in new content. Each scroll is only the height of a single row.

--- **Tip** --

Communicate community participation by periodically adding new content into the page.

_____

Considerations

There are a few issues to consider when using **Periodic Refresh**.

Visual noise

Netflix's Community section also uses the **Periodic Refresh** to spotlight recent member reviews (Figure 14-19).

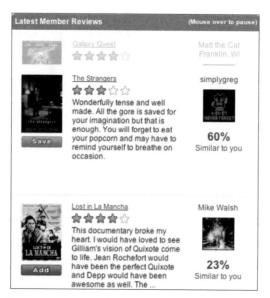

Figure 14-19. *Periodically, a new review is rolled in to replace the previous review; placing a mouse over the area pauses this feature*

One of the issues with the Netflix version is that each review is taller than a Digg Spy summary. This means each time a new review rolls in, it has to cover a distance equal to the height of a review. While Digg Spy is able to animate a new story into place in about a fourth of a second, Netflix reviews take closer to two seconds. An alternate approach would be to show collapsed review summaries. This would allow more reviews to be displayed and take less time to display each new review.

Pausing Periodic Refresh

For Netflix, placing the mouse over the area pauses the refresh. Digg Spy supplies a Play and Pause button.

Best Practices for Periodic Refresh

Here are some best practices to keep in mind:

- Use **Periodic Refresh** to keep a site's content fresh.
- Use **Periodic Refresh** to create a sense of relevancy.
- Don't update too often. Maintain a balance between readability and relevance.
- Allow the user a way to pause the automatic refreshes. This can be explicit or implicit. Implicit is usually the best approach. One method is to make any interaction with the area signal a pause.

Principles and Patterns for Rich Interaction

In the preceding chapters, we focused on designing for rich interactions.

The Principles

The six principles are simple and straightforward.

Make It Direct

The principle of WYSIWIG (What You See Is What You Get) has been proven over and over again during the last quarter of a century. Allowing users to directly edit content in context (**In-Page Editing**), control the interface with **Drag and Drop**, and directly manipulate objects (**Direct Selection**) all work toward creating an intelligent interface.

Keep It Lightweight

Respecting the user's level of effort is key to producing an effortless interface. Understanding the user's intent and providing just the right amount of interface (**Contextual Tools**) within the current context is critical to providing a lightweight experience.

Stay on the Page

Instead of breaking into the user's normal workflow with repeated page refreshes, we can now create an experience that more closely matches the user's flow. The proper use of **Overlays, Inlays, Virtual Space**, and **Process Flows** is integral to matching the way the user wants to work—not the way we forced them to work in the past.

Provide an Invitation

With an array of interactions at our disposal, it would be easy to have most of our features go unnoticed and unused. Throwing out contextual "welcome mats" within the page both statically and dynamically (**Affordance Invitation, Call to Action Invitation, Blank Slate Invitation, Tour Invitation, Hover Invitation, Drag and Drop Invitation, Inference Invitation,** and **More Content Invitation**) invites users to explore new idioms, improving their overall experience.

Use Transitions

Not just for those annoying mortgage ads, **Transitions** are necessary for both communication and engagement. With a wide variety of cinematic effects at our disposal (**Brighten and Dim, Expand/Collapse, Self-Healing, Animation, Spotlight, Lightbox Effect, Faceplate, Flip, Carousel, Accordion, Slide In and Slide Out,** and **Zoom**), we can either overwhelm our user with **Animation Gone Wild** or **Needless Fanfare**, or we can use these effects to explain happenings, show relationships, focus attention, improve performance, and create the illusion of virtual space.

Be Reactive

For every action there should be an equal and opposite reaction. This is the physics of our interfaces. Providing **Auto Complete, Live Suggest, Live Search, Refining Search, Live Previews, Progressive Disclosure, Progress Indicators,** and **Periodic Refresh** form the tools for creating a lively, reactive interface.

Staying Up to Date

The Web is constantly evolving, and it is impossible to always have the most up-to-date examples, and to capture emerging patterns in a book. We provide two resources to keep this work updated and relevant:

Designing Web Interfaces companion site
    Please visit *http://designingwebinterfaces.com* for up-to-date information on this book as well as updated examples, principles, and patterns. You can also contact the authors at this site.

Designing Web Interfaces Flickr site
    All of the figures are available on *http://flickr.com/photos/designingwebinterfaces/*. In addition, for many of the figures there are companion screencasts (movies) showing the interactions in action.

Index

M

Transitions, purpose of (*continued*)
maintaining context while changing views,
235–241
Accordion, 239–241
Carousel, 237–239
Faceplate pattern, 236
Flip transition, 236
Slide In and Slide Out effects, 235
showing relationship between objects,
244–245

U

Unfinished Invitation, 184
Upcoming.com, 13–14
upload status, 290
Use Transitions principle, 214–216, 296

V

Viewzi, 270
Virtual Pages, 103, 137–156
best practices
Carousel, 149
Inline Paging, 147
Virtual Panning, 151
Virtual Scrolling, 142
Virtual Spaces, 155
Carousel (see Carousel)
Inline Paging (see Inline Paging)
Scrolled Paging (see Scrolled Paging)
Virtual Panning (see Virtual Panning)
Virtual Scrolling (see Virtual Scrolling)
Zoomable User Interface (see Zoomable
User Interface)
Virtual Panning, 137, 149–151
best practices, 151
gesture-based interfaces, 151
Google Maps, 149–150
Natural Visual Construct, 150
Virtual Scrolling, 137–142
best practices, 142
desktop-style applications, 139
Google Search, 137
loading status, 139
Microsoft Live Image Search, 140
Microsoft Live Search, 141
PicLens, 141–142
progressive loading, 139–142
Yahoo! Mail, 138, 141
Virtual Space
best practices, 155
creating illusion of, 248

W

Wayfaring, 218
weather demo, 129
Webb, Matt, 214
Wine.com, 131
Wundrbar.com
Live Previews, 276–278
reacting immediately, 250–251

X

Xbox 360, List Inlay, 131

Y

Yahoo!
Personal Assistant tabs, 135
Unfinished Invitation, 184–185
Yahoo! 360, 11
Yahoo! Answers
Call to Action Invitations, 181
Live Suggest, 260–262
Progress Indicators, 289
Yahoo! Autos Car Finder tool, 130
Yahoo! Bookmarks, 64–66
Dialog Inlay, 126
Expand and Collapse, 222–224
Hybrid Selection, 72
Yahoo! Buzz, 86
Yahoo! Design Pattern Library, 6
Yahoo! Finance, 242
Yahoo! Foods, 115
Yahoo! for Teachers
Beta, 89
Drag and Drop Invitations, 200
Profile Card, 97
Refining Search, 273
Yahoo! Games, 211
Yahoo! Gobbler, 200
Yahoo! Health, 212
Yahoo! home page
Brighten and Dim, 219
More Content Invitations, 210–211
Tabs, 134
Tour Invitations, 188
Yahoo! Hot Jobs Call to Action button, 182
Yahoo! Mail, 49–51, 79
Auto Complete, 253
Beta, 74
Classic, 62
Toggle Selection, 73

About the Authors

Bill Scott is director of UI Engineering at Netflix in Los Gatos, California, where he plies his interface engineering and design skills. He is the former Yahoo! Ajax evangelist and pattern curator for the Yahoo! Design Pattern Library.

Bill has a long and glamorous history in the IT world, due mostly to his unique understanding of the technical and creative aspects of designing usable products. His ramblings and musings can be found at *www.looksgoodworkswell.com*.

Theresa Neil is a user experience consultant in Austin, Texas, where she designs rich internet applications for start-ups and Fortune 500 companies. Her work can be seen at *www.designgenie.org*.

Colophon

The image on the cover of *Designing Web Interfaces* is a Guianan cock-of-the-rock (*Rupicola rupicola*). Easily identified by the distinctive half-moon crest on its head, this bird is native to mountainous regions in northern South America, spanning the countries of Guyana, French Guiana, Suriname, Colombia, Venezuela, and Amazonian Brazil. Mainly fruit eaters, Guianan cocks-of-the-rock pass whole seeds through their digestive systems, thereby contributing to tree and plant diversity in the lowland forests they inhabit.

Adult cocks-of-the-rock reach heights of eight inches and have stout, round bodies. Males are typically smaller than females and have bright orange plumage with black and white accents, whereas the females are a muted brown. The males take advantage of their bright plumage to attract females as part of their elaborate mating ritual, during which they gather in a lek, spread their wings, strut, ruffle their tail feathers, and issue a series of unique calls. The birds are polygamous; successful males will mate with many females during breeding season. Females build cup-shaped nests for their eggs out of clay and plant matter inside cliff cavities or along rock faces, and they raise their chicks alone.

In the early 20th century, hunters trapped Guianan cocks-of-the-rock and sold them as pets. Today, the birds are popular among bird watchers, eco tourists, and fly fishermen (who use the colorful feathers to make fishing flies). Additionally, the Guianan cock-of-the-rock, with its prominent "mohawk" and vibrant plumage, has been featured on tourism brochures and stamps for several of the countries it inhabits. Although native tribes still hunt the birds for feathers and food, the species is not threatened or at risk of extinction.

The cover image is from *Johnson's Natural History*. The cover font is Adobe ITC Garamond. The text font is Adobe Minion Pro, and the heading and note font is Adobe Myriad Pro Condensed.

Related Titles from O'Reilly

Web Authoring and Design

ActionScript 3.0 Cookbook

Ajax Hacks

Ambient Findability

Creating Web Sites: The Missing Manual

CSS Cookbook, *2nd Edition*

CSS Pocket Reference, *2nd Edition*

CSS: The Definitive Guide, *3rd Edition*

CSS: The Missing Manual

Dreamweaver 8: Design and Construction

Dreamweaver 8: The Missing Manual

Dynamic HTML: The Definitive Reference, *3rd Edition*

Essential ActionScript 3.0

Flex 8 Cookbook

Flash 8: Projects for Learning Animation and Interactivity

Flash 8: The Missing manual

Flash 9 Design: Motion Graphics for Animation & User Interfaces

Flash Hacks

Head First HTML with CSS & XHTML

Head Rush Ajax

Head First Web Design

High Performance Web Sites

HTML & XHTML: The Definitive Guide, *6th Edition*

HTML & XHTML Pocket Reference, *3rd Edition*

Information Architecture for the World Wide Web, *3rd Edition*

Information Dashboard Design

JavaScript: The Definitive Guide, *5th Edition*

JavaScript & DHTML Cookbook, *2nd Edition*

Learning ActionScript 3.0

Learning JavaScript

Learning Web Design, *3rd Edition*

PHP Hacks

Programming Collective Intelligence

Programming Flex 2

Web Design in a Nutshell, *3rd Edition*

Web Site Measurement Hacks

O'REILLY®